W9-ASX-550

Walking
FOR BETTER HEALTH

EVERYTHING YOU NEED TO KNOW
TO WALK YOUR WAY TO BETTER HEALTH

BY
MAGGIE SPILNER

Health & Wellness Reference Library™

National Health & Wellness Club
12301 Whitewater Drive
Minnetonka, MN 55343
www.healthandwellnessclub.com

To the most influential people

in my walking life, with much respect and gratitude:

the late Robert Rodale, whose vision of global health and wellness

inspired me; Mark Bricklin, who had the instincts and

patience to mentor me as a writer and creative thinker;

and David Brotzman, my husband and lifetime walking partner,

who patiently put aside his needs for a year while

I pulled together this book.

CONTENTS

ACKNOWLEDGMENTS

Ever aware that I am only a messenger, I know that I owe many people in the walking world a debt of gratitude for the information presented in this book. I'd especially like to thank Suki Munsell, Ph.D.; Elaine Ward; Jake Jacobson; Suza Francina; Mike Cohen, Ed.D.; James Sunquist; Jeff Savage; Bonnie Stein; Sheree Meehan; and Martin Rudow. Whether or not they are quoted in these pages, they contributed much to my walking education and continue to inspire me because of their dedication to spreading the word about the importance of a healthy, active lifestyle.

I'd also like to acknowledge many other people whose work has helped to make this book complete. Special thanks go to Lisa Delaney, Dorothy Foltz-Gray, Susan Godbey, Sandra Salera Lloyd, Jordan Matus, Holly McCord, Peggy Morgan, Marty Munson, Mary Nagle, Emrika Padus, Cathy Perlmutter, Steve Schwade, Michele Stanten, and Alice Trevor.

Thanks also to editors Ed Claflin and Susan Berg for giving the manuscript their time, attention, and polish; to copy editor Karen Neely for ensuring the consistency and accuracy of the text; and to Carol Angstadt for creating an energizing and reader-friendly book design.

And finally, thanks to all of my loyal readers during my 12-year reign as *Prevention*'s "walking queen." I am profoundly grateful for their interest, their stories, their inspiring letters. May the wind be ever at their backs—unless, of course, they want to burn more calories!

FOREWORD

When I was asked to write a foreword for this book, I fairly jumped through the phone in anticipation. There are few people who have done more for walking, or who know more about walking, than Maggie Spilner. Writing a foreword gives me the opportunity to acknowledge what Maggie has done not only for me and my sport of racewalking but also for *all* walkers. She is one in 10 million!

My friendship with Maggie goes back to the early 1990s. At the time, I was very involved in the promotion of racewalking in southern California, serving as race director for an event in the Los Angeles area. Maggie already had several years' experience as *Prevention*'s walking editor, and I quickly realized that she was a key player in the fitness walking world.

Since then, our paths have crossed many times, and our professional partnership and personal friendship have grown. I remember one particular conversation in which I told Maggie how practicing racewalking techniques had cured my knee problem without surgery and virtually eliminated pain in my shoulders and lower back. She expressed concern that most fitness walkers, especially women, equate racewalking with competition. So they steer clear of the sport because they're not competitive.

I then told Maggie a story about my noncompetitive 78-year-old mom. After my father passed away, I taught my mother how to racewalk for something new to do. Within a month, she was telephoning to tell me how fast she had walked her 2-mile loop. Every time she shaved off a few seconds, she got more excited. She was obviously enjoying competing with herself, so I asked her why she said she wasn't competitive. She replied, "I don't like competing with others."

Maggie loved the story, and I could see her writer's mind at work. She has a gift for taking anecdotal information like this, as well as her own experience, and relating it to the problems and concerns of her readers. She is quite simply walking's best communicator. Her relaxed, easy writing style always speaks to each of us personally. It makes this book a pleasure to read.

As *Prevention*'s walking editor, Maggie has had a major impact on the promotion of fitness walking in the United States. For the magazine's July 1996 issue, she wrote an article called "The Easiest Way to Get Fit after 40," in which she gave the phone number of my organization, the North American Racewalking Foundation. We received more than 1,600 calls over the next 3 months! The phone rang literally day and night—and much of that interest was generated by Maggie.

Walking for Better Health is an outstanding resource for all walkers. If you want the best information on how to walk off those extra pounds, you'll find it here, enlivened by Maggie's accounts of her personal "battle of the bulge." If you want pointers on buying walking shoes or on weatherproofing your workouts in summer and winter, you'll get plenty of practical advice within these pages. If you want to train for a 5-K or for an upcoming hiking trip, you'll find information to help you do just that. With topics ranging from Volkswalking to marathoning, from Dynamic Walking to racewalking, this is truly a walking encyclopedia for the new millennium.

Whether you're a beginning walker or a seasoned veteran, use this book as a reference and companion. May you enjoy all the lifelong benefits of walking for fitness and sport.

Elaine Ward
Founder and director of the North American Racewalking Foundation

A Walker's Attitude

I woke up early today, excited about the day ahead. My health and well-being are important, and it is my job to decide to take care of myself. It's up to me to find the time and the place and the reasons to go for a walk.

Today I can complain because the weather is rainy, or . . .
I can be thankful that my skin will be blessed with moisture.

Today I can feel sad that I have so many other things to do, or . . .
I can be happy that I'll have so much more energy to do them when I'm done walking.

Today I can grumble over the temperature, or . . .
I can be thrilled that I've got the right clothes to deal with it.

Today I can lament that I have too many responsibilities, or . . .
I can feel grateful that I have a family and a job to stay healthy for.

Today I can cry because the roses on my path have thorns, or . . .
I can celebrate that those thorny bushes have roses.

Today I can mourn my lack of walking partners, or . . .
I can revel in my quiet time alone.

Today I can whine because I have to find the time to walk, or . . .
I can shout for joy that my body is able to keep pace with my spirit.

Today I can grumble about the time it takes to stretch, or . . .
I can delight in the sheer pleasure of my limbs reaching to the sky.

What my health and fitness will be like is, in great measure, up to me. I get to choose my level of well-being. I get to lay the plans for a daily walk.

Have a great walk today . . . unless you have other plans.

—Adapted by Maggie Spilner from *The Sculptor's Attitude,*
author unknown

ON THE ROAD
TO BETTER
HEALTH

WALKING IS POWERFUL MEDICINE

Whether you're just starting a walking program or you're already a regular walker, your health likely played a role in your decision to get fit. Maybe you want to lose a few pounds or protect your heart from disease or keep your bones strong and your joints limber. Walking can do all this and more.

But when we talk about walking for health, we must look beyond the physical benefits. After all, health is a rich fabric spun from physical, mental, emotional, and spiritual threads. If one of these threads becomes frayed for any reason, it can weaken the entire fabric. What you eat, how much you sleep, how you handle your personal and professional relationships, how you view the world and your place in it—all of these things influence whether or not you feel vital and strong. They also have a real impact on your body.

The same can be said of walking. It supports health in every sense—physi-cally, mentally, emotionally, and spiri-tually. It enriches and balances your life. And it just plain makes you feel good. No wonder the Greek physician Hippocrates (460–377 B.C.) deemed walking to be "man's best medicine."

BOOSTING IMMUNITY, ONE STEP AT A TIME

To get a complete picture of how walking supports good health, you must start at the cellular level. A daily walk keeps certain cells—your im-mune cells—tuned up for action, ready to whip viruses and battle bacteria. In fact, some experts believe that walking may be one of your best weapons for fighting off infection and disease and getting on the road to recovery fast.

Strong statement? Maybe. But a number of studies have shown that a moderate walk not only relieves the stress that may trigger or aggravate an illness but also stimulates your immune system, your body's main defense against disease. In one such study, a 45-minute walk (about 3 miles) increased the activity of certain immune cells by about 57 percent. The cells' activity level returned to normal about 3 hours after the walk.

Now researchers don't know for sure whether walking can make you heal faster, but some studies suggest that people who walk consistently (meaning, every day, which is what you and I strive for) develop fewer illnesses than people who are sedentary. The fact that walking is a moderate activity may be key to its immune-enhancing effects. Indeed, other studies show that long bouts of intense exercise—like an hour of pavement-pounding, heavy-breathing running—can actually suppress your immune system and make you more susceptible to infection.

This brings up a question that I often hear from fellow walkers: When you're under the weather, should you continue your walking program or take off a few days until you feel better? One expert recommends this rule of thumb: If you have a headache or runny nose, or if you're sneezing, you're okay to walk as long as your temperature is normal. In cases of fever, sore throat, or coughing, you should rest until your symptoms subside.

Even if you feel well enough to continue walking, skip the marathons, races, and fun walks for the time being—unless you have your doctor's okay to participate.

GAINING GROUND AGAINST CANCER

If walking has a beneficial effect on the immune system, then might it have some protective effect against any type of cancer? The research so far seems promising.

In one study, laboratory rats were given a chemical that induces breast cancer. Half of the rats were put in cages that allowed them free access to an exercise wheel. The rats could run on the wheel any time they got the urge, and they did so frequently. Compared with the rats that didn't have a wheel, those that did developed one-third fewer cases of breast cancer. What's more, their tumors appeared much later.

Exercise in general keeps cropping up as a factor in cancer prevention and treatment. Scientists don't yet understand how exercise might deter tumors, but they do know that people who work out regularly seem to get cancer less often than those who don't.

For instance, three separate population studies found that men with physically demanding jobs, such as carpenters, plumbers, gardeners, and mail carriers, are less prone to colon cancer than men who sit all day. In another study, Harvard University researchers determined that men who engage in about an hour of vigorous activity every day reduce their risk of prostate cancer by 47 to 88 percent. And researchers at the University of Iowa Cancer Center in Iowa City found that women over age 65, a group that accounts for 50 percent of all breast cancer cases, are less likely to get the disease if they exercise moderately. In fact, the more active these women are, the lower their chances of being diagnosed with breast cancer.

While no one can say for certain that walking every day protects against all kinds of cancer, enough evidence has been uncovered to persuade the American Cancer Society to recommend regular exercise as one possible way to reduce your risk. And if you or someone you know is receiving treatment for cancer, walking may be the ticket to a steady recovery and the speedy return of strength and energy.

Maggie's Log

SAVE YOUR LIFE ON PAPER

TEN YEARS AGO, I read an article in the *Baltimore City Paper* about how you can "save your life" by keeping a diary. The author talked about the importance of recording daily events as a way of staying in touch with yourself and as a tool for looking back and seeing how you've changed.

That got me thinking about how a walking log really is a save-your-life diary. Think about it: You might be protecting yourself from all manner of physical ills by walking every day. Documenting those daily walks shows you just how far you've come, mile by mile, hour by hour.

Many people have said that keeping a walking log helps them stay motivated. Watching those miles add up on paper is tangible evidence of the sometimes hard-won internal battles of "to walk, or not to walk."

It's also great to look back over the months and say, "Yep, I remember that walk around Trout Creek Park. It was drizzling and foggy, but the mist of the stream was eerily beautiful. Rainy-day walks are great!"

There are several ways in which you can enhance your record-keeping and make it more motivating. Keep track of your daily weight or your resting pulse. What's your time for a mile? How do your feet feel?

You can add more subjective words about your thoughts, moods, and feelings. What daydreams drifted through your mind? What problems did you solve? What relationship did you hash out? Your log can remind you of how creative and helpful your walks are.

Another great thing to do is record your routes. If you enjoy walking the same route, what changes do you see from day to day? Increase your powers of observation. If you alternate routes, document them so that you can go back there or take a partner to the best routes. There's no better way to get to know a town than to walk through it.

You may find "saving your life" on paper to be a fun way to spend a few minutes every day—with healthful results.—*M.S.*

For example, walking may counteract the fatigue and weakness that are associated with high-dose chemotherapy. Traditionally, patients have been told to rest to recuperate from chemo. But extended bed rest leads to loss of muscle strength and cardiovascular fitness, which only worsens fatigue and weakness—so much so that they can linger for years after treatment. So a team of German researchers tried a different approach: They encouraged patients to exercise regularly after completing chemotherapy. People had not only more energy but also a more positive attitude toward recovery.

The benefits of exercise for cancer patients are psychological as well as physical. One study of women being treated for breast cancer showed that their levels of depression and anxiety dropped dramatically after 10 weeks of regular exercise—30 to 40 minutes, 4 days a week. This finding is especially encouraging because breast cancer survivors face a significant risk of depression and anxiety.

WHAT ELSE CAN WALKING DO FOR YOU?

To be sure, scientists have only begun to scratch the surface in understanding the benefits of exercise—not only for fighting cancer and boosting immunity but also for enhancing all aspects of human health. Interestingly, most studies of exercise use walking as the activity of choice. And they have revealed some extraordinary information about what this most fundamental of workouts can do.

- It supports weight loss and weight maintenance.
- It reduces the risk of heart disease and stroke.
- It fends off diabetes by improving the body's ability to use insulin.
- It eases the pain and stiffness of arthritis.
- It keeps bones strong, which prevents osteoporosis.
- In women, it relieves premenstrual and menopausal discomforts.
- It improves sleep.
- It builds strength, flexibility, and stamina.
- It enhances mental function.
- It counteracts anger, depression, and anxiety.

We'll take a closer look at some of these benefits in the chapters that follow. But as you can see, you have a lot to gain just from lacing up a pair of walking shoes and putting one foot in front of the other.

CHAPTER 2

THE SECRET OF A HEALTHY HEART

You probably already know that walking and other forms of exercise can help keep your heart in prime pumping condition. But here's something that may be news to you: Exercising may be *more* important to your heart health than losing weight.

I mention this because weight loss is the reason that many people launch a walking program in the first place. Even if the number on your scale remains unchanged, it doesn't mean that walking isn't doing you any good. It surely is, though in ways you may not be able to see. That's why I always tell people to think in terms of walking for their health, not just for thin thighs.

Make no mistake: Overweight and obesity are risk factors for a number of ailments, including heart disease. And the more extra pounds you carry, the greater your chances of illness. Doctors have been saying this for years. But newer studies suggest that an active lifestyle, one that may involve regular walking, actually overrides certain risk factors for heart disease, including family history, smoking, and overweight.

FITNESS OUTWEIGHS FATNESS

Leading the way in this groundbreaking research is the famed Cooper Institute for Aerobics Research in Dallas. A team of scientists there, led by Steven Blair, P.E.D., confirmed that fitness is a fabulous overall health protector, even for those of us who are carrying around extra pounds.

For 8 years, Dr. Blair and his colleagues tracked the health status of more than 25,000 men and 7,000 women. The researchers monitored each person's body weight and fitness level (as measured in exercise stress tests) and periodically evaluated blood pressure, blood sugar, and cholesterol levels. They also documented any family history of heart disease as well as smoking habits.

Based on the data they collected, Dr. Blair's team concluded that death rates from all causes, including heart attacks, were lowest among men and women who were moderately to highly fit, regardless of weight (and other risk factors, such as smoking, high cholesterol, high blood pressure, and family history). Sedentary men and women fared worse, regardless of whether they were fat or thin.

DON'T COUNT OUT POUNDS

According to Dr. Blair, it's true that people who are thin generally are more active and fit, and therefore healthier, than people who are overweight. But as his research suggests, thinness without fitness won't protect you against illness or help you live longer. On the other hand, if you weigh more than you should but you walk or engage in some other physical activity on a regular basis, you're a step ahead healthwise of all those thin couch potatoes.

That's not to say that your weight doesn't matter at all. On the contrary, extra pounds put you at risk for all sorts of health problems, including high blood pressure and diabetes. What you need to keep in mind is that even if you don't lose all the weight you'd like,

you still boost your chances of a long, healthy life by being active and fit.

"Virtually every system of your body is affected in some way by regular exercise," Dr. Blair says. "Carbohydrate metabolism improves, and blood sugar levels normalize. There are positive changes in blood fats and blood pressure. Plus, people who exercise regularly simply have stronger hearts."

"Over time, regular exercise slows your resting pulse rate," adds William P. Castelli, M.D., medical director of the Framingham Cardiovascular Institute in Framingham, Massachusetts. "The faster your resting pulse, the shorter your life."

To determine your resting pulse rate, check your pulse first thing in the morning, before you even get out of bed. Place two fingers over the carotid artery, located on either side of your neck. Count the beats for 10 seconds, then multiply by 6 for the number of beats per minute. Seventy beats per minute or less is considered healthy. As you become more fit, you may see your resting pulse rate drop. If you get sick or experience some type of stress, your resting pulse rate may jump up.

Proof That Exercise Helps Hearts

IN A STUDY INVOLVING 5,000 doctors who had experienced heart attacks, those who exercised at least twice a week were 40 percent less likely to die from any cause and 50 percent less likely to die from heart problems.

In a separate study, 4,000 nurses between ages 40 and 65—all with diabetes—reduced their chances of developing heart disease by 28 percent just by walking regularly. More vigorous exercise lowered their risk another 5 percentage points.

THE SKINNY ON BELLY FAT

Perhaps the most significant health benefit of regular exercise such as walking is a reduction in intra-abdominal fat. This type of fat collects around internal organs, rather than under the surface of the skin as it does on the hips and thighs. Because of its location,

IN STEP WITH
STEPHEN PETRAKOVICH

HE'S ON THE ROAD TO A HEALTHIER HEART

STEVE PETRAKOVICH STOOD AT the bottom of the steep hill at the New Age Health Spa in Neversink, New York, and sighed. The year before, he'd have walked up it easily. But after two heart attacks and two angioplasties, he felt reluctant to even try. While others walked, he climbed into a van, feeling despondent and embarrassed.

At age 56, Steve finally experienced the heart problems that had stalked the rest of his family, killing his father, mother, aunt, and nephew. Angioplasty cleared away the obstructions inside Steve's arteries, but no one seemed interested in how two heart attacks had damaged his emotional well-being, leaving him feeling hopeless, frightened, and alone.

"My doctor focused on my physical symptoms, not my emotional vulnerability," Steve recalls. "At checkups, when he asked me how I felt, I said, 'Fine,' because I figured I was fine in the terms he was asking about. I didn't have chest pain. But I felt afraid to do anything, afraid to go places alone, to walk, to drive, to lift anything heavy. I was a wreck inside."

After 3 months of despondency, Steve decided to participate in a Healthy Lifestyles pilot program at the New Age Health Spa. Participants spent a week learning about exercise, healthy eating, and stress reduction. For Steve, it was a real turning point.

"I needed a fresh start. I needed to build confidence in my abilities again, to find new ways to cope with old problems," he explains. "I became more aware that there was a lot that I could gain control over."

Perhaps the most important thing Steve learned was how to take things one step at a time, at his own pace. "The program designer and leader, Bill Bakey, spent one-on-one time with me. He took the time to get into my head and to understand what I was feeling," Steve says. "Bill told me it was okay if I couldn't keep up with everybody else when I walked. He told me to stop and smell the roses instead of worrying about being a burden. He helped me pay attention to my body's signals. If I get tired or feel chest tightness, I can stop, take a few deep breaths, and enjoy the scenery. When I feel rested, I can keep walking. I know that sounds simple, but I really needed someone to take me through that process."

By the time Steve left New Age, he was walking up and down that steep hill twice a day. "And I was beginning to feel like I could get my life back," he adds.

intra-abdominal fat can contribute to serious health problems, including heart disease.

Through studies involving both men and women, researchers at the University of Alabama at Birmingham determined that the primary way exercise lowers heart disease risk is by trimming intra-abdominal fat. In fact, you may be losing this fat even when the number on the scale doesn't change.

That's why Jean-Pierre Despres, Ph.D., director of the Lipid Research Center at Laval University in St. Foy, Quebec, suggests that you trade in your scale for a tape measure. Take an initial measurement of your waist for comparison, then periodically recheck that measurement as you advance in your walking program. Or forget about the tape measure and keep tabs on your waist size using your favorite belt. With every notch you tighten your belt, you know you're making progress.

In several studies, Dr. Despres found that he was able to significantly reduce patients' internal belly fat and almost normalize certain disease risk factors through a combination of regular aerobic exercise and a low-fat diet. The exercise consisted of a 1-hour walk every day.

"Aim for at least 45 minutes, 5 days a week," Dr. Despres suggests. "Even 30 minutes a day will help." If you're not up to a brisk pace, walk slower but longer. It's not the speed but the total calories burned that counts.

THE BEST MEDICINE FOR HIGH BLOOD PRESSURE

There's another way in which exercise may help keep your heart healthy and strong. In combination with proper diet, it appears to lower high blood pressure.

This is important because high blood pressure is one of the many conditions for which doctors frequently prescribe medications. And these medications, like most, can have unwanted side effects.

Yet many people accept prescriptions from their doctors without question. Understandably, they feel uncomfortable challenging the course of treatment recommended by a medical professional—even when other, nondrug options exist. So some doctors get on a sort of medication merry-go-round: They prescribe one blood pressure drug, and if it doesn't work as well as expected, they prescribe another.

When eight prestigious physicians' groups, including the American College of Cardiology and the American College of Preventive Medicine, looked into the treatment of high blood pressure in this country, they found that doctors favor medication over exercise and diet. Often that's because doctors overlook high blood pressure until medication becomes a necessity.

EARLY INTERVENTION IS BEST

In the United States, an estimated 50 million people have high blood pressure. Yet 50 percent of all cases are either inadequately treated or undetected. The condition is sly and sneaky. There's no pain or other symptoms as your arteries gum up with fatty debris and your heart strains, weakens, and enlarges.

While blood pressure screenings are routinely performed during visits to doctors' offices, the readings themselves tend to get short shrift. That's because family practitioners and internists, who do those initial screenings, may not have the expertise necessary to properly interpret readings. They may not see high-normal blood pressure as significant, even though it tends to get higher over time. So 5 years down the road, patients who might have controlled their blood pressure through exercise and diet end up on medication instead.

"Most doctors don't spend enough time up front convincing patients that the way to reduce their risk of heart attack and stroke is to lower their blood pressures," says Ray Gifford Jr., M.D., professor of internal medicine at Ohio State University College of Medicine and Public Health in Columbus. "Doctors need to talk to their patients about making lifestyle changes that are almost certain to bring down blood pressure, so medication may never be necessary."

Dr. Gifford believes in early intervention, when a person's blood pressure reading reaches 130 to 139 systolic (the top number in a reading) and 85 to 89 diastolic (the bottom number). At this stage, he says, blood pressure can be reined in—before it gets out of control—with some simple lifestyle changes.

But those changes must be supervised. "You can't tell people to start a low-salt diet and an exercise routine and to come back in 6 months," Dr. Gifford asserts. "Patients need a physician who is willing to keep reevaluating them once they're on a program." Ideally, people should see their doctors three times within the first 6 months to make sure that their lifestyle changes are on track.

Of course, one of the most important changes a person with even mildly high blood pressure can make is to launch an exercise routine. Aerobic activities such as walking have been shown to lower blood pressure when they're done for 40 minutes at least three times a week. They seem to have the greatest effect on the systolic number in a blood pressure reading. They also tone your heart and other muscles in your body.

Besides regular walking, other lifestyle changes can help lower your blood pressure to where it should be. Your doctor may advise you to quit smoking, restrict your salt intake, and limit your alcohol consumption to no more than two drinks a day.

If you've already been diagnosed with high blood pressure, or if you suspect that you have the condition, see your doctor for a checkup before you begin a walking program. In fact, anyone over age 40, regardless of whether they have high blood pressure, should get a physical evaluation before starting an exercise regimen, especially if they have been sedentary for years.

A PRESCRIPTION FOR HEALING YOUR HEART

Even for people who already have heart disease or who have experienced a heart attack or undergone heart surgery, a walking program can work wonders. When you walk regularly, the conditioning effect enhances the pumping ability of your heart, so it's less likely to become overtaxed when you're exerting yourself. In addition, walking may lower your blood pressure, improve your cholesterol profile, and short-circuit the depression that often follows heart surgery.

Because your heart is in a weakened state, you need to be especially careful when starting a walking program. You may have all kinds of questions about what you can and can't do: "How fast should I go?" "Are hills okay?" "Should I walk after a meal?" "What about walking when it's hot, cold, or humid?" "What if I feel pain?" "Can I safely walk alone?"

Since every person's situation is unique, you should discuss these and other questions with your doctor *before* you begin walking. Your doctor may even recommend a specific walking routine for you as part of a comprehensive, supervised cardiac-rehabilitation program.

The following general guidelines can help make walking a safe, effective activity while your heart is on the mend. Again, some of these tips may not be appropriate for you, depending on your medical condition. Be sure to review all of them with your doctor.

Make walking part of a plan. Walking is a fabulous activity, but it can't heal your heart on its own. You need to make other lifestyle changes, too. So follow your doctor's orders. If you smoke, quit. Adjust your eating habits. Learn and practice stress-management techniques.

Have your doctor set your limit. One of the most important things for you to do is to identify the point of exertion at which you are putting yourself at risk for a heart attack. Pain may not be the best indicator, as some heart attacks are painless. By using an electro-

---

Take Symptoms Seriously

IF YOU'VE BEEN DIAGNOSED with heart disease, high blood pressure, or another heart-related problem, memorize these three warning signs.

- Shortness of breath when you're exercising at your normal level of exertion
- Excessive fatigue, even though you're taking your usual walk
- Any kind of chest discomfort

If you experience any of these symptoms, contact your physician immediately. If your chest pain does not subside with appropriate nitroglycerin therapy, call your local emergency number or have someone take you to the nearest hospital emergency room.

cardiogram (EKG) to track your heart rhythm during an exercise session, your doctor can tell you how hard you can push yourself before you put yourself in danger. He can also tell you how to stay within a safe range of exertion.

The challenge is to find a duration that's beneficial but safe. You may have to start at 5 minutes a day. But you'll want to work up to at least 30 minutes a day, at least 5 days a week, with your doctor's approval. Most people can monitor themselves on the basis of how they feel. You may not need to check your pulse or wear complicated pulse-monitoring equipment during workouts.

Maintain a moderate pace. "People should work up to a comfortably brisk pace, where they can still carry on a conversation," says Dean Ornish, M.D., author of *Dr. Dean Ornish's Program for Reversing Heart Disease*. His advice may seem simplistic, but it's based on sound, scientific evidence.

You really don't need to worry about going fast enough. The benefits of walking kick in at just 45 percent of your maximum heart rate, so a moderate pace is more than adequate. You do need to be careful about going too fast or too hard, which may do your heart more harm than good. As a rule of thumb, don't walk so speedily that you become breathless or can't carry on a conversation. If you enjoy intense exercise and want to take up race-walking or speedwalking, be sure to work closely with your doctor.

Disregard distance. Remember, it's how long you walk, not how far, that matters most. The "right" distance is what you can cover comfortably within 30 minutes—and that includes returning to your starting point.

Take it easy after eating. Forgo a brisk walk after a big meal, when blood is being shunted away from your heart and toward your stomach. Allow 2 to 4 hours after eating before engaging in vigorous exercise. A postmeal stroll is okay; in fact, it may help burn calories and enhance digestion. But wait about an hour after eating before heading out, if only to avoid indigestion. (Walking after a light meal generally poses no problems.)

Check out the thermometer. Temperature extremes may put your heart at risk. If it's cold outside, take time to warm up before walking. If it's hot, slow your pace and drink plenty of water en route. Or consider going to the nearest mall when the temperature goes too high or too low. The climate-controlled environment is perfect for people with heart problems.

Don't fear going out on your own. Unless you have unstable angina (a condition characterized by severe chest pain) or some other health problem that could trigger a medical emergency, you should be fine to walk by yourself. Teaming up with an exercise buddy, perhaps your spouse or a friend, may make walking more pleasurable and help you stick with your program. But it isn't a medical necessity.

Bag the hand weights. Many experts advise against them. And for people with heart problems, they may pose a serious risk by raising blood pressure.

Stay on level terrain. If a hill is steep enough to make your heart rate climb fast, you should probably avoid it. If that isn't possible, stop as often as necessary during your ascent to rest and allow your heart to recover. Don't press on and tough it out.

Pay attention to how you feel. If you feel as though you're pushing yourself too hard, slow your pace. Or take a brief break, then start walking again. (People with a condition called silent ischemia need to consult their doctors for pulse recommendations. They may be told to wear a heart monitor and to keep their pulses within a specific range when they work out. They can have heart attacks without experiencing pain or even breathlessness.)

You may have heard that stopping too quickly without first cooling down is dangerous for your heart. If you've been walking at a moderate pace, the degree of change should not have any negative effects, such as triggering an irregular heartbeat.

In case of pain, remember the "3 by 5 rule." Keep your nitroglycerin tablets with you at all times. If you experience any chest discomfort while walking, sit down immediately. Then follow what one cardiac rehabilitation center calls the 3 by 5 rule. If your pain doesn't subside within 1 minute, take 1 nitroglycerin tablet under your tongue. Wait 5 minutes. If your pain persists, take another tablet, for a total of 3 tablets over the course of 15 minutes. You can start walking again as soon as your pain goes away. If it doesn't let up within 15 minutes, call the local number for medical emergencies or have someone drive you to the nearest hospital emergency room.

The Buddy System Packs Triple Benefits

FRIENDS AND WALKING GO together like love and marriage. They're all predictors of longer, healthier lives.

Since a Swedish study gave strength to the theory that lack of social support is a risk factor for heart disease in women (other research had already confirmed such a correlation in men), having an exercise buddy would seem to make walking even better for you. How so?

- An exercise buddy provides social support, a predictor of heart health.
- Having a buddy increases the likelihood that you'll stick with your walking program.
- Walking in pairs or with a group makes you less vulnerable to robbery or attack.

While there may be times when you want or need to walk alone, know that stepping out with a partner may provide extra protection for your heart and your health.

THE BEST DEFENSE AGAINST DIABETES

For some reason, the word *diabetes* doesn't seem to strike fear in the hearts of most Americans. But it should. About 16 million of us have some form of the disease, half of whom don't even know it.

That's a serious problem because diabetes is the fourth leading cause of death in this country. By the time we find out we have it, it has been wreaking havoc in our bodies for several years, gumming up blood vessels, damaging organs, and starving our bodies of energy. Left untreated, diabetes can set the stage for a host of health problems, including heart attack, stroke, kidney disease, blindness, impotence, and limb amputation.

Do I have your attention? Good! Because there's one more fact that you need to know: Even if you already have diabetes, you can control the disease and avoid many of its consequences. "If you come close to doing the right thing, there's no reason you shouldn't live out a normal life," says Gerald Bernstein, M.D., associate clin-ical professor of medicine at Albert Einstein College of Medicine of Yeshiva University in Bronx, New York. "To me, normal means age 90."

And what's the "right thing" that Dr. Bernstein alludes to? You can probably guess: Eat better and *exercise*.

THE EXERCISE-INSULIN CONNECTION

The combination of a healthy diet and regular physical activity can help you slim down—an important benefit since overweight is a major risk factor for diabetes. (By medical standards, you're considered overweight if you exceed your ideal weight by more than 20 percent.) For some, dietary changes alone—that is, switching to low-calorie, low-fat foods eaten as small but frequent meals throughout the day—may be enough to reduce both blood sugar and body weight.

That's not to suggest that you can do without physical activity. On the contrary, exercise fights diabetes in ways other than weight loss. Studies are just starting to show the preventive power of fitness.

The famed Nurses' Health Study, for example, found that women who worked up a sweat more than once a week reduced their risk of developing diabetes by 30 percent. And Chinese researchers determined that people with high blood sugar who engaged in moderate exercise (and made other lifestyle changes) were 40 percent less likely to develop full-blown diabetes. "It wasn't really vigorous exercise either," notes Richard Eastman, M.D., director of the diabetes division of the National Institute of Diabetes and Digestive and Kidney Diseases in Bethesda, Maryland. In other words, brisk walking would do the trick.

Quick Tip

Take a vitamin E supplement. One small study found that taking 800 IU of the vitamin a day may help control blood sugar. Do check with your doctor before beginning supplementation.

To what does exercise owe its protective effects? Besides helping you get rid of extra pounds, it actually increases the number of insulin receptors on your cells. Insulin helps blood sugar move into cells, where it needs to go. Otherwise, it just sloshes around in your bloodstream, gumming up the blood vessel walls like a little kid who has dunked his hands in a jar of honey.

If you've already been diagnosed with diabetes, regular exercise can help control the progression of the disease. People who take insulin may be able to reduce the amount of medication they need, as physical activity enables their bodies to use insulin more efficiently.

As a bonus, regular exercise can help keep your brain sharp. Scientists have observed that older people with diabetes sometimes have problems thinking clearly. In one study, physical activity appeared to stimulate just the type of brain activity that had become impaired. Exactly what it is about physical activity that revs up the brain hasn't been determined, and being a regular walker won't turn you into an Einstein. But some experts theorize that exercise-related brain activity could be part of the reason why some folks say they are able to solve sticky problems while they are ticking off minutes and miles on their treadmills.

For all of these reasons, exercise may be one of the best diabetes therapies around. And one of the best forms of exercise is walking.

MAKE WALKING WORK FOR YOU

Before you begin a walking program, check with your doctor, especially if you already have diabetes. Your doctor can tell you whether you need to take any special precautions when you work out.

According to Dr. Bernstein, you must exercise for at least 30 minutes, three times a week to enhance your body's use of insulin. If your goal is to lose weight, however, you would do

HE GOT OFF MEDICINE
WITH EXERCISE

WHEN RICHARD DALY STARTED his walking program in the early 1980s, he had the best of intentions. But he didn't account for the brutal winters of his native Michigan. Each year, when the temperature dropped in late fall, he'd pack away his walking shoes until the following spring. His winter workouts consisted primarily of reaching for Twinkies and other treats.

"Every spring, I'd lose 18 pounds. Every winter, I'd gain about 30," Richard says. "You don't need a math degree to figure out what was happening." Unfortunately, he failed to make the calculations. Over the years, his weight climbed to 244 pounds.

That wasn't the only problem. Richard noticed that he felt tired all the time, and he had an almost unquenchable thirst. One night in April 1996, he drank eight colas in less than an hour. "The next thing I knew, I was in the hospital," he recalls. "I was diagnosed with diabetes."

Richard spent 5 days in the hospital learning how to give himself insulin shots to control his blood sugar. He also attended diabetes-education classes, which taught him the importance of a healthy lifestyle. "Those classes inspired me to take control," he says.

On his first morning home from the hospital, Richard started a real walking program. "Every day, rain or snow, I walked for at least 35 minutes," he says. "When the weather was really bad, I walked at a local mall or on a treadmill I had bought. I also walked the 2 miles to work and home again."

Along with walking on a daily basis, Richard made some changes in his eating habits. He ditched those Twinkies and began buying whole foods such as fruits, vegetables, and whole-grain breads. He also started eating oatmeal and bran cereal, with skim milk and raspberries or blueberries for flavor.

"I'd eat three meals a day, then snack on fruit, cottage cheese, carrots, or a bagel," Richard says. "I'd indulge once in a while, but I'd make up for it at the next meal by choosing something light and healthful."

The payoff was enormous. Within a month of his release from the hospital, Richard was off insulin and taking only a small dose of another medication. Within 2 months, he was off all drugs. He began slimming down even faster. "I actually had to add food to my diet to keep from losing too much weight," he says. "Then I started strength training three times a week."

A year after leaving the hospital, Richard was down to a lean and fit 170 pounds. His waist was 10 inches smaller. Even better, his blood sugar dropped below 100 from its highest of 290.

"My doctor still shakes his head in amazement at what I've accomplished," Richard says. "I've never felt better!"

well to walk five to seven times each week. But of course, you will want to work up to that level slowly, especially if you have been sedentary. If you skip a day, don't try to make up for it by walking twice as fast or twice as far during your next workout. Vigorous exercise can actually cause blood sugar to rise, especially in people who have insulin deficiencies.

If you have diabetes, the timing of your walks can help regulate your blood sugar level. People with non-insulin-dependent (type 2) diabetes may benefit from exercising *before* meals, which helps control appetite and promote weight loss. For those with insulin-dependent (type 1) diabetes, it's best not to exercise on an empty stomach. These folks should plan their walks for about an hour or so after a meal, when blood sugar levels are at their highest.

There are times when exercise can send blood sugar plummeting. This reaction is most common among people who use insulin. Ask your doctor how much exercise you can tolerate before you need to replenish your store of carbohydrates. And carry a healthy snack—like a piece of fresh fruit, dried fruit, or some peanuts or trail mix—with you for just this purpose.

TAKE CARE OF THOSE TOOTSIES

If you've been diagnosed with diabetes, your doctor has likely told you the importance of taking care of your

---

Put Your Feet to the Test

PEOPLE WITH DIABETES NEED to be extra-vigilant about foot care. A common side effect of the disease is a loss of sensation (called diabetic neuropathy) that can allow minor injuries to turn into major problems.

"If you can't feel a blister, you may not treat it properly," explains Linda Haas, R.N., certified diabetes educator and president of the American Diabetes Association. "The wound can become infected, which may lead to ulcerations and even amputation."

There's a home test kit that can help you discover if your feet are at risk for injury. Offered by the Lower Extremity Amputation Prevention (LEAP) program free of charge, the kit contains a reusable monofilament (something like a fishing line) that you press against your foot. If you can't feel the monofilament, you may be losing sensation, and you should see your doctor.

In one study, the monofilament test was accurate 87 percent of the time. To order your kit, write to Free Filament, LEAP Program, 2070 Chain Bridge Road, Suite 450, Vienna, VA 22182.

In addition to using the monofilament test, you should continue to visually inspect your feet for blisters on a daily basis and especially after walking.

feet. Not only is it important, it's imperative. Any small blister or callus can turn into a life- or limb-threatening condition.

Unfortunately, people with diabetes often have difficulty feeling problems on their feet because of nerve damage associated with the condition. To complicate matters, they're also more prone to infection. Even the slightest irritation left undetected and untreated can lead to major complications.

So if you're launching a walking program, you want to do what you can to keep your feet healthy. Above all else, that means investing in comfortable socks and great-fitting walking shoes. Keep them free of rough spots and foreign particles to prevent irritation and injury.

Inspect your feet on a daily basis, and apply baby powder to keep them dry and to discourage the formation of blisters. If you do notice any irritation or injury, consult a physician or podiatrist immediately—meaning, within 24 hours.

If there's any good to be found in diabetes, it's that the condition can motivate you to lead a healthy lifestyle that includes walking regularly. And that means not only better health and greater longevity but also increased enjoyment of life.

CHAPTER 4

A SURPRISING RX FOR ARTHRITIS

For years experts believed that exercise might be bad for people with osteoarthritis. The most common form of arthritis, it's characterized by the gradual breakdown of cartilage, the spongy material that cushions and protects joints. Over time, this wearing away produces joint stiffness and pain.

Millions of Americans have osteoarthritis, and many of them are understandably reluctant to take the plunge into a program of regular exercise. After all, it's reasonable to assume that walking every day might set the stage for the condition or aggravate existing symptoms.

But now we know that's not the case. In fact, research suggests that walking can prevent or relieve arthritis symptoms. With every step, walking literally cleanses and feeds your foot, knee, and hip joints.

"Cartilage has no blood supply, so it depends on your movement to squeeze out waste products," explains physical therapist Marian Minor, Ph.D., associate professor at the University of Missouri School of Health-Related Professions in Columbia. "Between steps, your cartilage sponges up fresh nutrients from the fluid surrounding it."

Imagine that! Every time you walk, it's like taking your joints to the laundromat.

FITNESS FIGHTS WEAR AND TEAR

There is no evidence that exercise is the culprit behind arthritis. On the contrary, exercise may be the perfect salve for arthritic joints.

For one study, Stanford University researchers recruited 51 men and women who ran for about 3 hours a week. Some of the runners cut back on their workouts during the study, while the rest either maintained or increased their levels of exercise. When the researchers compared knee x-rays of the study participants taken over a 2-year period, they found no significant differences in the number of tiny, lumpy joint growths that are a telltale sign of osteoarthritis.

Study author James Fries, M.D., associate professor of medicine at Stanford University, says that in 25 years of working with runners who log a whopping 40 to 100 miles a week, he found that they're better off, much better off, than their couch-potato counterparts. "You'd expect the x-rays of runners to be worse than those of nonrunners," he says. "But they're not. They're exactly the same. Yet runners have *less* pain and disability than people who are sedentary."

And if running doesn't accelerate the deterioration of joints, walking certainly won't. That should warm you up to the idea of starting a walking program.

STRATEGIES FOR PAIN-FREE PERAMBULATION

If you have osteoarthritis and you haven't been exercising regularly, Dr. Minor recommends that you start out by walking at a moderate intensity 4 to 6 days a week. (Moderate intensity means that you should be able to sing a song as you go along, without becoming breathless.) Your goal is to accumulate at least 30 minutes of exercise a day, every day. Of course, you'll have to work up to that. In the beginning, you may want to break down those 30 minutes into 10-minute segments, spread over the course of a day.

Each time you walk for 30 minutes, spend the first 5 to 10 warming up with an easy stroll. Once you're warmed up, take time to stretch. (You can use the Dynamic Body Exercises described in chapter 38.) Stretching creates space in your joints, which eases discomfort. Then you're ready to pick up your stride until you reach a comfortable pace. As you near the end of your workout, slow your pace a bit to cool down. If you have time, stretch again.

EXTRA HELP FOR HURTING KNEES

If walking proves to be more of a pain than you can tolerate, don't pack up your walking shoes. Give your joints time to adjust. You may need to take an over-the-counter or prescription pain reliever to ease any discomfort. Ask your doctor to recommend a brand and dosage.

In addition, some of these strategies may help keep your walks pain-free.

Wrap your knees with adhesive tape. When British researchers tried this technique on 14 people with osteoarthritis in their knees, the participants reported a 25 percent decrease in pain. The researchers theorize that the tape may help properly align the kneecaps until people develop enough muscle strength to maintain alignment themselves. Have a physical therapist show you how to wrap your knees before trying it on your own. You need to use super-sticky adhesive tape, not an elastic bandage. The tape can be hard on your skin, so it isn't appropriate for everyday use. But you shouldn't need it forever anyway, once your kneecaps are tracking closer to where they should be.

Expand Your Exercise Horizons

FOR PEOPLE WITH ARTHRITIS, an activity such as yoga, tai chi, or water therapy can be a great complement to walking. The exercises gently move your joints through their full range of motion, so you don't feel stiff and sore when you walk.

Water therapy, in particular, has been popular as an arthritis treatment for many years. Exercising in water helps take some of the pressure off aching joints. In addition, the warmth of the water may have a relaxing effect.

In one study, British researchers had 35 people with arthritis move around in a tub of hot water for 30 minutes twice a week. After 4 weeks, the participants reported that their joints felt less stiff. And the effect lasted for months.

I visited a "walk in water" class at a local YMCA several years ago, and I had a chance to speak with the participants. Many said that they started their walking programs in the pool, then moved onto dry land as they got stronger and more flexible. But they still love their water workouts.

Experiment with magnets. Although there's no conclusive scientific evidence that magnets help reduce pain, many people, including lots of athletes, swear by them. Just remember, the kind that you stick on your refrigerator won't do the job. Therapeutic magnets, which are available in many drugstores and department stores, are specially designed and have greater strength than ordinary household magnets.

Pick up some walking sticks. Using two walking sticks, held like cross-country ski poles, can take pressure off your knee joints. As a bonus, doing this increases your calorie burn and helps build your upper-body strength. (For more information on walking with poles, see pages 94–95.)

Unload the excess baggage. Because of your body's mechanics, every extra pound of body weight feels like another 8 to 10 pounds to your hips, knees, and ankles. So lose 5 pounds of fat, and you gain 50 pounds' worth of pain relief.

Sign up for a class. The Arthritis Foundation offers an Arthritis Self-Help course that, among other things, shows participants how to exercise properly. In one study, people who enrolled in the class reported an 18 percent reduction in their pain. The course costs between $25 and $35, which covers six 2-hour sessions. For more information, contact the Arthritis Foundation office nearest you (the telephone number is listed in the blue pages of your phone directory).

Quick Tip

If you're concerned that a long workout may take you too far from home—and that you'll be hurting too much for the return trip—choose a short, circular route around your neighborhood. You can still walk for 30 minutes, but you'll never be more than a block away from home.

CHAPTER 5

GOOD NEWS FOR BAD BACKS

Time was when an aching back could lay you up for days, if not weeks. But not anymore. While a day or two of bed rest might be part of your pain-relief prescription, most doctors want you to get on your feet as soon as you can. And often they recommend walking to help you do it.

In fact, walking is so good for bad backs that it has become an integral part of the treatment programs at most back-pain clinics. It strengthens the muscles that support good posture and triggers the release of chemicals called endorphins, which subdue pain and encourage relaxation. What's more, it conditions and tones your entire body.

People who have consistent walking programs tend to recover faster from back injuries than those who don't. Plus, walking helps them keep their weight in check, making them less likely to develop back pain in the first place. So if you're not yet a walker, you have another reason to become one.

Of course, even the fittest among us are vulnerable to back injury—whether from lifting a heavy object improperly or straining to retrieve a book from a too high shelf, from playing 36 holes of golf or coping with a stressful situation that sends back muscles into painful spasms. One year I missed a *Prevention* Walker's Rally after spreading 2 yards of mulch in my garden and straining my back so badly that I could barely move the next day. While everyone else was walking, I was laid up in the hospital.

That wasn't the first time my back brought me to my knees—nor was it the last. But over the years, I've learned that with proper care I can beat the pain. And walking has everything to do with my recovery.

GIVE YOUR BACK A BREAK

When you hurt your back, the first decision you must make is whether or not you need medical attention. Get yourself to your doctor or the nearest hospital emergency room if you experience any of the following:

- Your pain is so intense that you can't move around at all.
- You lose control of your bladder or bowels.
- Your pain is accompanied by fever, nausea or vomiting, sweating, or discomfort when urinating.
- Your pain is associated with some kind of trauma, such as a car accident.
- Your leg or foot feels numb or tingly.
- Your pain radiates to your buttock, thigh, or leg.

If you have none of the symptoms above, then you're probably dealing with garden-variety back muscle spasms. In that case, you're a good candidate for self-care.

Depending on the severity of your pain, you may want to just stay in bed until you feel better. Rest is a good way to start off your recovery—as long as you limit it to a day or two, as I mentioned earlier.

Lie down with your knees bent and your back flat. Put a pillow or towel under your knees if you need to. This keeps you from straining your back muscles. To pass the time, you can read, watch television, listen to music, or talk on the telephone. Whatever you do, avoid sitting in a chair, because that position is extremely hard on your back muscles. You may even want to eat standing up.

And remember: Rest means just that. If your dry cleaning is waiting to be picked up or your dog needs to go for a walk, ask someone else to do it. Refrain from lifting heavy objects. Being a martyr is noble, but it won't help your back heal.

While you're on the mend, you can take an over-the-counter anti-inflammatory, such as aspirin or ibuprofen, to help relieve pain and reduce any swelling. You can also apply ice to the sore spot. Wrap an ice pack in a towel, hold it against the affected area for 20 minutes, then take it off for 40 minutes before repeating.

Most doctors recommend using ice for the first 48 hours, then switching to heat. A warm to comfortably hot shower may do the trick.

BEGIN WALKING WITH BABY STEPS

During those first couple of days after you hurt your back, you can afford to put your walking program on hold. Such a short break won't cause you to lose muscle tone or aerobic conditioning. At the same time, don't expect to walk a 5-K as soon as your ache quiets down.

Once you're ready to start moving

Quick Tip

When a back injury puts you to bed for a day or two, take care whenever you get up. Support yourself by rolling onto your side and pushing yourself up with your arms. This minimizes strain on your back muscles.

TURN YOUR BACK ON PAIN

I'VE BEEN DEALING WITH back pain ever since I was a teenager. My first episode was a simple case of muscle strain, brought on by carrying heavy dish-laden trays in my job as a waitress. As I got older, things became a bit more complicated.

In the early 1980s, I lifted an air conditioner from a bedroom window. Feeling like Supermom, I was amazed at my strength. The next day, while out for a walk, I bent over to tie my shoelaces. That did it. I couldn't stand up straight for several days. I had two young children, a dog, and a cat to care for. My not being able to walk was a hardship for all of us.

In the mid-1990s, I was laying mulch and weeding my garden when I realized that, once again, I couldn't stand up straight. My mother-in-law found me pulling myself along on my elbows, trying to get to the house and a phone. I was in so much pain just trying to get up off the floor that I had to be taken to the hospital on a stretcher. I was there for 5 days, which meant that I had to orchestrate the Santa Fe Walker's Rally from my hospital bed.

A couple of years later, I was moving some heavy furniture, and again my back acted up. It happened just before a trip to Jamaica, a vacation that I had really looked forward to. I went anyway, despite the pain, using a cane to walk to the ocean's edge. There, I finally found relief, floating in the water under the blazing tropical sun.

These days, what amazes me most is not that I keep having bouts of back pain, but that I can get over them so completely. I've had magnetic resonance imaging (MRI) showing damaged disks in my spine, leading my doctors to recommend surgery. (Current research indicates that many people have bulging disks *without* pain, which suggests that disk problems aren't the sole source of back trouble.) I've had severe pain running down the side of my hip and buttock. I've had moments when I feared I'd never again walk without hurting. But now I know that those agonizing episodes don't indicate permanent damage. Now I know that I can be completely pain-free.

When I'm having a back crisis, I try anything and everything to help myself through it. I've gotten relief from chiropractic adjustments and acupuncture. I've slept on a magnetic mattress pad, which seemed to work wonders. I've taken painkillers and muscle relaxants when necessary. I do yogalike stretches in the morning—well, not every morning, but whenever I feel at all stiff. I even had special orthotics made to correct a foot problem that caused me to change my walking gait.

And after every flare-up of pain, I get right back into walking as soon as I'm able. Every step seems especially delicious when I've experienced agony just going from the bedroom to the bathroom. To walk with a brisk gait—standing tall, swinging my arms, feeling the wind rush by, letting the fresh air fill my lungs—that's the essence of feeling alive to me.

Back pain may get you down from time to time. Don't let it keep you down.—*M.S.*

around again, you need to spend a few days just getting used to being on your feet. Your first goal is to sit or stand comfortably for 20 minutes. At that point, you're ready to take a short stroll.

Put on the most comfortable and supportive walking shoes that you own. Then choose a route that's easy and on level ground. (Hills make you lean forward, which puts strain on your lower back.) Walk around the outside of your house, out to your mailbox, or to the end of your block and back. Just keep it short.

Some people find that they have trouble standing completely straight when they're first getting back on their feet. If this happens to you, don't be too concerned. You'll likely be able to straighten up as you walk. Walking boosts your circulation, which may relax your back muscles.

On the other hand, if you feel tension building in your upper back as you walk, it may be because you're subconsciously trying to protect your lower back. In that case, consider wearing a lumbar support. It's a stretchy belt that wraps around your waist to relieve stress on your lower-back muscles.

As your back gets better, you may be able to take several short walks over the course of a day, with long periods of rest in between. This helps keep your back limber without straining it.

When you feel ready, you want to gradually increase the duration of your walks. You can expect to feel some pain initially. The question is, how much is too much? It's really a matter of trial and error. You may hurt for a few minutes, then limber up as you go along and feel fine the rest of the way. That's okay. But if your pain starts while you're walking and lingers for hours afterward, you're probably pushing yourself too hard too soon. You need to go a little easier your next time out.

At this stage, it's a good idea to stick with walking routes that continually take you past your door. That way, when the pain doesn't go away, you can head for home and lie down. The last thing you want to do now is reinjure yourself.

What if you can't walk without pain, but you can't sit still? Consider moving your walking workout to a heated pool at a gym or the local YMCA. The water supports your weight, minimizing demands on your back muscles. And the heat soothes any soreness.

Another option is to pedal a stationary cycle. Just be sure to sit in a position that feels comfortable for you.

POSTURE MAKES PERFECT

While walking is an important part of any back-care program, it can actually aggravate back pain if it's done with poor posture. Be careful not to hang your head, hunch over, or lean forward, all of which can push your body out of alignment.

People who are swaybacked (a condition called lordosis) or who have a flat lumbar curve in the lower back are especially vulnerable to back trouble. They may feel more pain, not less, when they take long walks because of the pressure put on the spine.

If you want a strong, healthy back that can support you for miles and miles, practicing good posture is essential. We'll discuss body position and movement in greater detail in part 8. But for now, these tips can help you keep your back pain-free while walking.

- Think tall. That old image of a wire attached to the top of your head, pulling it upward, works well.

- Keep your shoulders relaxed rather than throwing them back military-style.

- Imagine that your pelvic bone is tilting up toward your navel, creating a slight pelvic tilt.

- Allow your spine to move from side to side as you step from one foot to the other. Don't stiffen your lower back.

- Use short strides, not long ones. The farther you reach forward, the greater the impact on your spine.

STOP PAIN BY STRETCHING

Besides practicing good posture, one of the easiest ways to prevent back pain while walking is by stretching. When your muscles are tight, they can actually constrict blood vessels and impede circulation. And without good circulation, you're more vulnerable to muscle spasms and back injury.

In part 8 of this book, you'll learn stretching exercises that target muscles in your calves, shins, thighs, buttocks, and lower back—all of which support your every step. The following stretches are designed specifically for people with chronic back pain. Do 10 repetitions of each stretch every day. If your pain worsens, discontinue the exercises and see your doctor.

PARTIAL SITUP. Lie on your back with your knees bent and your feet flat on the floor. Position your hands behind your head. Lift your shoulders off the floor, hold for 5 seconds, and lower.

PELVIC LIFT. Lie on your back with your knees bent and your hands behind your head. Lift your pelvis off the floor. Extend your right leg so that it's at a 45-degree angle to the floor. Be sure to keep your midback on the floor. Hold for 5 seconds, then lower. Repeat with your left leg.

TABLE POSE. Get down on all fours. Lift your left arm and right leg so that they're in line with your spine. Hold for 5 seconds, then lower. Repeat with your right arm and left leg.

CHAPTER **6**

A STEP AHEAD OF STRESS

What makes you want to walk?

When we posed that question to members of a walking club a few years back, we expected to get answers like "to lose weight" and "to get in shape." But we were delighted by the number of people who commented on walking's emotional benefits, in particular, its ability to relieve stress.

Aerobic exercise of any kind has the power to calm jangled nerves and improve bad moods. And when it's done every day, it can enhance self-esteem and combat depression. Indeed, research has shown that a brisk 20- to 30-minute walk can have the same calming effect as a mild tranquilizer.

Why is walking—or any physical activity, for that matter—such a potent stress reducer? Many experts cite its ability to trigger the release of endorphins, potent brain chemicals that relieve pain and stimulate relaxation. Simply put, the higher your level of endorphins, the greater your sense of calm and well-being. No wonder walking can make you feel so good.

STROLL TOWARD RELAXATION

To reap the stress-busting benefits of walking, you don't need to pound the pavement or push yourself really hard. In fact, at least one study has shown that a comfortable stroll can be just as effective as a brisk walk. The key is to use your mind while you're moving your body.

For the study, researchers recruited 135 volunteers and divided them into five groups. Three of the groups took up walking—one at a brisk pace, the other two at a low-intensity pace. The fourth group practiced mindful exercise, which is based on the principles and movements of tai chi. The fifth group served as controls—meaning, they were asked not to change anything about their lives.

In addition, one of the groups assigned to walk at a low-intensity pace learned a simple meditation technique to practice while exercising. All they had to do was pay attention to their footsteps, counting "one, two, one, two" and visualizing each number in

Why Walking Works

THE VERDICT IS IN: Walking is a top-notch stress-buster. That's what folks told us when we posted an informal survey about stress on the Web.

Whenever you're feeling too overwhelmed to work out, take a moment to read through these real-life testimonials on the benefits of walking. I bet you'll be instantly inspired to slip on your walking shoes and head out.

"I've learned that stress is energy. I have to deal with it physically, and walking is the best approach for me. I use a treadmill about 95 percent of the time, and nothing feels better than hopping on, working up a good sweat, and talking to myself. Sometimes I drive to a nearby small town, go for a walk, and have a nice long chat with myself. Before I know it, I've covered 3 or 4 miles, and I've gotten to know myself better!"

"Walking definitely calms me down. It helps me connect with the natural world in all the different seasons. I usually walk at night, after dinner. All the tensions of the day melt away, plus I like moving after I've eaten a big meal. Walking allows me to let my mind wander. My thoughts become more random, and I notice how the moonlight colors a tree. Sometimes I window-shop downtown. At bedtime, I often write about what I feel or see on my evening stroll."

"I commute 2 hours to and from work each day. I am so stressed by the time I get home, the first thing I do is grab an apple or pretzels and my walking shoes. I can usually convince my dad to come with me. All I need is a good, brisk 35- to 40-minute walk, and I feel great again."

"Walking at a fast pace really seems to relieve my stress. The first few minutes feel stressful. But after my body gets going, I feel a burst of energy, and the tension falls away. It's worth the effort!"

"Walking seems to make everything about me better. I'm much more calm and in control than when I started my program 7 months ago. Other people have noticed the changes in my personality as well as the physical changes!"

"Walking is more than a healthy habit. It is mentally therapeutic. Walking helped me through a traumatic divorce and through writer's block. Every day, it improves my state of mind."

"Being outdoors for 30 to 60 minutes, walking, clears my head and lets me focus on things that are really important rather than on the petty things that have annoyed me during the day. Walking frees pent-up energy that I've had to hold back at work. And I feel terrific when I'm done!"

"Walking is the only way I know to calm my mind. I have a good life, but with a home, three daughters, and a husband with multiple sclerosis, it sometimes gets tough to keep my head clear. I've tried other types of exercise, but this is what works for me!"

"When I first started walking, it was slow going. But eventually, I could do 2 miles in 30 minutes. Between exercising daily and making some changes in my diet, I have lowered my cholesterol by 65 points, reduced my blood pressure, and lost 45 pounds. I know that this has saved my life. . . ."

their minds as they went along. If they found their thoughts drifting to other matters, they simply said, "Oh, well," and resumed counting their footsteps.

The combination of meditating and low-intensity walking produced dramatic results, according to cardiologist James Rippe, M.D., who has written several books on the health benefits of walking.

During the 16 weeks of the study, the people who meditated while they walked reported decreases in anxiety, along with fewer negative and more positive feelings about themselves. In fact, the benefits were equal to those associated with brisk walking. Even better, they were evident after just one session, and they lasted for the duration of the study.

By comparison, the people who walked at a low-intensity pace but didn't meditate showed no improvements until the 14th week, and even then, the effects weren't as significant. On the other hand, the people who engaged in mindful exercise experienced results that were very similar to those reported by the walking-plus-meditation group, suggesting that other mental techniques could yield stress-busting benefits.

According to Dr. Rippe, one of the most impressive findings from this research is the immediacy with which walking can relieve stress. The study also provided good news for those who aren't able to engage in high-intensity exercise: They can capitalize on walking's destressing effects just by practicing meditation or another mental technique during their strolls. And for those who find relaxation exercises tedious or boring, the study proved that a brisk walk can do just as good a job of short-circuiting stress.

KEEP WALKING . . . NO MATTER WHAT

By participating in a regular walking program, you can offset the long-term health implications of stress—and there are many. Research has linked stress to a host of physical ills, from back pain and stomach upset to high blood pressure and heart disease.

Of course, when you're under pressure, whatever its source, going for a walk may be the last thing on your mind. You're not the only one who feels that way. When researchers tracked the exercise habits of 82 women for 8 weeks, they found that the women worked out less often during weeks that were filled with stressful events. At those times, exercise was "just one more thing to do."

When walking starts to feel like a stress *producer* instead of a stress reducer, making some adjustments in your workout can help. Here's what to do.

Adopt the right attitude. Tell yourself that taking a walk will help you accomplish more on your "to do" list. Exercise makes you feel better and think more clearly, so you become more productive.

Aim for the A.M. Walking first thing in the morning, before anyone else is out and about, gives you an opportunity to focus on yourself, says Suki Munsell, Ph.D., director of the Dynamic Health and Fitness Institute in Corte Madera, California. "When my day looks hectic, with lots of decisions ahead, an early-morning walk brings answers and clarity," she notes.

Seek out new scenery. Choose a walking route that takes you down quiet streets or through a beautiful park. The more appealing your surroundings, the calmer you'll feel. Walking on busy streets, in unsafe neighborhoods, or after dark only adds to your stress.

Slow your pace. Pushing yourself to go faster or farther only adds to your stress. During tense times, keep your walks leisurely.

IN STEP WITH
MELISSA AND MERLE KNAPP

WALKING KEEPS THEM WORRY-FREE

WHEN A PERSONAL CRISIS turned their world upside down, Melissa and Merle Knapp took up walking to help them cope. It turned out to be their salvation.

"My husband and I weren't always walkers," Melissa explains. "He felt that walking was no fun and not worth his time."

That was before financial disaster struck. Suddenly, the Knapps found themselves faced with the possibility of losing their home—something they had worked so long and hard for. The strain became almost too much to bear.

"Anyone who has endured an emotional trauma knows that it can be devastating to the body as well as to the mind," Melissa says. "The stress felt like tentacles squeezing my heart. I had constant headaches. And my husband lost his appetite."

Then one morning, Merle asked Melissa if she wanted to go for a walk, explaining that he had to do something to release his tension. Melissa agreed, suggesting that they go to a park that was just far enough from home to seem new to them.

Once there, they found a 2.8-mile loop with a breathtaking view of Washington's Puget Sound. The path was beautiful, with a varied terrain.

"That very first walk performed magic," Melissa recalls. "I don't know whether it was the soothing colors of nature or the rhythm of walking, but I do know that we felt better, even though our problems hadn't changed." They decided to walk the trail every day.

Besides relieving their tension and taking their minds off their financial situation, walking gave the Knapps an opportunity to connect with the world around them. They came to recognize other regular walkers on the path, and they seemed like kindred spirits. "It felt good to smile and say, 'How are you today?'" Melissa says. "We hadn't done much smiling for a while."

These days, the Knapps are happy to report that their finances have improved, and their stress is under control. "And we still walk every day," Melissa says.

Break up your workout. If your schedule is so busy that you can't find one chunk of time for your walk, take advantage of spare minutes throughout the day. Head outdoors for a stroll before or after lunch or between appointments. Even 5 minutes of walking is enough to recharge your batteries.

TURN YOUR BACK ON TENSION

While maintaining a regular walking program can counteract the physical effects of stress, you don't have to wait until your nerves are in knots to let walking work its magic. Here are some ways that you can incorporate walking into your daily routine—and derail stress before it gets the best of you.

Opt for a 10-minute trot. At work, pass up the break-time doughnut and coffee and go for a walk instead. Research has shown that walking briskly can give you a bigger energy boost than eating a sugary snack. If you're able to go outside, the fresh air and sunshine can clear out those mental cobwebs and brighten your mood. If you can't get out, cruise the hallways of your workplace or climb a flight of stairs. You'll arrive back in your work area refreshed and ready to concentrate.

Take the show on the road. Nervous about a meeting with your boss, a coworker, or a client? Suggest making it a walk-and-talk session. Walking can relieve your tension and anxiety, so you're more at ease. And you're not face-to-face with the other person, so you avoid the constant eye contact that can be stressful in itself, especially if the topic of your conversation is upsetting or unpleasant.

Walk away from a dilemma. Sometimes you're faced with a knotty problem that can leave you feeling knotted up as well. That's when thinking less and moving more can be a real asset. Drop what you're doing and take a stress-free stroll, letting your mind wander as you do. By the time you return to face the problem at hand, the answer that you were racking your brain for may seem obvious.

Use your feet to run errands. It's an all-too-familiar scenario: You hop in your car early Saturday morning and head for the bank or the drugstore, hoping to beat the long lines. Instead, you spend a half-hour circling your destination in search of a parking space— and by the time you find one, you're fit to be tied. Next time, try leaving your car at home and doing your errands on foot. You'll avoid the aggravation of clogged streets and parking lots, and you may even save time.

Park prudently. Cars pulling in and out, shopping carts rolling about, and people rushing in every direction—a parking lot seems like an accident waiting to happen. If you must drive in one, do what you can to keep yourself out of the fray. Park as far from other cars and the entrance as you can. If you can safely do so, walk around the perimeter of the parking lot before heading inside. Then you can face the crowds without feeling frazzled.

CHAPTER 7

THE PIONEERING PROS OF WALKING

When a salesman is trying to sell you a new car, you're more likely to believe what he's saying if he drives the same make that he's pitching to you. After all, who wants to buy a Chevy from a guy who tools around town in a Toyota?

Likewise, when your doctor tells you that you need to exercise, you're more inclined to heed his advice if he's following it himself. These days, he probably is.

Now more than ever, physicians and other health professionals are practicing what they prescribe, especially in terms of exercise. And often their activity of choice is walking.

Over the years, I've been fortunate enough to meet many of these health practitioners and hear their inspiring stories. Now I'd like to share a few of those stories with you. Read them and see if you aren't just a bit more convinced that walking can do wonders for your health and well-being.

HELPING A CITY SLIM DOWN

Herman Frankel, M.D., founder of the Portland Health Institute in Portland, Oregon, "discovered" walking some 25 years ago. Back then, he was a busy pediatrician with an especially stressful schedule in a hospital nursery.

At the end of one particularly rough day, Dr. Frankel decided to take a walk. He felt so much better that he vowed to make walking part of his routine. Every morning before he went to the hospital, he walked for 45 minutes. Within a year—without making any other changes in his lifestyle—he lost 15 pounds.

The experience piqued Dr. Frankel's interest in the effects of low-intensity exercise on body composition. He had always believed that only heart-pounding, sweat-producing workouts could provide any benefit. Now he had firsthand evidence that walking at a moderate pace could burn fat.

Five years later, he would put his theory to the test in a very public arena.

He and the staff of a Portland-based television show launched a program called "Fight against Fat." Six female volunteers, chosen from hundreds, went on a weight-reduction plan that emphasized a low-fat diet and regular walking. The women appeared on the TV show once a month to share their experiences with viewers. In turn, viewers could write to the show for self-help packets that included graphs to chart their own daily walks. By the time the program ended, all six women—and hundreds of the people who had watched their progress—lost weight.

"Fight against Fat" was considered such a success that it won the United States Secretary of Health and Human Services Award for Excellence in Community Health Promotion and Disease Prevention. As for Dr. Frankel, he continued his personal regimen of walking regularly and eating healthfully. The last time I spoke with him, his weight was holding steady, just 5 pounds more than his weight at age 26, when he was a national-level volleyball player.

FITNESS IS HIS PRESCRIPTION

When I interviewed Neil Block, M.D., the family physician from Orangeburg, New York, told me that he had taken up walking to ease his back pain and maintain his weight. He figured that the regular workouts would help fend off heart disease, too, a healthy bonus. He managed to work up to a speedy 12-minute-per-mile pace, exercising for 40 to 60 minutes, three or four times a week.

Because of his busy schedule, Dr. Block fit in his walks whenever he could—even if it was just before bedtime. Some people say that late-night workouts overstimulate them and keep them awake. But Dr. Block found that he not only slept very well but also fell asleep faster.

In his practice, Dr. Block advised almost all of his patients to walk, even one gentleman with emphysema who had been relying on others to drive him everywhere. Eventually, this man was able to walk to stores and to the library on his own. "You can't grow new air sacs (in your lungs), but you can make sure that your diaphragm and other muscles that support respiration are strong," Dr. Block explained.

To help his patients follow his walking prescription, Dr. Block sometimes walked with them—around a nearby lake in the summer, at a local mall or health club in the winter. "Walking is part of a healthy lifestyle," he observed. "My business card says, 'Family Practice—Lifestyle Changes.' Correct habits create health. Walking creates health."

SETTING AN EXAMPLE THROUGH EXERCISE

You might say that Ross Stryker, D.D.S., was an orthodontist with a mission. He had seen so many out-of-shape adolescents in his Missouri dental practice that he planned an 8-day walk to celebrate his personal commitment to fitness (and to have some fun). On November 8, 1998, he set out on a 250-mile journey along the Katy Trail, which runs from Clinton to St. Charles, Missouri.

The Katy Trail is a converted railroad bed, perhaps the longest and the flattest in the country. Dr. Stryker arranged to stay in bed-and-breakfasts along the way. His wife, Mary, sent care packages to the innkeepers, so he could walk relatively unencumbered. "Although I was trying to make a statement about the importance of exercise, such as walking, mostly I just enjoyed myself!" he says.

During his walk, Dr. Stryker wore a bright orange vest with flashing lights.

Hunting season had arrived, and lots of hunters were out early in the morning. "I would start walking at 6:30 A.M. in total darkness," he recalls. "Slowly, the sun would come up—first a small hint of light, then a glow in the clouds on the horizon. It was the perfect time of day for me, and a great time to spot wildlife on the move."

A dedicated 50-mile-a-week walker, Dr. Stryker displays mementos from his Katy Trail trek in his office to generate interest among his patients. He hopes that they'll be motivated to take up walking and make it a lifetime activity.

For more information on the Katy Trail, you can call the Missouri Department of Natural Resources. The toll-free number is available through 800 directory assistance.

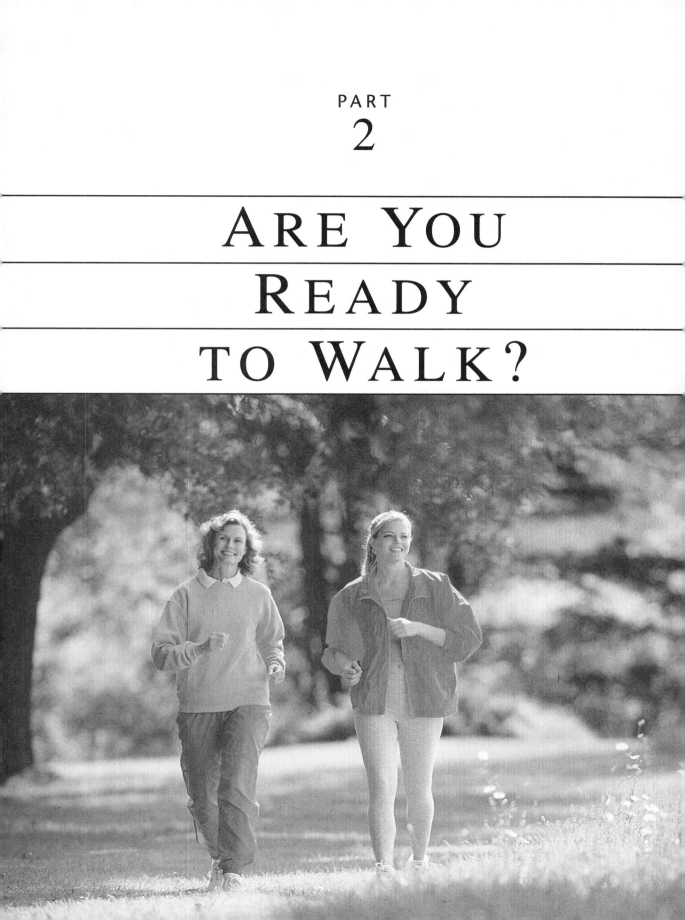

ARE YOU
READY
TO WALK?

CHAPTER **8**

SHOES: THE FACTS ABOUT FIT

If you are going to be a walker, you need one very important piece of equipment. Well, actually two: a pair of good walking shoes. They will be your best walking buddies—for 6 months to a year, anyway. So choose them with care. And when you find that perfect-fitting style, stay with it.

There is a shoe out there for every-body—or, more precisely, for every foot. You just need to know a few facts so that you can get the right fit. An expensive shoe that's the wrong size or shape won't serve you as well as a moderately priced shoe that ac-commodates the contours of your foot, bending where your foot bends and giving your toes ample wiggle room.

If you're like me, once you find a great pair of walking shoes and you discover what real comfort feels like, you may not want to subject your feet to anything else. These days, I wear heels maybe once or twice a year. All of my work shoes are designed for maximum comfort.

Actually, finding a pair of shoes that is comfortable as well as stylish has gotten a lot easier in the past year or two. More and more footwear manu-facturers are realizing that many con-sumers—women, in particular—will no longer sacrifice comfort and foot health for fashion.

So how do you find the perfect match for your feet? Let's get down to some shoe-buying basics.

LEARN THE LINGO

Before you go shoe shopping, take a few minutes to familiarize yourself with the following terms. The sales-person you deal with should under-stand this terminology, too. Believe me, it can make a world of difference in the quality and fit of the shoe you take home.

EVA: A shock-absorbing foam that's soft, light, and flexible, EVA is found in the soles of many good walking shoes. It compresses on long walks but springs back after a day of rest. Some shoes have dual-density EVA, which simply means that the material has two different compression rates.

Heel-strike: This is the point where your heel makes contact with the ground if you're using proper walking technique. You need to consider heel-strike when selecting a shoe, because your heel takes a pounding with each step—and that may happen thousands of times when you're out walking. Look for a shoe that provides stability, with a slightly beveled heel and plenty of cushioning.

Last: This is the mold on which a shoe is formed. The last—and, therefore, the bottom of the shoe—can be straight, semi-curved, or curved. For a good fit, make sure that the shape of your shoe matches the shape of your foot.

Medial support: Sounds fancy, but don't let the term confuse you. It simply means arch support.

Overpronation: This means that your ankle rolls inward when you're walking, which puts way too much pressure on your arch and nearby ligaments and tissues. Over time, overpronation can lead to heel pain and other problems. A good shoe supports and stabilizes your ankle so that it doesn't roll inward.

Sockliner: Every good shoe has one of these inserts, which cushions and protects your foot from the shoe's "guts." Without a sockliner, you would feel stitching or little lumps of glue when you walk.

Toebox: This is the part of a shoe that encases your piggies. It should be roomy, both in width and in height. And it should somewhat resemble the toe-end of your foot. No more pointy toes.

SIZE MATTERS— BUT THAT'S NOT ALL

To ensure that your shoes fit well, you need to learn a bit more about your feet. What I'm going to explain now may surprise even some shoe salespeople. But that's okay. Armed with this information, you can help yourself.

The Great Shoe Debate

FOR AS LONG AS I've been writing about walking—more than 12 years now—there has been some controversy over whether running shoes are acceptable for walkers. Remember, running shoes came first. Before 1986, you couldn't even buy walking shoes. Stores carried "comfort shoes" or canvas shoes with rubber soles, what baby boomers know as sneakers.

Walking shoes have come a long way since then. They've gotten a lot better. At first, they looked like nurses' shoes or orthopedic shoes. Now they're engineered with just as much technical know-how as running shoes, and they have lots of product testing behind them.

Running requires far more cushioning and stability than walking, but that doesn't mean you can't wear running shoes for walking. The fit is what counts.

Running shoes tend to be flashier than walking shoes in design and color. And they're usually more plentiful than walking shoes, so you have more brands and styles to choose from. On the downside, running shoes tend to have thicker soles than walking shoes. They'll make you taller, but they'll also make you more prone to tripping. So be careful!

The point I like to make is that walking shoes are specifically designed to help propel you through the heel-toe motion of the proper walking technique. While runners land flat-footed, walkers land on their heels. So the heels of walking shoes are often beveled to increase stability. And that stability is equally important when you roll your foot forward and push off with your toe.

Personally, I recommend walking shoes for serious walkers. I've worn both types of shoes, and except when I have sore feet from overtraining, I really prefer walking shoes.

But if you can't find a walking shoe that fits, by all means, try a running shoe. But go to a store where a knowledgeable salesperson can assist you in selecting a brand and style.

If you're a racewalker, you will have to search until you find a walking shoe that is flexible enough to meet the demands of your sport. Try grabbing the shoe at both ends and bending it. If it doesn't flex easily and you want to go really fast, then shop around for another brand. Some racewalkers prefer running flats, a type of running shoe that is very flexible and has a very thin sole.

For a shoe to fit properly, it has to match your foot type—that is, its flexibility—and curvature. You can easily assess these characteristics on your own in a few simple steps.

Flexibility refers to whether your foot is rigid, neutral, or flexible. To find out, do the following:

1. Sit in a chair, with one foot resting across the opposite knee. Measure the elevated foot from the heel to the tip of the longest toe (usually your big toe) by holding a ruler against the sole. Be careful not to press on the ruler, as that will skew the measurement. Write down the number, then do the same with your other foot.

2. Lay the ruler on the floor and stand on it with one foot. Measure from the heel to the tip of the longest toe. Write down the number, then switch feet and repeat.

3. Determine your foot type based on these descriptions.

• If the measurements taken when seated and when standing are about the same, your feet are rigid.

• If the measurements differ by about ⅛ inch, your feet are neutral.

• If the measurements differ by about ¼ inch, your feet are flexible.

Now that you know your foot type, you're ready to determine your foot *curvature*—that is, whether your foot is straight, semi-curved, or curved. Here's what to do.

1. Sit in a chair, with a piece of paper on the floor in front of you.

2. Put your left foot on the paper so that it's pointed straight ahead. Lift your toes upward to stabilize the shape of your foot.

3. Either by yourself or with someone's help, trace the outline of your foot on the paper.

4. Pick up the paper and fold the outline of your foot in half, bringing the heel up over the toe. Then fold the heel-end back down, so the heel is visible.

5. Compare your outline to the three below. Select the one that matches yours.

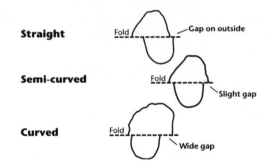

THE RIGHT SHOE FOR YOUR TYPE

Armed with your foot type and curvature, you're ready to do some shoe shopping. Give the information to a knowledgeable shoe salesperson, and he should be able to recommend just the right shoe for your foot. Or you can do the matching-up yourself.

To find a shoe that has the proper curvature, or last, cut out the foot outline that you traced and take it with you when you go shopping. Hold the outline against the bottom of each shoe that you like. You'll be able to tell which shoe is going to fit your foot comfortably. (You'll also be able to check to see whether a shoe is long enough and wide enough for you.)

To make sure that a shoe is appropriate for your foot type, look for the following features.

Rigid: Rigid feet are very stiff and tend to have high arches. They're stable, but they don't handle impact well. For this foot type, you need a shoe that is very well-cushioned, because your arch is not going to flex and provide much cushioning for you. You also need an upper that has a lot of volume, or space, to accommodate your high instep. You may have tight Achilles tendons (at the backs of your ankles), so you'll want your shoe to have a bit of a heel. Most rigid feet are curved, so a shoe with a curved last will fit better.

Neutral: This foot type is the easiest to fit. A neutral foot has normal mobility, which means it lengthens or spreads about half a shoe size when bearing weight (when you stand up, for example). It absorbs shock well and has good stability. You can get by with less support, although a little extra won't hurt either. For a neutral foot, a shoe with a semi-curved last should fit well.

Flexible: Of the three foot types, flexible feet are the most complicated and most difficult to fit. They absorb shock well because they are so mobile, but that mobility tends to make them unstable. They change one whole size when bearing weight. They also tend to be flat and have a low instep. If you have flexible feet, look for shoes with low volume—meaning, little distance from the laces to the soles. You don't need a lot of cushioning, but you do need a lot of support. You also need a low heel, which will do a better job of stabilizing your foot. You may feel most comfortable in a shoe with a straight last, as your foot tends to flatten and straighten out when you walk.

Quick Tip

Ask other walkers or runners where they buy their shoes. Runners often know the best stores. Their feet take a lot of abuse, so if they want to run for long, they need really great-fitting shoes.

BRANDS THAT MEASURE UP

As I said before, there is a shoe out there for every foot. So don't settle for less than a perfect fit. Expect to pay between $55 and $85 for a good-quality, good-fitting pair of walking shoes. If the price seems high, consider the cost of an appointment with a podiatrist or orthopedist. You're worth the expense, and so are your shoes.

Go to a store that carries a wide variety of brands and styles, so you have the best chance of finding the right shoes for your feet. Once you've selected a pair, you can go to

Shoe-Shopping Strategies

IN THE MARKET FOR a new pair of walking shoes? Follow these shopping guidelines, and you're guaranteed to find the perfect match for your feet.

- Shop at the end of the day, when your feet are largest.

- Wear your walking socks. Some styles are really thick, and you may need to go a half-size larger with your shoes to accommodate them.

- Get your feet measured if possible. As you get older, your feet tend to flatten out. Also, they swell when you walk, and they need room as they go through the walking motion. All of these factors may affect your shoe size. So be kind to your feet and buy big-enough shoes. Footwear that's too small can cause all kinds of problems. A few years ago, a study by the American Podiatric Medical Association revealed that most foot problems among women result from wearing too small shoes.

- When you try on shoes, make sure that there's plenty of room—at least a finger's width—beyond the end of your longest toe (usually the big toe). Measure when you're standing up rather than sitting down. When I do walking clinics, I often have people check each other's shoes to see if everyone has enough room up front. Most folks don't.

- Spend some time in the shoes you are trying on. Walk around the store. If you're in a mall, ask if you can take a few laps around the inside corridors. The shoes should feel great. In addition, a skilled shoe salesperson should be able to watch you walk and assess whether the shoes are giving you enough support.

other stores to see if you can get the same brand and style for less. Keep your eyes peeled for sales and discounts.

I'm not going to tell you my favorite brands and styles, because they may not be the best for *your* feet. But I can tell you a little about some of the major manufacturers.

New Balance is considered to be a leader among manufacturers of footwear. They make lots of sizes and widths to fit all kinds of feet. They also have styles for every foot type.

Easy Spirit is for women only. Their shoes are best for rigid or neutral feet, with styles that tend to be a bit softer and more flexible than those of other brands.

Saucony walking shoes are known for their ability to keep people from overpronating. They have a special insert that acts like a soft orthotic, which provides great arch support. (An orthotic is a device that holds your foot in a biomechanically correct position.)

Other big names in the walking-shoe industry include Rykä, Etonic, Naturalsport, Nike, Reebok, Adidas, Wilson, Brooks, Rockport, and Asics. Some of these brands, like Nike, are available only in B widths. Other brands are available in a variety of widths, but stores don't bother to stock them. If a store doesn't carry the style that you want in the width that will fit you best, don't hesitate to order a pair. You still get to try them on when they come in. Don't let an overeager salesperson try to persuade you otherwise.

So, wise consumer, go forth with your new shoe knowledge and shop. Once you've gotten your feet into some serious walking shoes, you're ready to begin a serious walking program.

Maggie's Log

IF THE SHOE DOESN'T FIT, DON'T WEAR IT

MANY YEARS AGO, I met a man named Charlie Smith. A Virginia resident, Charlie was a *professional* shoe fitter. He even used the initials P.S.F. after his name.

Charlie was on a kind of crusade to make the public aware that a lot of the foot problems were simply the result of wearing too small shoes. He had helped hundreds of people—many of them literally hobbled—to get better by fitting them properly. He told me that as far as he could tell, most podiatrists don't even look at shoes. They just look at feet.

Ten years after I spoke with Charlie and wrote about his cause in *Prevention* magazine, the American Podiatric Medical Association produced a study that cited too small shoes as the cause of most foot problems, especially among women. The study verified just about everything that Charlie had told me. I don't know whether he was around to hear the news, but if he was, I bet he was thinking, "It's about time!"

Long before that study came out, I experienced the wisdom of Charlie's advice firsthand. Well, maybe secondhand. My sister Paula had always worn a size 6 shoe. She told me that she was having a lot of pain in her knees and she couldn't understand why. I noticed that the black Reeboks she was wearing (the shoe of choice among New York City walkers at the time) were way too small by Charlie's standards. Her big toe was poking way out in front. When I pointed that out, she said, "But my feet don't hurt."

I told her that didn't surprise me. Charlie explained it by saying that sometimes the foot contracts to keep the toes from banging against the front of the shoe. When that happens, the discomfort may be felt in the ankle, the calf, or even the knee or hip.

I took my sister to a shoe store to try on larger sizes, starting with a 6½. By the time we found a shoe that allowed ½ inch of wiggle room beyond her longest toe, she was wearing a size 8!

I convinced Paula to buy that pair. Was it the first time she ever listened to her little sister? You bet! And within a few days, her knee pain was gone.—*M.S.*

CHAPTER **9**

GETTING ALL GEARED UP

Besides a good pair of walking shoes, what else might you need to dedicate yourself to a regular walking program? Actually, not much. Of course, you can always find stuff to buy—more gear, more gadgets—and some of it is lots of fun. But if you're a beginning walker, most of what you need you probably already own. And what you don't own you should be able to buy relatively inexpensively.

EXTRA PROTECTION FOR YOUR SOLES

When I was a teenager, socks were completely uncool. My friends and I wouldn't have been caught dead in them. Now I can't fathom wearing my walking shoes without them.

Next to your shoes, your socks are your most important piece of walking gear. A lousy pair of socks can make a great pair of shoes feel absolutely awful. On the other hand, an okay pair of shoes can feel a lot more tolerable when they're worn over a fantastic pair of socks.

The sock market has exploded in the past 10 years, beginning with a brand called Thorlo. As far as I know, Thorlo was the first company to realize that since human feet lose their fatty padding as they get older, folks would appreciate a little cushioning in their socks. Thorlo walking socks are thick and luxurious, with extra padding in the ball and heel. You feel as if you're walking on a cloud, provided your walking shoes are big enough to accommodate all that fluff. Otherwise, you just feel cramped.

Like any good athletic sock, Thorlo walking socks are synthetic. They wick away sweat from your feet, dry quickly, and retain their shape, softness, and resiliency. As a rule, socks made from synthetic fabrics are best. A little cotton is okay, but all-cotton socks get soggy, lose their shape and softness, and wear through faster.

These days, Thorlo has lots of company in the walking-sock category. Many stores carry dizzying displays of socks in all brands, colors, sizes, and styles. Some are thick; some are thin. Some support your arch; others pad your bunion. Many footwear manufacturers offer socks bearing the same brand names as their shoes.

My suggestion is to try a variety of brands and styles until you find one that you really like. Then buy a whole bunch, so you always have a clean pair waiting for you. Nothing feels better than slipping on fresh, soft, padded socks first thing in the morning.

When you're going for a long walk—say, more than 4 miles—you may want to carry an extra pair of socks with you. Then if your feet get hot or wet, just change socks. You'll feel totally refreshed and revitalized.

IN CLOTHING, COMFORT BEATS FASHION

Now that you have your feet properly attired, what about the rest of you? Let the temperature outside be your guide when you're deciding what to wear.

For warm-weather walking, you need a pair of comfortable shorts that won't ride up the inside of your legs. I prefer stretch shorts, like those worn for cycling. On top, a T-shirt is fine. I like the kinds that are cotton-polyester blends. They're softer than 100 percent cotton shirts, and they don't shrink.

Everyone owns T-shirts these days. As you become more involved in walking and attend events or races, you'll get more Ts than you know what to do with. I had 20 of mine made into a beautiful memory quilt that hangs in my bedroom.

For cooler weather, sweatpants or stretch pants are great. Choose a fabric that breathes and wicks away sweat, such as Lycra spandex. Make sure that your pants allow for a full range of motion. Avoid those that are too tight around the waist. You need to breathe. On top, you may want a long-sleeved T-shirt and a lightweight jacket, depending on the temperature. (If you're heading out in really cold weather, check out the tips in chapter 13.)

A HEADS-UP FOR GOOD POSTURE

To complete your walking outfit, you'll want to have a hat, a visor, or a pair of sunglasses. It's not just to protect your eyes from the glare of the sun or to save your skin from wrinkles— though those are nice bonuses. When the sun is shining brightly, many people tilt their heads forward to avoid a glare directly in their eyes. Walking in that position creates extra strain in the neck and upper back.

What's more, looking down at the ground is more likely to leave you feeling down. When you wear a hat, a visor, or sunglasses, you keep your chin up, literally and figuratively.

I own several visors from a company called DesignWear. Sold under the brand name Scrunchvisors, they have an ultralight, supersoft foam brim that rolls up and can easily fit in a pocket or fanny pack. They come equipped with a Velcro closure, so they can be adjusted to your head size and hairstyle. Sometimes I wear the closure over my hair, sometimes under—depending on how hot or windy it is. The visors have sewn-in sweatbands and are completely washable.

DesignWear also makes scrunchable baseball caps. For more information or to place an order, write to DesignWear at 8955 South Ridgeline Boulevard, Suite 100, Littleton, CO 80129.

THE PERFECT PACK FOR PERAMBULATING

When you're walking, you want to be able to swing your arms freely. For this reason, you really shouldn't carry anything, not even a water bottle or a cassette player. But you may have a few items—your house or car keys, money, medication, or tissues—that you want to keep with you. That's when a fanny pack can come in handy.

Hanging loosely around your waist, a fanny pack is wonderful. I own about five, and I always wear one when I'm traveling to hold my money and my glasses. It helps me avoid what I call purse-strap posture, when I hunch one of my shoulders to hang on to my purse strap.

Some fanny packs are designed to accommodate water bottles. In fact, L. L. Bean makes one that holds two bottles.

When fanny packs first became popular, they were worn behind the body, over the fanny (hence their name). I still prefer that placement when I'm walking briskly. But when I'm shopping or traveling, I wear the pack on the front of my body. It's more secure and more accessible in that position.

If you're going for a walk and you don't need to carry more than a key and your ID (which you should *always* have with you), you might be able to make do with a wrist wallet. Some styles are made from terry cloth, with Velcro closures that secure around your wrist. These wallets are useful if your workout wear doesn't have any pockets.

KEEPING THE PACE WITH YOUR TIMEPIECE

You may not think of your watch as walking gear. But it can become an indispensable part of your workout—and not just for showing you when it's time to turn around and head for home. Using your watch, you can determine your pace—that is, how fast you cover a mile.

If you're walking on a measured course, you can time each mile of your workouts and use that to track improvements in your speed and strength. Plus, as you get to know how it feels to walk at a certain pace—to cover a mile in a certain number of minutes—you'll be able to judge fairly accurately how far you've gone, based on how much time you've spent walking.

If you cover a mile in 20 minutes, you're moving at a pace of 3 miles per hour. That's a comfortable speed for anyone who is in good health and exercises a couple of times a week.

If you walk a mile in 15 minutes, you have a pace of 4 miles per hour. That's considered brisk. Most people need to work up to a 15-minute mile. Going that fast feels somewhat challenging and exhilarating. You're breathing noticeably faster, but you're most likely able to carry on a conversation. You just can't sing an aria.

If you cover a mile in 12 minutes, you're cruising at a pace of 5 miles per hour. At that speed, walking starts to become inefficient from a biomechanical standpoint. It just feels very hard. In fact, running would be easier if you can tolerate the pounding on your joints. If not, you may have to use some sort of special technique, such as racewalking, to keep up.

As you might imagine, increasing your pace—going from a 20-minute mile to a 15-minute mile, for example—takes effort. If you slack off, you'll have to work to regain your strength and endurance. At one time, I regularly did 10- and 11-minute miles,

listening to music of a certain tempo to keep my legs moving fast enough. I could slack off so easily without realizing it!

At those speeds, you will make great strides in fitness. But going fast isn't necessary if your main goal is better health. These days, I usually do between 15- and 20-minute miles, and I'm very comfortable at that pace.

But who knows? I may decide to train for a 5-K and start pushing myself harder . . . for the fun of it!

THE PROS AND CONS OF PEDOMETERS

Personally, I put pedometers in the "frill gear" category. But lots of people like these gadgets. They work by counting the number of steps you take, ticking off a step every time you move your leg. Then they multiply that figure by the length of your stride to get your mileage.

The problem is, your stride changes when you encounter hills. You may lengthen your stride going uphill and shorten it on the way down. But a pedometer can't make that same adjustment. So if a group of people went walking, with everyone wearing the same type of pedometer, they may end up with different mileages for the same route. Hopefully, each pedometer would be within 1/4 mile of the correct mileage.

If I had to use a pedometer, I'd choose one that is totally mechanical.

Treadmills: The Ultimate Walking Gear

A TREADMILL MIGHT BE a worthy addition to your walking program. While you don't want to walk inside all the time, using a treadmill may be the only way for you to exercise with the consistency necessary to achieve the health and fitness benefits you desire.

Treadmills range in price from $500 to $5,000. How much you spend depends on how many functions and features you want. For $500, you can get a decent-quality machine with some basic gadgetry. More expensive models usually come loaded with an array of electronic extras, plus they have great stability and durability. They're able to meet the demands of even the most punishing walkers.

I'm not going to recommend specific models here because brands and styles change so rapidly. I would advise against buying a treadmill that doesn't have a motor. Though these machines tend to be cheaper and much quieter than motorized models, most people who try them just don't like the effort required to start them and keep them going.

The kind of motorized treadmill that will serve you best depends on your age, your fitness level, and your goals. Keep these guidelines in mind when you're shopping around.

- Basic functions and features: good deck stability (the deck is the part of the machine that you walk on), comfortable adjustments for starting and stopping, smooth speed changes, easy-to-use programs, at least one interval-training program to vary your routine, heart rate monitor

- Needs for people age 50 and over: quick and easy manual modes for getting started; gradual and gentle starting, stopping, and pace changes; simple electronics; large, easy-to-read screen displays

- Needs for people under age 50: quick start and program override functions, more variety in programs, customizable programs, wide range of speed and incline changes

Personally, I enjoy walking on a treadmill the most when I have a full-length mirror in front of me. I find watching my form far more productive than trying to keep up with a TV program. But it's fun to listen to music, too; sometimes I even sing along. When my voice starts to falter a little, I know I'm getting into my target heart rate range.

For first-timers, walking on a treadmill can take some getting used to. To help you start out smoothly and safely, use this step-by-step approach suggested by Mark Bricklin, former editor-in-chief of *Prevention* magazine and an avid 'miller.

That way, I wouldn't have to worry about replacing batteries. Besides, mechanical models are easy to read, and they don't have all those buttons and functions that basically just confuse me.

With any pedometer, the tricky part is setting it to your stride length. Here's the best way I know.

1. Plant your feet on the side rails and grip the handrails. To avoid motor strain, don't step on the belt until the speed reaches about 1 mile per hour (unless your directions tell you otherwise).

2. Keep a light grip on the handrails for a while. Many beginners feel unsteady or disoriented with the belt moving beneath their feet. Once you're comfortable, let your arms swing naturally at your sides.

3. Slowly increase the speed until you're walking at a comfortable, no-hurry pace—like you would when you're at the mall.

4. After a few minutes, with the incline set flat, increase the speed a tad. Keep swinging those arms. You've left the mall, and now you're walking in the park.

5. Position yourself so that the control panel is within easy reach. Never let yourself drift backward; some people have been flipped off the back of these machines.

6. Listen to your feet: Are they going *poom, poom, poom*? If so, you're landing flatfooted. That's a no-no. Try landing on your heel and rolling your foot forward. Less noise means better form.

7. Check where your feet are pointing. If they're aiming outward, try to position them so that they're straight ahead. Why walk in two directions at once?

8. If you're in front of a mirror, watch your head. If not, have someone else watch and give you feedback. Are you bobbing up and down, like a bicycle with square wheels? If so, your stride is probably too long. Shorten it and aim for a smooth, gliding walk.

9. Make sure that you're not leaning forward from your waist. It only strains your back.

10. Maintain a pace that leaves you feeling invigorated—not panting or aching or sweating a lot.

11. If your treadmill has an incline function, use it to add oomph to your workout in short bursts—anywhere from 30 seconds to 3 minutes. When walking becomes laborious or you start losing good form, return to a flat position. Or you can slow your pace to adjust to the incline, just as you do when you're walking outdoors.

12. When you're ready to stop, ease up your pace and walk slowly for a few minutes. Then step onto the side rails and turn off the treadmill. When you get off, you're going to feel a little dizzy. It's natural. Grab a drink of water and allow yourself a few minutes to regain your "shore legs."

1. Mark off a level 20-foot path.

2. Walk that distance, counting the number of steps you take. Give yourself room for a walking start, so you're using a relaxed, normal gait by the time you reach the marked-off path.

3. Divide the distance (20 feet) by

Low-Tech Pulse-Checking

KEEPING TABS ON YOUR heart rate is easy—and you don't need a heart monitor to do it. A watch with a second hand works just as well.

First, you need to find your pulse. Place the index and middle fingers of one hand against the carotid artery, located at the front of your neck. Press just hard enough that you can pick up the sensation of your pulse. Count the beats for 10 seconds, timing yourself with your watch.

If you've been walking really fast, keep moving slowly while you check your pulse. Stopping suddenly can cause your heart to skip beats, which can be very stressful for anyone with a heart problem.

Once you've counted the number of beats, compare it with the 10-second heart-rate range for your age group. In the chart below, all of the ranges have been calculated to reflect 70 to 80 percent of your maximum heart rate. Memorize your 10-second range, so you'll know what to aim for when you're working out.

Keep in mind that 70 to 80 percent of your maximum heart rate is a high-intensity workout. If you're within your target range, that's great, but you can still get a good workout at a lower heart rate.

As a general rule, you should be able to carry on a conversation while you're walking, even if you have to huff and puff a little to do it. If you're breathless, you're going too fast for your fitness level.

Age	Exercising Heart-Rate Range	Range for a 10-Second Count
35–39	130–148	22–25
40–44	126–144	21–24
45–49	123–140	21–23
50–54	119–136	20–23
55–59	116–132	19–22
60–64	112–128	19–21
65+	109–124	18–21

the number of steps to determine your stride length. For example, if you took 10 steps, divide 20 by 10 for a stride length of 2 feet.

4. Repeat this process three times. Then use those results to calculate an average stride length.

5. Set your pedometer to that stride length.

FOR THE HARDWORKING HEART . . .

With all the technological advances now taking place, the day will come when you can buy endless varieties of devices to track not only your pace but also your heart rate, your respiration rate, and maybe even your blood sugar level while you walk. But unless you have a specific health problem that requires you to constantly monitor your vital signs, such features certainly aren't necessary.

These high-tech gadgets might be helpful for someone who is recovering from a heart attack or who has a heart problem, for example. But if you're a beginning walker who is otherwise healthy, simple pulse-taking techniques should provide all the monitoring you need.

That said, if you'd like to bump your fitness level up a notch or two, or if you want to burn more calories while you walk, a heart monitor can be a great tool to help you along. You can set the monitor to beep as soon as you drop below your target heart rate range, alerting you to pick up your pace. Likewise, if you exceed the high end of your range, the monitor will beep to let you know that you're pushing too hard, which only tires you out more quickly.

Some heart monitors fit on a finger; others are strapped around the chest or fitted into a special bra. Basic models begin at $70 and are available in sporting goods/fitness equipment stores, health clubs, and some department stores.

CHAPTER **10**

FINDING THE BEST PLACE AND THE BEST TIME

We've already addressed the "what" of walking: what you need and what you don't. So let's move on to the next most-pressing questions: when and where?

The simple answer is, you can go for a walk any time you want, anywhere you want. That's what makes walking such a great activity: its convenience.

But if you're just starting a walking program and you're trying to make it a habit, then you need to do a little more planning. You can't rely on a spur-of-the-moment urge to take a walk, unless you naturally get those urges every day.

LOCATION MAKES A DIFFERENCE

When you're deciding where to do your walking, the best place is the one that you find most attractive *and* most convenient. These two qualities are inseparable.

You may know a wonderful trail through a beautiful park across town. But if driving there takes you 20 minutes, are you willing to make that trip every day or several days a week? Or perhaps there's a path close to your workplace, but it's littered with trash and so close to traffic that you'd be inhaling exhaust fumes instead of fresh air. Do you really want to give up your afternoon coffee and doughnut for that—even if walking on your break time would be a healthier and more reliable pick-me-up than snacking?

If you can walk out your front door to a sidewalk that takes you safely around your neighborhood, I think that's great. But if you live in an area like I do—with no sidewalks and cars going around blind curves at 50 miles an hour—you'll have to get creative.

I walk around the border of my property, around a neighboring cornfield, and around adjacent football and soccer fields. I just keep going until I have spent 20 to 30 minutes walking briskly. I do go out on the country roads sometimes, but I'm very careful to stay alert for cars.

If you can't walk close to home, or you simply prefer not to, consider these venues instead.

Municipal parks: You may find that the best place to walk is in a nearby municipal park. These usually provide bathroom facilities and water fountains. And many have mileage markers, so you can monitor your distance and check your pace. Just try to avoid parks where walkers and cyclists share the same paths. Mixed-use trails can be very hazardous, especially for walkers who are talking or wearing headphones and don't hear cyclists speeding up behind them. A collision can cause serious injury or worse to everyone involved.

County and state parks: Check out other local natural resources, too—some may be closer than you think. For example, many county- and state-run parks have great walking and hiking trails. Call your local parks and recreation department to request maps. Also find out whether the trails are considered safe for solitary walkers or you're better off with a partner. In general, if lots of people use the trails, there's safety in numbers. If a park is all but deserted, you might want to think twice before going there on your own.

Tracks: High school and college tracks are great when you want to work on your walking technique, when you are trying to improve your speed, or when you just want to get in your miles and go home. If you're on a track for the first time, you may want to see how long it takes you to do a mile—that's four laps—at a comfortable pace. Also, check whether your local YMCA or health club has an indoor track, ideal for days when you don't want to walk outside. If the track is sloped, be sure to change directions often to avoid straining one leg.

Malls: More walkers are taking advantage of the temperature-controlled, traffic-free environment at their local malls. Often these people are "regulars" who are looking for a little camaraderie as well as exercise. As a bonus, they have ready access to bathrooms, water fountains, telephones, and even food. Many malls open their doors early to walkers who want to get in their workouts before the stores open and shoppers arrive. To find out whether your local mall has such a policy, just call the administrative office.

CHANGE COURSE? IT'S YOUR CHOICE

Should you walk the same route every day, or should you switch routes

Quick Tip

If you're just beginning a walking program, choose a route that takes you in a short loop, so you're never too far from your house or car if you get tired. I know people who started out by walking to the end of their driveways and back, over and over, so they could build up their endurance. (Many of these folks had heart or respiratory conditions or were recovering from surgery; they really needed to go slowly.)

from one day to the next? That's really up to you. My advice is to do what keeps you interested. It makes sticking with a walking program a whole lot easier.

Some walkers prefer to stay on one route. They like to watch the changes from day to day or from season to season. Or they look forward to inter-acting with certain people or animals that they meet along the way. Or they ap-preciate the famil-iarity of the route because they can relax and let their minds drift, perhaps to mull over problems and come up with solutions.

Other walkers need to change routes to keep themselves stimulated and en-tertained. I'm always looking for new, convenient walking paths. On the weekends, I like to walk farther and longer, so I've come up with a whole list of possibilities: on the Delaware Canal towpath, through university ath-letic fields, along an 8-mile converted railroad bed. Sometimes I hike the paths of a nearby nature center.

For me, it's the excitement of won-dering what's around the next bend that makes walking so pleasurable. I get a kick out of discovering new paths. So think about your own likes and interests, then spend some time finding routes that suit your personal preferences.

TIMING IS EVERYTHING

Once you've settled on where you want to walk, you need to decide when. Most experts will tell you that if you want to be consistent, your best bet is to walk first thing in the morning. By getting it out of the way early, there's less chance of your workout being sidelined by other obligations that arise over the course of a day.

If this works for you, fantastic. Per-sonally, I find that an early-morning walk makes a great start to a produc-tive day. By the time I finish my workout, my energy level is up, and I feel relaxed and energized. Plus, if you get out the door early enough, you'll beat the early-morning commuters. That means there's less traffic and less car exhaust to deal with.

If you're not a morning person, don't force yourself to become one. You need to find a time to walk that suits your schedule and your lifestyle. As with choosing the right place, choosing the right time can make committing to a walking program much easier.

For you, lunch may be the perfect time to walk, especially if you work outside your home and you have young children or other responsibilities that keep you from getting out of the house early in the morning or after dinner. For working parents, a lunch-hour

The Mall Calls

FOR A SAFE, COMFORTABLE workout, no place beats the local mall. Like walking outdoors, walking at the mall is free. What's more, it burns extra calories.

In a study of 60 women and men who were timed with a stopwatch when they walked, researchers found that the women naturally walked faster in a mall than on a track. And the faster you move, the more calories you burn.

"Where you walk makes a difference," says study author Richard S. Cimbalo, Ph.D., professor of psychology at Daemen College in Amherst, New York. "Something about the mall—possibly that it's a familiar and safe place—may help women get a better workout."

But that's not the only advantage to walking in a mall. Here are some of the other reasons why you may want to take your exercise indoors.

You're too hot. When the temperature rises above 75°F, your heart has to work twice as hard to deliver blood not only to the muscles you're using but also to your skin to keep it cool. "Anybody who's at risk for heart disease shouldn't be exercising outdoors in those conditions," advises Bryant Stamford, Ph.D., professor of exercise physiology at the University of Louisville in Kentucky.

You're too cold. Cold presents its own problems, which may be complicated by icy or snowy sidewalks. Often, it's safer to drive than it is to walk. So drive yourself to the mall and walk there.

You're sneezing. In most malls, the air is filtered as well as cool and dry. So if you have allergies, you won't be bothered by pollen or dust as you would outdoors.

You like company. A growing number of malls sponsor organized walking programs, which may include group walks, special incentives, and even speakers and health fairs. To find out whether your local mall has such a program, call or stop by the administrative office.

You have trouble staying motivated. Mall-walkers are a fiercely devoted bunch. "If you stop showing up, they're going to call to find out where you are," says Sara Donovan, founder of WalkSport America, a Minnesota company that manages mall-walking programs such as the one at Mall of America.

You want security. A mall offers a smooth, even walking surface that's well-lit and well-populated. You can feel safe there. That's one of the big reasons why mall walking is becoming so popular, even in areas where the climate is mild.

You're short on cash. Walking in a mall is a lot less expensive than joining a health club or buying a treadmill.

workout can seem like a mini-vacation. It provides a great opportunity for you to destress.

One word of advice, though: Try to walk first and eat lunch afterward. That way, you can travel at a brisk pace without aggravating your digestive system. And you may find that you're less hungry by the time you get back— a bonus for those who are trying to lose weight. If you're starving by lunchtime, eat a small snack, maybe a piece of fruit, to tide you over until you've finished your workout.

If you and your spouse like to exercise together, you may prefer to take after-dinner walks. They're a wonderful opportunity for the two of you to spend time together and to discuss the day's events away from the dishes, the telephone, and the TV. I know many couples who describe walking as the balm that soothed a raw nerve in their relationships. Just plan on going at a leisurely pace. When you walk after a meal, your body is putting all of its energy into digesting food. If you walk too fast, you may end up with cramps or indigestion.

Depending on your schedule, you may have to do your walking just before bedtime. In my area, there's a group called the MoonWalkers that meets at 8 or 9 o'clock at night, after their children are in bed and they've taken care of their other obligations. They revel in the quiet of the evening and the safety of being in a group. They've been walking together for years.

Keep in mind that walking at night isn't for everyone. While some say that it's the perfect nightcap, others find it too stimulating. Safety is an issue, too. Experiment to find out whether it's right for you.

GET INTO THE GREAT OUTDOORS

JUNE 29, 1999—ANOTHER spectacular day in my home state of Pennsylvania! We've had a most glorious spring, with lots of warm, dry days and cool nights. The conditions are near-perfect for walking.

I've taken advantage of the mild weather to explore some new walking routes. One is on the grounds of Lehigh University in Bethlehem. I love it because it is secluded and has high weeds on all sides, so I can let my dog, Petey, off his leash. He gets to play while I walk, but he can't leave the trail because the weeds are well over his head.

Another is the towpath that runs along the Delaware Canal. Sometimes my husband and I go there in the evenings. We've spotted dozens of rabbits, a blue heron, bullfrogs, turtles, and even beavers. Wildflowers grow there in abundance. On the other side of the towpath is the Delaware River, the longest, continuously free-flowing river east of the Mississippi.

Both of these walking routes are fairly close by, within a 15-minute drive of my house. I just never took advantage of them before. They're really marvelous natural resources.

Think about the area where you live. Are there any parks that you've never visited? Any paths that you've never set foot on? Any mountains or lakes that you've never explored? Make a point of going to these places and rediscovering the splendor of the great outdoors.

GET IT IN WRITING

Choosing a time to walk is relatively easy. Sticking with it may be more of a challenge. These days, so many of us have such tightly packed schedules that we wonder how we can possibly add even one more item to our "to do" lists.

If you keep an appointment book, make walking one of your appointments. Or write a note on each day of your wall calendar: "Walk at 7:30 A.M." That way, you have a constant reminder of your commitment to exercising and getting fit.

And each time you go walking, don't forget to mark it off in your appointment book or on your calendar. It shows you not only that you scheduled your workout but also that you actually followed through.

If you're a more spontaneous type who squeezes in walks whenever you can, then write them down after the fact. That's what I do. I may walk in the morning one day, on my lunch hour the next, and on my treadmill the night after that. I keep track of my workouts in my daily planner. And if I notice that I'm skipping days, then I'll start scheduling my walks. That helps me remember how much better I feel when I exercise regularly. You can use the walking log on pages 237–40 as a record.

Think, too, about the activities you enjoy. Have you pedaled a bicycle lately? Or paddled a kayak or canoe? Activities like these are wonderful complements to walking—and they can bring new energy and pleasure to your interaction with nature.

Just this past Saturday, my husband and I joined some friends for an 8-mile canoe trip down the Delaware River. And on Sunday, we went on a 12-mile bike ride sponsored by the Friends of the Delaware Canal, stopping for a short history lecture and ice cream along the way. I've become so enamored with the canal and the river, which are only 3 miles from my home, that I even bought my own kayak. In the canal, there's very little current, so I can paddle down and back on my own.

Also at this time of year, I love touring public gardens, those big, complicated ones that I can't imagine growing in my backyard. I've purchased a couple of guides to gardens that are within an hour's drive of my house. Plus, I always check the Sunday newspaper because it often has a feature story about a garden that I've yet to visit. If I go there, I may take along my bicycle or my kayak and look for new trails, streams, or lakes along the way. I've gotten in the habit of looking everywhere for places to walk, ride, or paddle.

The older I get, the more precious each season becomes. I can't wait to get out and revel in the sights, the sounds, and the smells that surround me. I'm so grateful that I'm fit enough to enjoy all of it. And I have so much left to explore!

No matter what time of year you're reading this, take the opportunity to head outdoors and see what your corner of the world has to offer. It doesn't matter whether you're wearing walking shoes or cross-country skis, whether you're sitting on a bicycle or in a kayak. Just remember: *Carpe diem*—seize the day!—*M.S.*

CHAPTER 11

PAIRING UP FOR EXERCISE

To reap all of the physical and mental benefits of walking, you need to do it every day—or almost every day—for the rest of your life. That's a tall order, even for a dedicated walker like yourself. I know I have moments when I'm short on time, energy, or motivation, and I need a little extra nudge to put on my walking shoes. Of course, once I'm out walking, I feel great.

The fact is, as much as I enjoy the solitude of my walks, sometimes I need a buddy to get me going. Many walkers would agree. For us, teaming up with a partner keeps our motivation from sliding and our walking programs on track, even when we're convinced that we have other "more important" things to do.

Of course, you can undertake a walking program on your own if you want. But studies show that few people stick with a fitness routine of any kind unless they have a partner. We humans need social support. Even when we join walking groups, we usually do it with someone else.

Anyone can become your walking partner: a family member, a friend, a coworker, a neighbor, even a dog. Be open to whomever happens to come your way. You may not find one person who's willing to walk with you every day. But you can likely recruit two or three people, each of whom can keep you company at various times throughout the week.

To maintain your motivation, you and your most frequent walking partner should share the same agenda. Maybe both of you want to lose weight, improve your fitness level, or work off stress. Or maybe you enjoy bird-watching or window-shopping while you walk. Whatever your mutual goals or pleasures, they'll keep the two of you coming together for regular, consistent workouts.

STEPPING OUT WITH YOUR SPOUSE

When you're looking for a walking partner, you may want to start your search close to home. That way, each time you exercise, you have an opportunity to strengthen the relationships that are most important in your life, those that contribute to your sense of happiness and well-being.

If you're married, you may want to ask your spouse to walk with you. Some marriage counselors believe that walking together can improve the way that you and your significant other relate to one another. So you not only add miles to your exercise log, you also bring harmony into your home. Susan Johnson, Ed.D., director of continuing education at the Cooper Clinic for Aerobics Research in Dallas, refers to this phenomenon as sweat bonding.

How can walking strengthen marital ties? For one thing, it removes you from all the duties and distractions that take the fun and romance out of a marriage—things like paying bills and doing household chores. For another, when done outside in the sunshine, it raises levels of a feel-good brain chem-

IN STEP WITH
MARY NAGLE

GETTING FIT
ON THE BUDDY SYSTEM

LONG BEFORE WALKING BECAME America's favorite fitness activity, Mary Nagle was pounding the highways and byways around her country home. She tries to walk at least once every day.

What keeps the Zionsville, Pennsylvania, resident on such an ambitious schedule? "I always find a partner," she says. "My friends in the neighborhood are just as enthusiastic about walking, and we call each other the night before to set up a time and place to meet."

Mary first took up walking as a way to control her weight. But among her female companions, she soon found herself using her workouts to blow off steam. "Sometimes I just want to vent, and my women friends understand that," she says. "I'd never feel comfortable letting go like that in front of their husbands."

Over time, Mary's walks have become what she describes as a positive addiction. "If I can't go walking, for whatever reason, I find myself getting moody and anxious," she explains.

These days, Mary meets at least one of her walking buddies at 7:30 every morning—rain, sleet, or snow. "Actually, I love walking in the snow because I can always dress warm for cold weather," she says. "Staying cool is a bit more difficult, but I've figured out a way to do it. When the weather gets hot, I wrap ice cubes in paper towels and tuck them inside my bra."

For Mary, having a walking partner is key to sticking with her walking program. "I feel bored or lazy when I'm alone," she says. "But when I make a commitment and I know that Carolyn, Sarita, Ann, or Peggy is waiting for me, I'm always there."

ical called serotonin. Serotonin helps adjust your frame of mind, so you're better able to address any issues that you and your spouse might want to discuss.

Walking also stimulates the release of the mood-boosting compounds known as endorphins. You feel more optimistic, more upbeat—and if you're with your spouse, you may associate the good feelings with him or her. You may see the other person in a more positive light, which can help smooth over any anger or disenchantment with your relationship.

In fact, many couples say that they have an easier time communicating with each other when they're walking. They're more comfortable opening up to their partners because they're side-by-side rather than face-to-face. And because walking can release tension, they're more likely to feel calm while discussing sensitive or divisive issues.

If you and your spouse use your walks to reminisce about your relationship, the two of you may remember what brought you together in the first place. That's important, because as one marriage counselor points out, spouses today tend to think of themselves as married "singles" rather than as married couples. By walking together, you and your spouse may see each other as "we," not as "you and me."

CONNECTING WITH KIDS

If you and your spouse can't always walk together, ask your child or grandchild to join you instead. Kids can be great walking partners, provided you choose a destination that's of interest to them.

Don't just suggest going for a walk; there's a good chance that you'll be ignored. Instead, offer it as a trip to a video arcade, an ice cream parlor, a school playground, or a park. Most youngsters will gladly go the distance if the end goal seems enticing enough. But most important, you'll have lots of fun—and get plenty of exercise—en route.

If you're walking with very young children, remember: You're the one with the ability to adapt. Slow down to match the child's pace. Walk too fast or too far, and the child may not want to go with you again.

And don't view your stroll as an opportunity to lecture to a captive audience. Just smile and relax. Let the kids do the talking, and enjoy their company.

WALKING ON THE JOB

Outside your family, you may be able to find a walking partner or two among your coworkers. The workplace can be fertile ground for walkers. Everyone gets breaks, and using that time to go walking can do more to de-stress and reenergize you than coffee and a doughnut.

Try to block out at least part of your lunch hour for walking, too. You definitely don't want to skip your lunch completely, but save 10 to 15 minutes for a walk. It can be a great stress reliever. (Ideally, you should eat after

THE POWER OF TWO

I MUST HAVE WRITTEN it a hundred times in the past 10 or so years: If you have trouble sticking with a walking program, find a partner. To be honest, though, I never followed that advice myself. It just seemed too hard to find somebody who could walk when I wanted to. And if I was having a hard time motivating myself, I'd have to work twice as hard to motivate someone else.

My attitude began to change several months ago, when I met Connie. She told me that she really wanted to lose weight, and I toyed with the idea of training her to racewalk. When I mentioned it to her, she seemed really interested. We agreed to meet at 7 o'clock, two mornings a week, at a walking path halfway between our homes. We even set a date to start training.

Connie runs her own business. She's organized and committed. When she says, "I'll be there," she means it. The funny thing is, I found *myself* vacillating about whether I really wanted to go through with it.

"I'll be there, Connie," I told her on the phone one day. "Unless something comes up with my son. Or I don't feel well. Or I'm behind on deadlines, and I have to go into work early."

"You know, I get really uncomfortable when I make a commitment to walk with someone," I added, surprising even myself with my candor. "It feels kind of like I'm putting myself under pressure. But I *think* I want to do this with you."

I heard the tone of Connie's voice change from cheery to cautious. "Okay," she said. "Are you sure you want to do this?"

At that moment, I realized just how wishy-washy I was being. I wanted to walk, didn't I? Wouldn't pairing up with Connie help me get out more regularly? If I couldn't make a commitment to this enthusiastic person, was I *really* committed to my walking program?

"Yes, Connie," I replied. "Seven A.M. sharp. I'll be there, rain or shine. *You can count on me.*"

We've been walking together for months now. Every Wednesday and Friday, I roll out of bed, get dressed, drink some water, and head for the trail. I don't even think about it. I don't ask myself if I want to, if I feel all right, if the weather is too cold, too hot, too wet. The only thing that would stop me is a call from Connie saying that she can't be there. And she always calls the night before if she can't make it.

We walk briskly for 45 to 60 minutes, sprinting every once in a while. The time passes quickly. We stretch together. We push each other a little. We share healthy eating tips and confess our hot fudge sundae indulgences.

And every once in a while, we call each other on the phone and say, "Thanks for being there. It really helps." And it does.—*M.S.*

your walk, so you don't tax your digestive system. If you opt to eat first, keep your pace leisurely to avoid cramps and indigestion.)

Keep an extra pair of walking shoes and socks at your desk, so you can be ready at a moment's notice. For really brisk walking on warm days, you may want to change into workout clothes. But on cool days, just slip on your shoes and socks.

Try to choose a walking partner who is a good match for you in terms of fitness level, pace, and stamina. You may want to have several partners—one who likes to stroll for when you don't want to work up a sweat, another who's up for a half-hour of hill walking when you want more of a workout. Just don't push yourself to keep up with someone who walks a lot faster than you. It isn't worth the risk of injury. If you're gasping for breath while your partner carries most of the conversation, you need to slow down.

Walking with coworkers gives you an opportunity to get to know each other away from on-the-job pressures. You improve your rapport with fellow employees—and get a better-toned body to boot.

PARTNER WITH A POOCH

When you're in the market for a walking partner, don't overlook the four-legged variety. Walking with a dog isn't for everyone, and I certainly don't advise adopting a dog just for your walking program. Pet ownership is a big responsibility. But based on what I hear from walkers, I'm convinced that a pooch can be a most devoted and reliable walking partner.

The great thing about dogs is that they *always* want to go for a walk. They remind you when it's time to go, in case you've gotten too comfortable in front of the TV. And they make wonderful company: If you want to talk, dogs will listen without complaint; if you prefer to walk in silence, they won't feel slighted.

Some dogs need obedience training to prepare them for a walking partnership. But most are natural, able partners right from the start. If you have a dog that hasn't been exercising regularly, get him checked out by a veterinarian before you start working out. Ask the vet to recommend a training program to ease your dog into exercise.

If you don't currently have a dog and would like to adopt one, a veterinarian or kennel club can help you find the breed that best suits your lifestyle. Ideally, you want a dog that's friendly to other people and to other dogs, one that is strong and can tolerate the temperatures where you live.

If you just want a walking partner, not necessarily a full-time companion, ask friends and neighbors to "borrow" their dogs. Or contact your local animal shelter—often they're in need of volunteer dog-walkers.

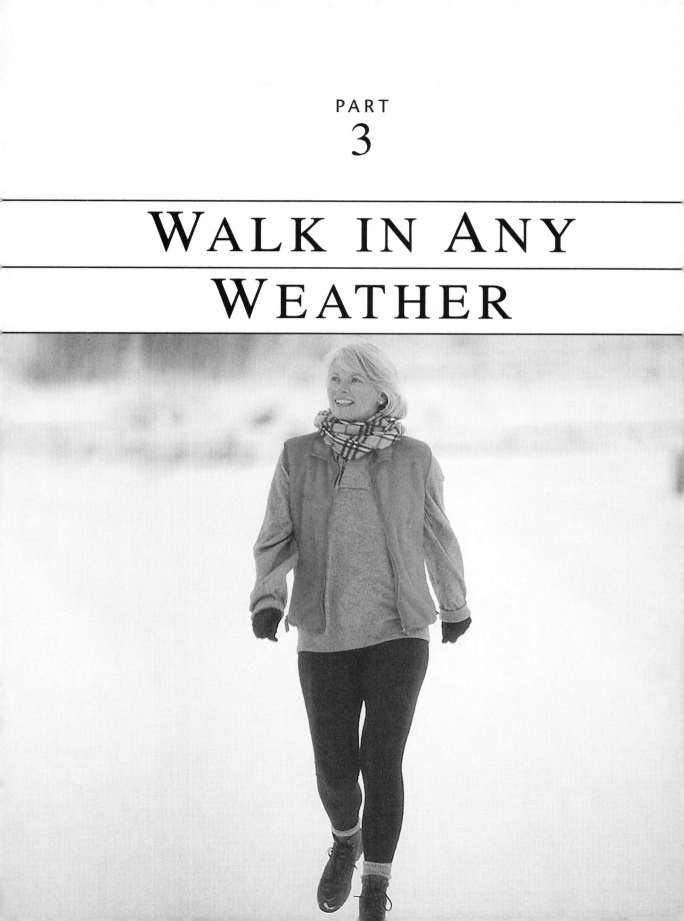

PART
3

WALK IN ANY WEATHER

KEEP YOUR COOL IN THE HEAT

As I write this chapter, the temperature outside is sizzling. The thermometer says it's about 99°F, but with the humidity, it feels like 110°. Definitely not a day for walking or doing much of anything outdoors.

When the heat is stifling, your best bet is to move your workout inside to an indoor track or a treadmill. Or you can do your walking in a pool if you have access to one.

The point is, heat can be dangerous. Some days it may be hotter than you think. No matter what the reading on the thermometer, the temperature can feel even higher to your body. And that can have serious consequences if you're not careful.

WHEN IS HOT TOO HOT?

Sometimes it's tough to tell when a nice, warm day is actually too hot for safe outdoor exercise. You've no doubt learned from experience that high humidity makes a high air temperature feel even more uncomfortable. The combination of humidity and air temperature is known as apparent temperature. And as it rises, so does your risk of heat exhaustion or heatstroke, which can be life-threatening.

Heat-related health problems most often affect those who are older and those who have chronic medical conditions. (If you have any kind of medical condition, you need to ask your doctor whether you should exercise indoors or forgo your workout altogether.) Young children are also vulnerable. But even the fittest among us can fall victim to the heat if we overexert ourselves or become dehydrated.

So when the mercury is rising, use "Your Hot-Weather Workout Guide" (on page 69) to determine whether to do your walking outside or inside (preferably in the air-conditioning). Once you find the day's apparent temperature, check it against the recommendations below.

• 90°F and below: Head for the great outdoors.

A Cool Place for Walking

WHEN THE TEMPERATURE IS rising, consider moving your walk to the nearest pool. You'll cool off, and you'll double your workout efficiency to boot.

Exercising in water provides 12 times more resistance than exercising in air, according to Carolyn Kyle, a certified water fitness instructor at Canyon Ranch health resort in Tucson. It works both halves of opposing muscle groups—for instance, the muscles on the front and back of your thighs. It conditions major and minor muscle groups and enhances your flexibility. And water's soothing, massaging qualities minimize the soreness that may occur when you exercise harder or longer.

Walking in water is easy. Just hop in the pool and start moving. You can work at any depth you're comfortable in—but the deeper the water, the more it will support your weight and massage your body.

Of course, if you can't touch bottom with your feet, you're not walking, you're treading water. That's okay. Treading water is a great workout, too.

- 91° to 104°F: Proceed with caution.
- 105° to 129°F: Consider indoor options unless you're acclimated to these conditions.
- 130°F and above: Stay indoors.

WAYS TO STAY COMFORTABLE

If you decide that the conditions outside are suitable for walking, you still want to make sure that you're prepared to handle the heat. Here are some great tips from veteran walkers who've weathered workouts on hot summer days.

Be an early bird or a night owl. Plan to walk in the early morning or early evening to avoid the steamiest temperatures. Direct sun can make the temperature feel up to 15°F higher than it really is.

Switch to cooler footwear. For warm-weather workouts, you need lightweight, ventilated walking shoes and socks that wick away sweat. If you have two pairs of shoes, alternate between them every day so that each pair has a chance to dry out completely between uses. This helps you avoid blisters, fungi—and stinky feet.

Dress lightly. The more skin that's exposed, the better sweat can evaporate, and that helps keep you cool. Of course, remember to wear sunscreen. Apply it underneath your shirt, as the garment may not block the sun's harmful ultraviolet rays. If it's really hot, or if you don't like wearing tank tops, mist your shirt with a water bottle. The dampness acts like air-conditioning when you're out walking.

Apply some friction protection. Reduce friction in areas where skin rubs against skin—between your toes, between your thighs, and under your arms—with a little petroleum jelly. Or use Runner's Lube, a nonstaining

Your Hot-Weather Workout Guide

TO DETERMINE THE APPARENT temperature on any given day, find the environmental temperature (that is, the temperature of the outside air) at the top of the chart and the relative humidity on the left-hand side. Then locate the number where the respective column and row meet. That's the apparent temperature.

Relative Humidity

Relative Humidity	Environmental Temperature (in Fahrenheit)							
	75°	80°	85°	90°	95°	100°	105°	110°
	Apparent Temperature (in Fahrenheit)							
0%	69	73	78	83	87	91	95	99
10%	70	75	80	85	90	95	100	105
20%	72	77	82	87	93	99	105	112
30%	73	78	84	90	96	104	113	123
40%	74	79	86	93	101	110	123	137
50%	75	81	88	96	107	120	135	150
60%	76	82	90	100	114	132	149	
70%	77	85	93	106	124	144		
80%	78	86	97	113	136			
90%	79	88	102	122				
100%	80	91	108					

cream made from lanolin, zinc oxide, and benzocaine that prevents itching and soreness. It's sold in many sporting goods stores.

Wear a hat rather than a visor. A visor protects your face, but your head can still get hot. Choose a hat that's made from a breathable fabric, such as cotton or a cotton-synthetic blend. If you can, soak it in cool water before putting it on.

Drink plenty of water. Keep a half-full water bottle in the freezer and top it off just before you head out. Take sips regularly while you're walking. Six to 8 ounces of water for every 15 minutes of walking should be enough. As an extra precaution against dehydration, weigh yourself before your walk and again afterward. If you've dropped a pound or two, drink up. You've lost fluid that is important to your body's cooling system.

Listen to your body. Your body will tell you when you can push yourself and when you need to coast. If you develop a headache or become dizzy or weak, stop exercising and head for a cool place. Drink plenty of cool fluids while you're resting.

SPORT DRINKS: BETTER THAN WATER?

You know that you need to increase your fluid intake when you exercise, especially in the heat. But you just can't get yourself to take more than a few gulps of water. Why not try a sports drink?

If something tastes good, you're bound to consume more of it. And sports drinks contain a small amount of sodium, which makes you want to sip even more. (If you're on a sodium-restricted diet, get your doctor's advice. You may have to limit your sodium intake from other foods and beverages.)

Sports drinks have other benefits besides tasting good. They supply less than half the calories of fruit juices. They're absorbed quickly into the bloodstream, so you can exercise longer and avoid post-workout fatigue. And they're easier on your stomach than beverages with higher concentrations of carbohydrates.

If you don't like the flavor of sports drinks either, try diluting your favorite fruit juice with water.

WINTERIZE YOUR WALKING PROGRAM

For most people, exercising outdoors may be safer in cooler weather than on hot, humid days. Your body temperature rises as you walk, so when it's sultry outside, you're getting a double dose of heat. When it turns cold, on the other hand, you can regulate your internal temperature more easily. If you get too hot while you're working out, just slow your pace, open your jacket, or take off your hat or gloves. You'll solve the problem instantly.

TAKE CARE WHEN THE TEMP DROPS

Even on chilly days, some of us need to take extra precautions before venturing out to exercise. If you have any kind of heart problem, for example, you should consult your doctor before working out in the cold. As the air temperature drops, your body responds by constricting blood vessels, a process that pulls blood toward the trunk to feed your internal organs. When this happens, exercising puts extra strain on your heart as it tries to pump blood to your extremities.

Walking can relieve some of this strain by dilating blood vessels in your legs. The trick is to warm up slowly, to allow your body to adjust to the coldness. If you don't warm up when it's freezing outside, you could set yourself up for angina (severe chest pain) or a heart attack, says Roger Fielding, Ph.D., assistant professor in the department of health sciences at Boston University. That's why people have heart attacks when shoveling snow.

When you warm up, do it indoors, before exposing your body to the cold air. This reduces the strain on your heart, because your blood vessels become dilated. You'll feel better about going outside, too, because you'll be warm already.

Cold-weather workouts can also be risky for people with diabetes. Because walking in the cold burns more calories to increase warmth, it steps up the body's demands for blood sugar (glucose). While this is a plus for most folks, it can cause those with diabetes to become hypoglycemic. If you have diabetes, ask your doctor for advice on managing your medications or your food intake to regulate your blood sugar level while you exercise.

You also need to be concerned about developing frostbite, as people with diabetes tend to have poor circulation in their extremities. Warm socks, gloves, and a hat are essential. If you experience loss of feeling in your feet or fingers while you're walking, head indoors as soon as you can and check whether your skin looks blue. This condition, called cyanosis, is the first sign of frostbite. You need to see your doctor immediately.

Frigid temperatures don't mix well with asthma either. If you have this respiratory condition, you already know that inhaling cold air can trigger an attack. (In fact, some people experience asthma-related breathing problems *only* when they work out in cold weather.) Wearing a mask or scarf over your nose and mouth can help prevent an attack by warming up the air before it reaches your bronchial tubes. That way, the tubes are less likely to go into spasm. If covering your nose and mouth doesn't help, consult your doctor for advice on adjusting your medication for cold-weather workouts.

In fact, if you have any chronic health problem, you may want to check with your doctor before you exercise in the cold. He can tell you what precautions to take, if any. Or he may advise you to do your walking indoors.

LAYERS KEEP OUT THE COLD

If you are heading outdoors, you need to dress for the chilly temperatures. Twenty years ago, that would have meant donning flannel underwear, a wool sweater, wool pants, a heavy wool coat, and thick wool socks to protect you from the cold. You'd be so bundled up that you could barely move.

These days, when you dress for wintry conditions, less is more. Thanks to an array of high-tech textiles, you can be warm and dry and still have freedom of movement. New fabrics insulate, block the wind, and wick away moisture without bulk or heaviness.

Still, dressing in layers is your best bet. That way, you can adjust your attire as you go, according to the weather and your level of activity. For the innermost layer (the one closest to your skin), choose light garments made from a synthetic fabric such as polypropylene, which wicks away perspiration from your body. That should be topped off with an insulating layer—a sweater, a sweatshirt, or a fleece pullover—for warmth. For the outermost layer, or shell, you want a garment that protects you from wind and rain. The fabric should be waterproof, as opposed to water-resistant

Get Snow-Tire Traction for Your Shoes

SLIPPERY SIDEWALKS KEEP MANY people indoors during the winter months. But you can venture outside safely, provided you have the right equipment.

Stabilicers are detachable soles that can make you so surefooted that you'd feel safe walking across a river of ice. Built like sandals with Velcro straps, they slide over your walking shoes quite easily. The top of the sole grips your shoe, while the bottom, which is imbedded with steel cleats, digs into ice and hard snow. They're perfect for winter walking or any slippery situation.

Stabilicers sell for about $40 a pair. You can buy them in many department stores and sporting goods stores as well as through mail-order catalogs.

(which is designed to keep you dry in a light mist). It should also be breathable—meaning that it allows water vapor to escape without actually letting water in.

The new synthetic fabrics do a better job of keeping you warm and dry than either wool or cotton. When you're shopping for cold-weather walking wear, read clothing labels and try on a variety of garments to get a sense what's out there. You'll be amazed at how comfortable you can be, even at extremely cold temperatures.

FOOTWEAR FOR NASTY WEATHER

To prepare your feet for winter walking, often all you need is a pair of walking shoes and a thick pair of socks. Then as you warm up, your feet warm up, too. Just make sure that your shoes can accommodate your socks, or your feet will get cold from lack of circulation.

For keeping your feet toasty on bitterly cold days or for navigating sidewalks that are wet, icy, or slushy, you may want more rugged footwear. One place to look is in the hiking-shoe display of your sporting goods store. Hiking shoes have heavy-duty soles that grip better on sloppy or uneven terrain. They have elevated foot beds (because of the thickness of the soles), so your feet are higher than the water or slush that you're walking through. They're often waterproof, or at least water-resistant. And their tough exteriors stand up to the elements better than the average walking shoes.

A pair of hiking shoes that's made for trekking dirt trails should provide enough flexibility for fitness walking. And if you're expecting to end up with a pair of big, clunky "stompers," you're in for a pleasant surprise. These days, you can choose from lots of low-cut styles that are very lightweight and comfortable. (To get a pair that fits well, follow the shoe-buying guidelines in chapter 8.)

EXPLORE WINTER'S WONDERLAND

ON THIS DAY, THE entire Northeast is in the grip of an awesome storm. Snow, sleet, and freezing rain have pummeled us for 2 days. Temperatures have ranged from 29°F to −20°F, with the windchill.

Now these might not seem like the best conditions for walking. Then again, weather like this is unlikely to repeat itself often. And if you're curious like me, you want to go outside and see what's up.

That's why I've decided to brave the elements. Besides, my dog, Petey, has to go out. So I don my fleece-lined, rubber-bottomed Kamnik boots, my fleece vest and down jacket, my wool hat and polar-fleece-lined gloves. Then I grab an umbrella and head out.

Petey and I walk together through snow and slush 3 inches deep, both of us making perfectly formed footprints that are likely to freeze in the next 24 hours to become temporary additions to the landscape. We tramp up to the field behind our house, where the wheat-colored grasses are bending and cracking under the weight of the ice. The 30-foot blue spruces that line one side of the field are crystallized into towering, glassy figurines. In fact, every branch, leaf, and tendril of every plant is encased in an icy coating. The sun isn't out today, but if it were, the scene would be even more dazzling.

Just as our footprints are so well-carved into the icy slush, so are the prints of other creatures. A big dog galloped through on a morning run. A deer trotted from one field to the next. A rabbit print trailed off into the briar batch. For lack of a better plan, I follow each set of prints until it disappears into a thicket or the street, curious how much time has passed since the animals wandered through. I wonder where they're holed up now to escape the steadily falling sleet and hail.

Even on this familiar land, 20 minutes of walking now feels like 40. My feet are slogging through heavy, wet snow, pushing my heart to work harder than usual. Finally, I reach a spot where I can look out over the football field across the street to the tree line and the valley below. Everything appears draped in white, with fog rising as the air meets the ice.

It's much quieter than usual. The drone of the highway is muffled, and the usual truck traffic is just a trickle, probably because of the weather. Winter storm warnings have kept lots of people at home, where they're safe and warm. I'm warm, too, except for my nose, which reminds me just how cold I'd be if not for my high-tech walking wear.

Venturing out in adverse conditions always makes me feel more connected to my surroundings. My senses are attuned to every sight, sound, and smell; for a short while, the inner dialogue goes quiet, and the distractions cease. I'm calm, centered, and at peace. It just plain feels *right.—M.S.*

SHOW OFF YOUR SKIN SMARTS

When you're walking in wintry conditions, protecting your skin is just as important as protecting your feet. Cold and wind are no kinder than heat and sun. All can be quite drying. And don't let the chilly temperature fool you: The winter sun has ultraviolet rays that are strong enough to cause sunburn, age your skin, and increase your risk of skin cancer.

During the winter months, your hands and face are most vulnerable to the elements. You may wear gloves, only to have your hands get all sweaty as they warm up. But if you take off your gloves and expose your wet hands to the cold air, they may become chapped. That's why you should wear two pairs of gloves: thick ones on top, thin ones underneath. Leave on the thick pair until your hands feel warm, then slip them off and wear only the thin pair to protect your skin.

To save your face from the effects of wind and cold, invest in a ski mask. A thin one made from silk might be most comfortable, but check what's available. New, lightweight fabrics keep popping up everywhere.

If wearing a ski mask irritates your skin or obstructs your vision, you can go without one. But do wear a hat to keep body heat from escaping through the top of your head. To protect your face from the elements, first apply sunscreen and allow it to dry, then add a thick layer of a protective moisturizer, petroleum jelly, or hand cream. Choose a sunscreen that's waterproof with an SPF of at least 15. Be sure to reapply both layers if you sweat a lot or wipe your face frequently.

If there's snow on the ground, you need to be extra-vigilant about your sunscreen use. Snow reflects 85 percent of the sun's harmful ultraviolet rays right back at you, nearly doubling your exposure. The average person gets about 19 hours of sun each week, regardless of the season. That exposure accumulates from routine activities, such as walking your dog and driving a car (UVA rays can penetrate most windows).

According to one dermatologist, if you don't wear sunscreen between September and May, the damage to your skin could be the same as if you spent about eight straight summer weekends on the beach. Unfortunately, while 52 percent of Americans wear sunscreen in the summer, only 2 percent bother to slather it on in the winter. So here's your chance to do something good for your skin.

CHAPTER 14

EXERCISING WITH ALLERGIES

By one count, some 20 percent of Americans have what doctors call seasonal allergic rhinitis. You and I know it as hay fever.

If you're among the sniffling, sneezing millions, you already know that hay fever can wreak havoc on your walking program. At best, your symptoms can turn a pleasant stroll into a red-eyed, nose-blowing ordeal. At worst, they may convince you to pack up your walking shoes and stay inside until allergy season ends.

In general, hay fever symptoms are most severe between August and October. That's when the big pollen-producers, such as ragweed, pigweed, and lamb's-quarter, are in full bloom over most of the country. Mold spores are also especially troublesome in August, when their levels, spurred by summer rains, tend to peak. Between them, pollen and mold spores account for most cases of hay fever.

So what can you do to stifle your allergy symptoms, short of giving up walking until the first frost? Plenty, as it turns out. But you need to find out *exactly* what's causing your allergies before you can take steps to keep your walks symptom-free.

THE SOURCE OF YOUR SYMPTOMS

If you've never been to an allergist, schedule an appointment with one. He can perform skin tests to determine exactly which substances, or allergens, are triggering your symptoms. Once you know the specific offenders, you can plan your walking program so that you avoid them.

If you're allergic to weed pollen, for example, you'll feel more comfortable if you do your walking later in the day. That's because weeds typically release their pollen early in the morning. And if you're allergic to molds, you'll be better off walking immediately after a rain. You have a window of a few hours from the time everything gets wet to the time the molds start producing spores like crazy.

Give Hypnosis a Whirl

IF YOU'RE OPEN TO alternative therapies, try using your mind to manage your allergy symptoms. A handful of studies have found that, for some people, hypnosis provides relief.

Does this mean that allergies are all in your head? Not at all. But the study results provide additional evidence that the mind has greater influence over the body and physical responses than anyone ever imagined.

To find a health professional who's trained in medical hypnosis, send a business-size self-addressed, stamped envelope to the American Society of Clinical Hypnosis, 130 East Elm Court, Suite 201, Roselle, IL 60172. This organization can provide a list of medical hypnotists in your area.

Heavy rains also help people with pollen allergies by washing away pollen, but light rains actually make things worse. They break large clumps of pollen into tiny particles, which tend to remain airborne longer.

If rescheduling your walks is difficult or doesn't reduce your allergy symptoms as much as you'd like, then you may want to try premedication—that is, taking medicine before you go outdoors. An over-the-counter antihistamine may be enough to keep you walking right through allergy season. Your doctor or pharmacist can help you choose the one that's right for you.

Antihistamines are preventive medications. So for maximum effectiveness, they should be taken $\frac{1}{2}$ hour before you go walking. Some antihistamines can cause drowsiness or jitters. You may be able to minimize or avoid these side effects by starting at one-quarter to one-half the recommended dosage and taking a little more every day, working up to the full dosage over the course of 3 to 4 days.

If an over-the-counter drug doesn't do the trick, you may want to talk to your doctor about prescription-strength antihistamines. They're available in several forms, including pills, eyedrops that relieve itchy eyes, and nasal sprays that prevent allergy-induced stuffy noses.

Depending on the severity of your symptoms, you may even want to try allergy shots. You must get the shots all year round. Discuss them with your doctor to find out whether they'd be right for you.

TIPS FOR AVOIDING ALLERGENS

Whether or not you go the medication route, you have plenty of other options for reducing your exposure to allergens while you're walking. Here's what some experts recommend.

Keep tabs on the pollen count. You can get daily readings on pollen and mold levels from newspaper, radio, and TV weather forecasts, as well as from the Internet. If they're predicting a bad day, consider moving your walk indoors. Work out on a treadmill or head for a mall, where you can walk in climate-controlled, pollen-free comfort.

Pay attention to pollution. A number of studies have shown that if you're exposed to air pollution, especially ozone, you become sensitive to lower levels of airborne allergens. No one knows why, but scientists suspect that pollutants irritate the lining of the respiratory tract. So keep an ear to the news. If there's a pollution alert, plan on working out indoors that day. If you're on allergy medication, you may want to talk to your doctor about increasing your dosage when pollutant levels are high.

Steer clear of trouble spots. Plants that give off pollen tend to proliferate in vacant lots and other areas that aren't mown regularly. To reduce your pollen exposure, you may have to find another route.

Warm up inside. If you stretch before you walk (and you should), plan to do your exercises indoors. That way, you spend less time out among the al-lergens. And the shorter your exposure to pollen or mold, the less severe your reaction will be.

Wear cool shades. Itchy, burning eyes are a hallmark of seasonal allergies. To keep pollen away from your eyes while you're walking, wear sunglasses. The bigger the glasses, the better their coverage. Wraparound and goggle-like styles are the best, because they cover more of the eye area. As a bonus, they block sun glare from the sides, so you can see where you're going.

Strap on a surgical mask. If your allergy symptoms are really bothersome, you may not mind looking like Dr. Kildare. A surgical mask offers some protection by filtering out pollen. Look for the kind that are designed for industrial workers and home renovators. They're available in hardware stores and home centers.

Clean up after your workout. By showering and shampooing after your walk, you can remove most of the pollen that you picked up while outside. If you can't fit a shower into your schedule, at least wash your hands and face.

PART
4

WALK OFF
YOUR
WEIGHT

PICK YOUR PERSONAL SHAPE-UP PLAN

Diet and exercise: They're the foundation of any sensible, successful weight-loss program. Whether you want to shed 5 pounds or 50, the only surefire way to slim down is to use up more calories through regular physical activity than you take in from food.

And one of the best all-around activities for weight loss is—you guessed it—walking.

Granted, other forms of exercise, like running, bicycling, and swimming, may burn more calories per minute. But studies have shown that people who take up walking actually stick with it, while those who pursue other activities tend to give up after the first few months. What's more, walking is gentle and low-impact, a plus if you've been sedentary for a while. And it's easy to incorporate into your daily routine. No packing a bag and driving to the gym.

To help you get rid of those unwanted pounds once and for all, I asked one of *Prevention* magazine's fitness experts to develop three basic programs for beginning to experienced walkers. Just read through the plans and choose the one that best matches your current fitness level, lifestyle, and weight-loss goals.

After 4 weeks of walking (the duration of each plan), you should notice the pounds melting away. How fast they disappear varies from one person to the next. If you're more than 50 pounds overweight and you've been sedentary for years, you may start losing almost immediately. If you've been losing but you seem be stuck at a certain number, you may need a bit more time to see results.

Remember, too, that the goal of walking is to get fit and healthy, not to be pencil-thin. Even losing 10 percent of your body weight can cut your risk of serious illness. Every step you take reduces stress and boosts your energy level. And that's definitely something to stride for.

THE GET-STARTED PLAN

Choose this beginning-level program if any of the following applies.

- You're severely overweight.
- You're recovering from illness or surgery.
- You have a chronic health problem that limits activity.
- You devote less than 60 minutes a day to "active" tasks like walking the dog, chasing after kids, or putting out the garbage.
- You spend your days sitting at a desk or in your car and your evenings lounging on the couch.

With the Get-Started Plan, you'll ease your way into a regular walking routine. It starts you out slowly, to build your confidence and reduce your risk of injury. Even at a moderate pace, you'll reap many benefits. ("Moderate" means you're moving fast enough to get your heart pumping but not so fast that you become out of breath.) Almost immediately, you'll notice improvements in your flexibility, your energy level, and your mood. After the second week of the program, your workouts will feel easier—a sign that your heart is getting fitter and your legs are getting stronger.

THE PLATEAU-BUSTING PLAN

If you agree with any of the following statements, this program is perfect for you.

- Your scale hasn't budged for the past month.
- You've been walking regularly for at least 6 weeks.
- You're bored with walking, and you're starting to skip workouts.

The Get-Started Plan

During week 1 of this program, walk at a speed that feels comfortable for you. Then in weeks 2 through 4, pick up your pace a bit, as though you're in a hurry to get somewhere.

Week	Duration (min)	Frequency (days/week)	Intensity
1	10	3	Moderate
2	15	4	Moderate
3	20	5	Moderate
4	30	5	Moderate

The Plateau-Busting Plan

This plan uses intervals—periods of brisk walking, followed by periods of recovery—to step up calorie burn and send those stubborn pounds packing.

Week	Program	Rate of Perceived Exertion
1 Exercise for 35 minutes, 5 days this week.	Warmup (5 min.)	10–11
	Normal walk (5 min.)	13
	Speed-up (5 min.)	15
	Recover (10 min.)	13
	Speed-up (5 min.)	15
	Cooldown (5 min.)	10–11
2 Exercise for 35 minutes, 5 days this week.	Warmup (5 min.)	10–11
	Normal walk (5 min.)	13
	Speed-up (5 min.)	16
	Recover (10 min.)	13
	Speed-up (5 min.)	16
	Cooldown (5 min.)	10–11
3 Exercise for 45 minutes, 5 days this week.	Warmup (5 min.)	10–11
	Normal walk (5 min.)	13
	Speed-up (5 min.)	16
	Recover (8 min.)	13
	Speed-up (5 min.)	16
	Recover (7 min.)	13
	Speed-up (5 min.)	16
	Cooldown (5 min.)	10–11
4 Exercise for 45 minutes, 5 days this week.	Warmup (5 min.)	10–11
	Speed-up (5 min.)	16
	Recover (5 min.)	13
	Speed-up (5 min.)	16
	Recover (5 min.)	13
	Speed-up (5 min.)	16
	Recover (5 min.)	13
	Speed-up (5 min.)	16
	Cooldown (5 min.)	10–11

Borg Scale for Rate of Perceived Exertion

6 7 8	Very, very light (lounging on the couch)
9 10	Very light (puttering around the house)
11 12	Fairly light (strolling leisurely)
13 14	Somewhat hard (walking normally)
15 16	Hard (walking as if in a hurry)
17 18	Very hard (jogging or running)
19 20	Very, very hard (sprinting)

• You don't have a formal exercise routine, but your days are active.

As its name suggests, the Plateau-Busting Plan is specially designed to jump-start a weight-loss regimen that seems to have stalled. Sometimes a simple change in your workout is all you need to start shedding pounds once again. It not only increases your calorie burn but also breathes new life into your workouts—a great way to combat boredom.

In the workout chart, you'll come across the phrase "rate of perceived exertion." It refers to the Borg Scale for Rate of Perceived Exertion (RPE), an easy, low-tech method of assessing how hard you're exercising.

To use RPE, simply do a mental scan of your body while you're walking. Is your breathing heavy? Are you sweating? Do your muscles feel warm? Are they burning? Based on your scan, rate your walk on the scale above. It tells you whether you're working hard enough.

THE MAXIMUM-CALORIE-BURN PLAN

Do any of the following statements describe you? If so, then this is your program.

• You think walking is too easy.

• You want to lose weight fast.

• You've been doing intervals—periods of brisk walking, followed by periods of recovery—for at least 6 weeks.

- You don't have time for longer walks, but you want to burn more calories.

In the Maximum-Calorie-Burn Plan, you'll be doing what's called a Power Pyramid. Basically, you work your way up to a brief but very high intensity walk or jog, then work your way back down. To make the intervals easier, you might want to record some favorite upbeat tunes and add voice cues every 30 to 60 seconds to indicate when to change pace. That sure beats constantly checking your watch.

Maggie's Log

NEVER TOO BUSY FOR EXERCISE

OF ALL THE FITNESS experts I've interviewed over the years, many have offered the same advice: To lose weight and get in shape, you must walk for an hour a day at least 5 days a week. That's 1 hour. Sixty whole minutes.

Now I don't know about you, but to me, that sure seems like a big chunk out of a short day. In fact, setting aside an hour for exercise once so overwhelmed me that I was ready to give up on slimming down. Then I discovered a simple solution: I could divvy up that hour over the course of a day.

That's right. While some were insisting that anything less than an hour of exercise wouldn't cut the fat, and others were throwing up their fanny packs in despair, researchers discovered that little bits of activity squeezed in throughout the day were just as good as one big chunk—and maybe even better.

As I read about these findings, I began thinking about how I could break down my own walking routine. Usually, I tried to squeeze in a 1-hour walk every morning, but it was difficult with everything else I had to do. So I decided to cut back to a short, 20-minute a.m. workout. I head for the nearest hill and go up and down twice. That done, I've fulfilled one-third of my daily walking requirement.

At lunchtime, I eat something light, then I step out for a brisk walking tour of the small town where I work. Twenty minutes is plenty to take in the sights. For the day, it's 40 minutes down, 20 to go.

Those last 20 minutes present the biggest challenge. I can take a short walking break in the afternoon or a lap around the block before my half-hour drive home or a quick spin on the treadmill once I get home. For me, the trick is to not feel smug that I've already gotten in 40 minutes, and that's good enough. For weight loss, often it's not.

The latest research suggests that short bursts of activity may cause your body to burn calories more steadily throughout the day. Seems to me that "incremental exercise" is an idea whose time has come. It works for me; maybe it will work for you, too.—*M.S.*

The Maximum-Calorie-Burn Plan

This workout features Power Pyramids, which pump up the intensity and, therefore, the calorie-burning capacity of your walking program. To do a pyramid, simply follow the instructions in the graph below.

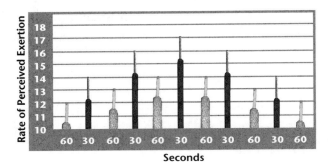

This graph shows you how to do a Power Pyramid. The numbers across the bottom indicate the length of each mini-interval, while the numbers on the left-hand side represent rate of perceived exertion (RPE). So for the first interval, which lasts 60 seconds, your RPE should be 120. When you complete one interval, move on to the next until you've worked through all of them. Then refer back to the chart below.

Week	Program	Rate of Perceived Exertion
1 Exercise for approximately 40 minutes, 5 days this week.	Warmup (5 min.)	10–11
	Pyramid	See graph
	Normal walk (7 min.)	13
	Pyramid	See graph
	Normal walk (6 min.)	13
	Cooldown (5 min.)	10–11

Week	Program	Rate of Perceived Exertion
2 Exercise for approximately 45 minutes, 5 days this week.	Warmup (5 min.)	10–11
	Pyramid	See graph
	Normal walk (5 min.)	13
	Pyramid	See graph
	Normal walk (5 min.)	13
	Pyramid	See graph
	Cooldown (5 min.)	10–11
3 Exercise for approximately 50 minutes, 5 days this week.	Warmup (5 min.)	10–11
	Pyramid	See graph
	Normal walk (5 min.)	13
	Pyramid	See graph
	Normal walk (5 min.)	13
	Pyramid	See graph
	Normal walk (5 min.)	13
	Cooldown (5 min.)	10–11
4 Exercise for approximately 60 minutes, 5 days this week.	Warmup (5 min.)	10–11
	Pyramid	See graph
	Normal walk (5 min.)	13
	Pyramid	See graph
	Normal walk (5 min.)	13
	Pyramid	See graph
	Normal walk (5 min.)	13
	Pyramid	See graph
	Cooldown (5 min.)	10–11

CHAPTER **16**

WHAT'S THE SPEED FOR SLIMMING DOWN?

A few years back, long slow distance—LSD for short—was all the rage for weight loss. Why? Because a few studies suggested that walking at a comfortable, moderate pace helps the body preferentially burn fat. For weight-conscious walkers, the mantra became "Slow down!" Going too fast uses up carbohydrates but not fat stores.

At first, the advice seemed to defy logic. After all, most of us were convinced that exercising hard *must* get rid of more fat by burning more calories. But perhaps because this new fitness philosophy meant that we didn't have to sweat to slim down, it went over big.

The fact is, as long as you use up more calories through physical activity than you take in from food, you'll lose fat *and* weight in the long run. Whether that physical activity is slow or fast doesn't really matter. At any speed, *calories burned are calories burned.*

FASTER IS BETTER . . . SOMETIMES

Of course, not everyone loses weight at the same rate. You probably know people who shed pounds like a duck's feathers shed water. They were inactive for years, yet ever since they started exercising, the fat has just melted away.

Other people—and maybe you're one of them—have worked out religiously for years. Even though they're in better shape and they feel great, the number on the scale has hardly budged. Obviously, these folks need to do something differently if they want to slim down. But does that mean they need to *slow* down?

Well, at least one study seems to challenge the long slow distance theory. Researchers at West Virginia University in Morgantown recruited two groups of volunteers—one to work out at a high intensity, the other at a

Calories Go, Fast or Slow

THE CHART BELOW, ADAPTED from *Sports Nutrition for the '90s* by Jacqueline Berning, R.D., and Suzanne Nelson Steen, R.D., compares the number of calories burned by an average 150-pound person while walking at various speeds. As you can see, the faster you go, the more calories you use per minute. But if you figure out the number of calories burned per mile, there's not that much difference between walking slow and walking fast.

For example, a 20-minute-per-mile pace burns 4.1 calories per minute, or 82 calories per mile (20 × 4.1 = 82). By comparison, a 12-minute-per-mile pace burns 8.2 calories per minute, or 98.4 calories per mile (12 × 8.2 = 98.4). That's just 16 calories more—and you can easily make up for that by walking an extra ¼ mile at the slower pace.

So if you're walking to lose weight, remember that you don't need to push yourself at top speed. Going slower but farther—long slow distance—can produce the same results.

Speed (mph)	Minutes per Mile	Calories Burned per Minute
1.0	60.0	2.3
2.0	30.0	3.2
2.3	26.0	3.5
3.0	20.0	4.1
3.2	18.5	4.7
3.5	17.1	5.1
4.0	15.0	6.4
4.5	13.2	7.1
5.0	12.0	8.2

moderate intensity. Both groups exercised for the same amount of time and the same number of days every week. Neither was asked to follow any specific dietary guidelines.

Over the 11 weeks of the study, the high-intensity exercisers reduced their body fat and improved their cardiovascular conditioning, while the moderate-intensity exercisers showed no changes. Interestingly, the high-inten-

sity exercisers reported that they automatically began eating less saturated fat and more carbohydrates. Apparently, their bodies naturally craved carbs for quick energy.

Does this mean that you *should* work out at a high intensity—that's 80 to 90 percent of your maximum heart rate—if you want to lose weight? (To find your maximum heart rate, subtract your age from 220.) "There do seem to be some advantages to working at high intensities," notes Randall W. Byrne, Ed.D., who led the study. "But there's no advantage if you hate walking fast and stop exercising altogether. Besides, for some people, such as those with heart disease, diabetes, or asthma, high-intensity exercise may not be safe."

One other point worth making: This study lasted just 11 weeks, a relatively short time in which to bring about weight loss through physical activity alone. In a longer trial, both groups may have shed pounds without altering their eating habits.

MAKING A CASE FOR MODERATE PACE

While brisk walking and long slow distance may have the same calorie- and fat-burning capacity over the long run, LSD has other advantages that may make it a better choice for you. For example, maybe you feel that sweaty, heart-pounding workouts should be reserved for Olympians and professional athletes. Or perhaps your physical condition makes brisk walking difficult, if not impossible. Or maybe you're the sort of person who would rather walk 5 miles at a moderate pace than racewalk around the block.

All of these are perfectly legitimate reasons to opt for long slow distance. Just remember that the slower your pace, the farther you need to go to burn the same number of calories that you would at a fast pace—hence the phrase "long slow distance." Makes perfect sense, right?

Over the years, I've met many fitness experts who swear by long slow distance. Among them is Rob Sweetgall, who has written a number of books on walking. He also created the Walking Wellness school curriculum, which helps teachers develop lesson plans that encourage kids to learn about their bodies and explore the world through walking.

Sweetgall became an expert on walking by . . . well, walking. In fact, he has trekked across the country seven times, including an 11,208-mile excursion that took him to all 50 states and lasted an entire year.

With almost two decades of walking experience to back him up, Sweetgall maintains that a moderate pace is the best pace for anyone at any age. "I'm convinced that the human body is a $3\frac{1}{2}$-mile-per-hour walking machine," he says. "Even slowing down from 4 miles per hour to $3\frac{1}{2}$ is better for most people. I've walked across America at both speeds, and I had much less soreness at the slower pace. Personally, I'd rather enjoy walking and *not* get sore."

Sweetgall believes that the purpose of walking is to keep yourself healthy and functional, so you can enjoy life to the fullest. You don't need to go fast to experience those benefits. "Of the thousands of people who attend my workshops, those who have the most aches and pains are almost always pushing themselves, trying to go a few gears higher," he says. "Don't get me wrong—I myself engage in intense exercise from time to time. But I can reach my target heart rate at just 2 miles per hour by Exerstriding (walking with poles) up a steep hill or climbing a ridge near my home in snowshoes."

IN STEP WITH
DICK BARR

HE HAD TO SLOW DOWN TO SLIM DOWN

PREVENTION WALKING CLUB VETERAN Dick "The Bear" Barr spent years trying to walk off some extra weight. But no matter how many miles he logged, he couldn't seem to slim down. Then he changed his attitude toward exercise— and he easily dropped 75 pounds in 18 months.

A resident of Edmonton in Alberta, Canada, Dick never got a driver's license. He relied on his feet to take him where he wanted to go. Yet even though he walked everywhere, he was carrying 260 pounds on his 6-foot-1 frame when he joined the *Prevention* Walking Club in 1986.

Back then, Dick found motivation in the club's patches, which were handed out for logging a certain number of miles. "I walked 8 to 10 miles a day, going to and from work—and I'd go out again *after* work," he recalls. "I rushed to get my miles in." And at *Prevention* Walker's Rallies, he always found his way to the front of the pack, so he could compete for first place with the fast walkers.

Unfortunately, Dick didn't realize that his high-gear approach to walking—and the hearty appetite that it produced—was undermining his efforts to slim down. In fact, over the next 10 years, his weight crept up to 284 pounds.

That's when he set out to do things a little differently. "I decided that my rushed way of walking was for the birds," he says. "I kept on walking, but I focused more on being healthy, as opposed to racking up miles. I threw out my bathroom scale because I didn't want the frustration of looking at the numbers every day. And I reread all my *Prevention* magazines and Walking Club newsletters for motivation."

Dick also began paying more attention to his eating habits. He ate only when he felt hungry, snacking on fruit in the middle of the day to tide him over until dinnertime. He slowed the pace of his meals so that he'd recognize when he was full and not stuff himself.

Dick's plan worked like a charm, as the pounds finally started melting away. "I was so surprised by how fast I lost weight that I went to my doctor just to make sure everything was okay," he says. "He told me that I was in great shape—and to keep walking!"

Dick remains an avid walker, only now he goes at a more leisurely pace. "I'm much more relaxed about it," he says. "And when I'm in a group, I've learned to love being at the back of the pack."

What about walking for weight loss? Sweetgall still thinks distance is more important than speed. The more distance you cover, he reasons, the more calories you're going to burn. "If you increase from a 17-minute mile to a 15-minute mile, you may use 9 percent more calories per mile. If you double your distance, you use 100 percent more calories. That's why I tell people to walk at their most comfortable pace and to stop worrying about whether they're going fast enough."

Ultimately, whether you choose brisk walking or long slow distance depends on your fitness level and your personal preferences. Do what feels right for you. And if your goal is to lose weight, know that you don't need to speedwalk to see results. Slow and steady sheds pounds, too.

CHAPTER 17

GREAT GADGETS FOR BOOSTING YOUR BURN

There was a time when I wouldn't even look at a gadget that promised to enhance the benefits of walking. I was a purist.

When hand weights were all the rage, I rejected them hands down. I knew that they could be harmful to my ligaments, tendons, and muscles. In fact, the first woman I knew to try them did a couple of miles with 2-pounders and ended up with a nasty case of bursitis in her shoulder. I was convinced: Hand weights are great for strength training at home or in a gym, but not while walking.

Then as I got older and my body began to change, my attitude toward gadgets began to change, too. I saw my once-svelte size 10 figure getting rounder and flabbier. Like many women and men my age, I was losing muscle and gaining fat—even though I walked regularly.

Frankly, I knew my eating habits needed an overhaul. But I also knew that my walking program was losing ground to a very busy and stressful schedule. I needed to get more from my workouts, and I had to do it with less time.

That's what prompted me to start looking a bit more seriously at equipment that promises to boost calorie burn. While I remain leery of hand weights, I have found two other gadgets that are especially helpful and fun to use: my walking poles and my PowerBelt.

I don't use these devices all the time because, to me, there's nothing more relaxing and stress-reducing than a nice long walk with my arms swinging freely and unencumbered. But a couple of times a week, I head out with my walking poles or my PowerBelt. I get a better cardiovascular workout without having to walk a lot faster, I burn more calories in less time, and I build upper-body strength. Who can argue with those benefits?

PUMPING IRON
WITHOUT THE IRON

When I first read the promotional materials for the PowerBelt, I laughed out loud. "Another silly walking gadget," I thought. Then Joshua Corn, president of Inergi Fitness (which manufactures the belt), sent me one to try. And you know what? I loved it!

The PowerBelt is a portable fitness machine that you wear around your waist, just like a belt. It has two handles that you hold while you walk, swinging your arms back and forth. (Surprisingly, you can move your arms in close-to-natural fitness-walking or racewalking form.) The handles are attached to cords, which are wound around spring-action disks. The disks provide resistance when you pull on the handles. This not only increases your heart rate but also tones the muscles in your shoulders, arms, and back.

Unlike hand weights, the PowerBelt doesn't strain your wrists. If your arms get tired, just let go of the handles—they pop right back into place on the belt. No need to lug them around. Once your arms have rested a bit, just grab the handles and start swinging.

The PowerBelt comes with special attachments, called PowerPaks, that progressively increase the resistance you feel when you pull on the handles. The PowerPaks can be added anytime. Sometimes I don't use the attachments; other times, I carry them in my fanny pack and add them when I want to do intervals (periods of brisk walking followed by periods of recovery).

Actually, you don't need the Power-Paks to get a good workout. Researchers at the University of Wisconsin–LaCrosse found that walking with the PowerBelt set at its lowest resistance burns 48 percent more calories than walking at the same speed without the belt. That's an impressive gain, even without the extra resistance.

While you walk, you can experiment with the handles, too. For example, you can give your shoulder and arm muscles more of a workout by pulling the handles out to the sides or up over your head. When you order your PowerBelt, you get a video that shows you different ways to use it. It's great for walking on treadmills, too.

At the time of this writing, the PowerBelt is selling for about $70. You may be able to find it in a sporting goods or fitness equipment store. If not, you can order it directly from the company: Inergi Fitness, 304 Tequesta Drive, Tequesta, FL 33469. For a toll-free number, call 800 directory assistance.

USING POLES
TO INCREASE INTENSITY

Ten years ago, at a *Prevention* Walker's Rally, I met a former cross-country skier by the name of Tom Rutlin. For a long time after, he hounded me to try a pair of walking

Another Plus for Poles

IF YOU HAVE OSTEOARTHRITIS or another joint disease, or if you're on the mend from a knee injury, walking poles can help you ease into exercise by reducing the force of your footsteps. According to Michael Torry, Ph.D., of the Steadman Hawkins Sports Medicine Foundation in Vail, Colorado, walking with poles can reduce the accumulated force by about 6 tons over the course of a mile. That way, you keep your workouts low-impact and pain-free.

poles that he had developed. He called them Exerstriders.

Rutlin is in his fifties now, but he looks years younger. He swears that he hasn't lifted a weight or used an exercise machine in 15 years. He attributes his trim waist and muscled arms and legs to walking with poles. "It allows me to work all of my muscles with one total-body activity," he explains.

Rutlin feels that total-body exercise such as walking with poles is the key to weight loss and overall fitness. It not only boosts aerobic capacity but also builds muscle strength and endurance. "Most people don't have time to do aerobic exercise *and* strength training," he explains. "Walking with poles combines both."

Swimming, rowing, and cross-country skiing are also forms of total-body exercise. But depending where you live, you can't do any of these activities year-round unless you have access to an indoor swimming pool or a rowing or cross-country ski machine. That's what makes walking with poles an ideal workout for so many people.

"Exerstriding (walking with poles) is a simple, safe, enjoyable activity that uses almost all of your muscles in a single exercise session," Rutlin says. "If done properly, it builds muscle in both your upper and lower body while providing enough of an aerobic workout to melt away fat. In fact, walking with poles burns 20 to 50 percent more calories than walking without poles at the same pace."

Needless to say, Rutlin's enthusiasm for his Exerstriders finally won me over. I agreed to give them a try. I must admit, I felt a bit strange walking with them at first. I stayed on little-used paths just so I wouldn't have to deal with all the odd looks and the "Where's the snow?" comments.

Now I keep my Exerstriders in the back of my car for spur-of-the-moment workouts. They're like having an extra pair of feet for support. They're also a nice piece of insurance, should I encounter any aggressive dogs on my walks. (I live out in the country, where dogs are often left to roam unattended.)

The Exerstriders come with a booklet that shows you stretching exercises you can do with the poles. In fact, one of my favorite things about walking with poles is being able to stop every few minutes to stretch my upper body and back. By propping myself up with the poles, I can rest and balance more easily.

If you order Exerstriders, you'll also get a video that shows you exactly how to use the poles to get the most from your workout. Rutlin even sings a tune to give you an idea of the proper pace.

At the time of this writing, the Exerstrider walking poles cost $69.95 per pair, plus $8.95 for shipping. To order, write to Exerstrider, PO Box 3087, Madison, WI 53704. If you prefer, you can get the company's toll-free number through 800 directory assistance. Either way, you'll need to specify your height, so you get the right-size poles. There is a 30-day return policy.

CHAPTER **18**

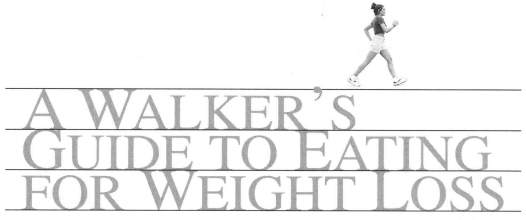

A WALKER'S GUIDE TO EATING FOR WEIGHT LOSS

No doubt about it: Walking can do wonders for your body, helping you to stay fit and healthy. But if your goal is to slim down, walking is only part of the equation. You need to eat right, too.

I know this from experience. As I approached my forties, I finally had to admit that I could no longer walk off my dietary indiscretions. And the older I get, the more those indiscretions affect my waistline.

Of course, what constitutes "eating right" depends on which expert you're asking. At one end of the spectrum is the ultra-low-fat diet recommended by Dean Ornish, M.D., president and director of the Preventive Medicine Research Institute in Sausalito, California. At the other end is the high-protein, very-low-carbohydrate diet proposed by Robert C. Atkins, M.D., in his book *Dr. Atkins' New Diet Revolution*. Between the two, you'll find all kinds of dietary strategies, each one promising to get rid of those extra pounds fast.

The middle-of-the-road plans seem to fall into two basic camps. One advocates a diet that is high in complex carbohydrates and low in fats, treating proteins more or less as a condiment. The other swears by what has become known as a 40-30-30 diet, where carbohydrates, proteins, and fats are always in balanced proportions. (The numbers refer to percentages of daily calorie intake: 40 percent carbs, 30 percent proteins, and 30 percent fats.)

Both eating plans are said to promote weight loss, and both claim to be heart-healthy. While the high-carb, low-fat diet has the most support within the medical and scientific communities, the 40-30-30 diet is winning raves from a growing number of believers who are finally taking off pounds after years of feasting primarily on carbohydrates. Some experts say, however, that this diet is dangerously low in carbohydrates if you are exercising daily.

Ultimately, which eating plan helps you slim down depends on your biochemistry, your food preferences, your lifestyle, and lots of other factors. The plan that took 50 pounds off your best friend may not do a thing for you, and vice versa. You'll need to experiment with different programs until you find one that you're comfortable with and that gives you the results you want. You may end up combining strategies from several programs into one customized eating plan.

Just be wary of diets that focus on a single food to the exclusion of virtually all others. Sure, you may lose a few

FINDING THE RIGHT REASON TO CHANGE

MANY PEOPLE LAUNCH A walking program because they want to lose weight. That's as good a reason as any. But sticking with any exercise routine can be a challenge. Add dietary changes to the mix, and anyone can feel overwhelmed by the prospect of slimming down.

For me, exercise has always come easy because I enjoy walking so much. Improving my eating habits was another story, until recently. That's when a series of events changed my attitude and helped to solidify my commitment to getting rid of the 30 pounds I had gained since age 40.

It all started when I happened to see Rush Limbaugh on television. At first, I barely recognized him. He had lost so much weight that he looked about 20 years younger. When the interviewer asked how he managed to stay so disciplined, he replied, "It's not about discipline. It's about desire. It's about passion. It's about belief and faith that if you pay your dues, you'll get the payoff. Discipline implies conflict and struggle. If you're trying to discipline yourself to eat well and exercise, then you're still in conflict."

His words struck me somewhere between my brain and my stomach. I had to become truly *passionate* about wanting to lose weight. Merely educating myself about healthy eating wasn't enough. It wouldn't give me the strength I needed to look at a bowl of ice cream and an apple and make the nutritious choice.

When I had this revelation, I happened to be staying at the Cloisters in Sea Island, Georgia. I was in a fabulous room overlooking the ocean, and I had a room-service menu filled with delicious treats. Somehow I managed to forgo the Death by Chocolate pie for a turkey sandwich with a dill pickle.

The next day, as I walked around the beautifully lush property, I noticed many older couples, perhaps in their late seventies. Some of them looked frail, some stooped, some overweight. I wondered how much they could actually enjoy their stays at such a lavish resort when they didn't seem fit enough to participate in many of the activities that were offered there.

pounds. But once you go off the diet, they'll come back. The same happens with crash dieting, which drastically cuts calories.

Always keep your food choices and calorie intake sensible. If you need guidance, consider consulting a nutritionist or a nutrition-minded physician.

SHEDDING POUNDS STARTS WITH YOUR PLATE

Personally, the eating plan that I like best isn't really a plan at all. It doesn't involve counting calories or calculating percentages of carbohydrates, protein, and fat. It's much simpler than that. You just need to redesign your dinner plate.

On my flight home that day, I picked up a magazine and by chance opened it to a photograph of a man named Bob Delmonteque. Then in his late seventies, he still had a magnificent physique—even washboard abs! He worked long and hard for that body, but he seemed to be having a lot of fun. To me, he looked so much more youthful than the people I had seen the day before, even though he was the same age as they.

Then when I arrived home, I came across a similar story in *Parade* magazine. This one described a woman in her late seventies who had decided to take up bodybuilding. She, too, looked incredible, as though she were rippling with energy. And she had been working out for only a few years.

This chain of events replayed in my mind for days. As far as my own weight-loss efforts, I could never muster much motivation from fitting into a smaller dress size or achieving what someone else had defined as the "perfect" body. But capturing the energy and vitality of Bob Delmonteque and his seventy-something female counterpart—now that inspired me!

Slowly but surely, I began to make changes in my eating habits. I chose foods more carefully, and I wrote down everything that went in my mouth. I felt more passionate about my decisions, and that translated into a sense of control that I had never experienced before. I found that I could pass up the ice cream in favor of the apple and not feel a single twinge of remorse. In the supermarket, I could walk right past the sweets on my way to pick up a can of artichoke hearts and not even flinch.

Never had I been so resolute about eating healthfully. And it showed: Within 4 weeks, I lost 5 pounds—a major accomplishment!

As I write this, I've kept off 8 pounds for 6 months. I'd like to lose more, but I'm focusing on getting fit. And I'm feeling so good that I'm able to do walk/runs.

Incidentally, I cut out the photos of those two bodybuilding seniors and hung them in my office. Looking at them every day reminds me that eating healthfully and exercising regularly aren't just about fitting into a size 10 dress. They're about getting healthy and being able to live life well.—*M.S.*

You've seen those paper plates that are divided into sections, right? If you were to use one of those to serve a typical American meal, the largest section—about half the plate—would be filled with meat. The other two sections would hold mostly fats and refined carbohydrates. Those proportions just don't fuel the body optimally.

In fact, we Americans eat some 839 *billion* calories of fat every year. That translates to about 35 percent of total calorie intake—a megadose compared with the 25 percent recommended by experts. And all that fat is leaving little room for nutrient-dense vegetables and other wholesome foods.

To trim your fat intake and create more balanced meals without measuring, just change the proportions on your plate. Going back to that divided paper plate, instead of putting the meat in the largest section, trim the portion so that it fits in one of the small sections. That's about a 3-ounce serving, roughly the size of a deck of playing cards, the amount considered healthy by nutrition experts.

As for the rest of the plate, fill the largest section with vegetables and the remaining small section with grains. Actually, you can let the grains spill over into the veggies if you want. And as you lose weight, you can adjust the portions even more, so the grains and vegetables are about equal. This increases your calorie intake a bit without adding on pounds.

Reconfiguring your dinner plate in this way makes healthy eating easy. It provides the right mix of nutrients while automatically slashing calories and grams of fat. And because your plate is full, the portions look adequate and appealing, so you won't feel deprived. That's key to making permanent changes in your eating habits.

To complement your healthy meals, use your snack times to nibble on your choice of fresh, juicy fruits. Try papayas, mangoes, kiwis, and other exotic options that you might normally pass by.

FILL UP, NOT OUT

Bet you didn't think eating for weight loss could be so simple. But it is! To keep meal preparation fast and your foods nutritious and tasty, just follow this advice.

For veggies, outsmart the seasons. Some vegetables, such as summer and winter squash, cabbage, lettuce, and tomatoes, taste best fresh. Most others are quite good frozen. So when fresh isn't available or convenient, reap the bounty of your supermarket's frozen-foods section. In particular, look for carrots, corn, green peas, green beans, and broccoli.

To bring frozen veggies back to life, try steaming them on the stovetop or cooking them in the microwave. Use as little water as possible, to preserve the nutrients. Prepared properly, frozen vegetables are just as nutritious as fresh.

Keep your grains whole. Whole grains are not only packed with vitamins and minerals, they're also loaded with fiber. And fiber makes you feel full, so you eat less—a big boost to weight loss.

One of the tastiest grains is rice—not the white instant rice, but brown and other varieties. Each has its own subtle flavor. Also shop for whole-wheat pasta, barley, millet, bulgur, multigrain dinner rolls, and 12-grain breads.

Jazz up your meats. Worried that you can't survive on a smaller portion of meat? Intensify the flavor with herbs and spices, and you'll feel completely satisfied. You can do the same with your fish and poultry, too. At Canyon Ranch health resort in Tucson, culinary experts add crushed fresh herbs to 1 teaspoon of melted butter to create a richly flavored sauce for broiled fish. (While you should try to limit your intake of butter, which is pure saturated fat, using just a teaspoon wisely can make a big difference in your enjoyment of your meal.)

Keep in mind, too, that in terms of your sense of satisfaction, meal presentation is just as important as preparation. Foods should be as pleasing to your eyes as to your tastebuds. Three ounces of beef doesn't look paltry when it's sliced and arranged on your plate.

If you simply can't stop with 3 ounces, go ahead and help yourself to a larger serving. Then make your next meal vegetarian. To lose weight, you want to make dietary changes that you can live with.

CHAPTER 19

THEY'RE LEAN AND LOVING IT

Sometimes it takes a good story to get us off our duffs and into walking. We like to hear that a person with whom we can identify worked out to lose weight and succeeded.

That's why I decided to collect several of my favorite "walking makeovers" and present them to you here. Between them, the four women whom I've profiled lost a total of 271 pounds. But it's not just their now-slim physiques that I find impressive. To me, each woman embodies the exhilaration of committing to a goal and achieving it. Success has changed them inside as well as outside.

These stories never cease to inspire me. I hope they inspire you, too. Enjoy!

SLIMMING HER BODY, HEALING HER MIND

In 1997, Carol Fisher took up walking to slim down. Two years later, she was 35 pounds lighter. But that doesn't even compare to the weight of the stress that had been lifted from her shoulders, thanks to exercise.

"Back then, I was a newly single mom, working 60 to 70 hours per week just to provide the basic necessities for my three daughters," Carol recalls. "Eating was my main source of pleasure, a means of managing my stress. Only it didn't work."

Carol remembers sleeping poorly at night and being tired during the day. She felt like a failure, and it was crushing her spirit.

"My family had lost so much—our life, our home, our dreams," Carol explains. "There was no extra money for roller skates, bicycles, music lessons, or new clothes. I always dreamed of being a writer, but I no longer had the time, inspiration, or energy to write."

Carol hated the way she felt and looked. She knew that she had to do something, but what? Fitness centers and exercise equipment were out of the question—they were too costly. So were weight-loss programs.

Carol mentioned her dilemma to a

friend, who suggested that she start walking. After all, it was free—no expensive equipment or special clothing to buy, no diet pills to pop.

"That first morning, though, I would rather have faced a grizzly bear alone in the dark than dragged myself out of bed an hour early just to walk," Carol laughs. "As I headed out the door and down the sidewalk, I struggled with the idea that I had completely lost my sanity. Or that I might die from lack of sleep. Yet by the time I returned home, I hated to go back inside. It seemed like ages since I had breathed fresh air and heard the sounds of nature."

Getting up early never got easier for Carol, but that didn't stop her from becoming hooked on walking. Within several weeks of starting her exercise program, she realized that she was losing weight. "I no longer felt the need to eat so much," she says. "Even better, I was gaining energy and feeling less achy."

Walking also gave Carol the private time she needed to vent her grievances, clear her head, and pray for guidance. She began to think more clearly and to rediscover her life's dreams. Eventually, she decided that she wanted to go back to college. And she did.

Before Carol began walking, there was so much weighing her down, emotionally as well as physically. Today, she uses walking to keep her life on track. "If I feel my goals are slipping out of sight or becoming too hard to achieve, I take a walk," she says. "If I

have issues that challenge and confuse me, I take a walk. When I need to talk or listen to God, I take a walk."

Yes, walking helped Carol to lose 35 pounds. But along the way, it also helped her to find herself.

MAKING WEIGHT LOSS PERSONAL

For Vicky Hager, losing and gaining weight was a way of life. She tried Weight Watchers and NutriSystem, once shedding more than 100 pounds. But the pounds were back within a few years.

By June 1995, Vicky's weight had crept to 264 pounds. "That's when I decided that I'd been fat long enough," she says. She was determined to slim down, and she'd do it on her own terms.

She combed through books and magazines, gathering information on weight loss. From that, she created her very own eating plan, breaking down her usual "three squares" into five mini-meals a day and counting grams of fat.

Once she got a handle on her eating habits, Vicky decided to add exercise to her weight-loss program. She couldn't do much at first, but eventually, she was walking several miles a day.

"Near my home, there's a lake with a 2-mile path around it. My sister and I walked there at night," Vicky says. "At lunch, I'd do a 1-mile loop around town near my workplace." Once winter arrived, she moved her lunchtime workouts indoors, to the enclosed sky-walks that crisscross downtown. In the evening, she'd stride on her treadmill or pedal her exercise bike.

"Eventually, I joined a fitness class that met on my lunch hour," Vicky says. "I never dreamed that I would join a fitness class at work!"

In May 1996, 11 months after launching her weight-loss program, Vicky entered a 10-K with a partner. "We were the first to finish!" she says. "We were so proud."

The next month, Vicky traveled to Germany to visit her brother. "He was shocked by how good I looked and how fit I'd become," she smiles. "While I was there, we participated in four Volkswalks" (noncompetitive group walks).

Between her walking routine and her healthy eating habits, Vicky managed to lose 98 pounds in 1 year. At the time she shared her story, she wanted to lose 30 more. To help her reach her goal, she joined a weight-loss support group. She also formed a group that gets together almost every day at lunch to walk.

"Right now, I walk 4 to 6 miles a day," Vicky says. "I feel great. I have lots of energy. And I do so many things that I never used to."

58 POUNDS LIGHTER, HEALTHIER THAN EVER

At age 34, Lisa Baker seemed to be losing control of her health—and her life. She weighed 177 pounds, too much for her 5-foot-4 frame. She was on insulin to control her diabetes, a condition she'd had for 25 years, as well as medication for high blood pressure, an underactive thyroid, and sore feet. She took quinine for nighttime leg cramps and another drug for esophageal reflux. On top of all that, she developed a drinking problem.

Tired of feeling sick when she woke up in the morning, Lisa confided in a colleague, who referred her to a treatment program. As she began to feel better, she came across information about the *Prevention* Walking Club. "The club inspired me to take my first walk around the block to lose weight," she recalls. "Three years earlier, I had managed to shed 30 pounds. But all of it came back, and then some."

Over time, Lisa's trips around the block extended to 4- to 5-mile daily excursions around several blocks, up hills, and over bridges. "Each day, I would try to walk just a little bit farther," she says. "Not so much that I felt uncomfortable, just enough to make a difference by the end of the week." Sometimes she'd listen to tapes of her favorite music, which helped to relieve stress. She also began lifting weights to build her upper-body strength.

Because she has diabetes, Lisa has very specific dietary guidelines to follow. But she taught herself to be more creative with her meals. "I used the American Diabetes Association diet as my guide," she explains. "For breakfast, I'd have bran cereal, half a pita, or a whole-wheat bagel, plus a piece of fruit. Lunch might be turkey breast with low-fat cheese or salad greens or homemade lentil soup. On weekends when I had the grill out, I'd cook vegetables on it for a bit of variety."

Finally, Lisa was doing something good for herself, and it paid off handsomely. Within 2 years, her weight dropped to 119. Her nighttime leg cramps and reflux problems went away, and she no longer needed medication for blood pressure or painful feet. Her doctor reduced her insulin dosage from 38 units to 18. And she became alcohol-free.

Lisa never imagined that walking could have such profound effects on her health. "I feel so much better, and I look better, too," she says. "That first walk around the block taught me an invaluable lesson: All things that seem insurmountable really do begin with a single step."

STAYING TRIM THROUGH TEAMWORK

As captain of the Buns and Roses walking team from Portland, Oregon, Jackie Lord is accustomed to rallying her teammates for competition. But it's her teammates that keep her motivated to walk and committed to fitness. She credits them with helping her to maintain an 80-pound weight loss for the past 4 years.

Jackie didn't always have a weight problem. In fact, as a high school student, she was a lean running machine. At 5-foot-11 and a mere 125 pounds,

she was fast enough to earn a spot in the Junior Olympics. But even then, despite her athletic prowess, she didn't pay much attention to eating right.

Years later, Jackie wed and began raising a family. The combination of a troubled marriage and a less-active lifestyle took a toll on her waistline. Eventually, she weighed 204 pounds. "When I turned 30, I joined Weight Watchers, where I lost 60 pounds," she says. "But as my marriage faltered, I got off track. I not only gained back the 60 pounds, but I added 60 more."

Jackie went back to Weight Watchers, but this time, she couldn't make it work. "I was having financial problems, and I just couldn't rationalize paying the fees," she explains. "So I decided to increase my activity level and watch my diet as best I could." On her own, she lost 80 pounds.

Suddenly, Jackie found herself facing a new dilemma. As thrilled as she was with her newly trim physique, she was terrified that all those pounds would come back. She knew she had to do something to stay motivated.

Jackie read several articles about walking and decided that it might help her trim and tone her body even more. At the time, her coworkers were looking for an organized activity that could help them shape up, too. So Jackie suggested that they form a team and enter the Portland to Coast Relay, a 125-mile walking event held every year in late August. They called themselves Buns and Roses and appointed Jackie captain.

In the relay, team members take turns walking 5- to 7-mile segments of the route. The entire event takes 20 to 24 hours to complete. "The first year we completed the relay, I cried for days afterward," Jackie says. "I couldn't believe that after years of abusing my body by gaining and losing weight, I was still able to accomplish such an athletic feat."

The experience proved emotional for another reason as well. "I remember coming down the promenade, about 300 yards from the finish line, when I spotted my daughter Kelly," Jackie says. "Kelly was our first-aid volunteer, but she's a star athlete in her own right, a state competitor in track and water polo. As I passed her, I could see that she was crying. She gave me a high five and told me that she was proud of me."

Kelly still calls her mom her hero, a title that Jackie treasures. It's one reason why she continues to enter Portland to Coast each year. Another is the camaraderie of her teammates. "We depend on each other for emotional support as well as physical motivation," Jackie explains. "In my case, the team keeps me committed to watching my weight and staying healthy. For others, the team has helped them to overcome weight problems, deal with divorces and the passing of loved ones, and confront emotional issues that deeply affect their lives."

Jackie, who's now married to a former member of the Buns and Roses volunteer support crew, says that her weight still fluctuates a bit. "But my doctor is thrilled with my cholesterol and sugar counts," she adds. "He says that I'm reducing my risk of diabetes, which runs in my family. And I feel as if I owe it all to Buns and Roses!"

STRENGTH TRAINING FOR WALKERS

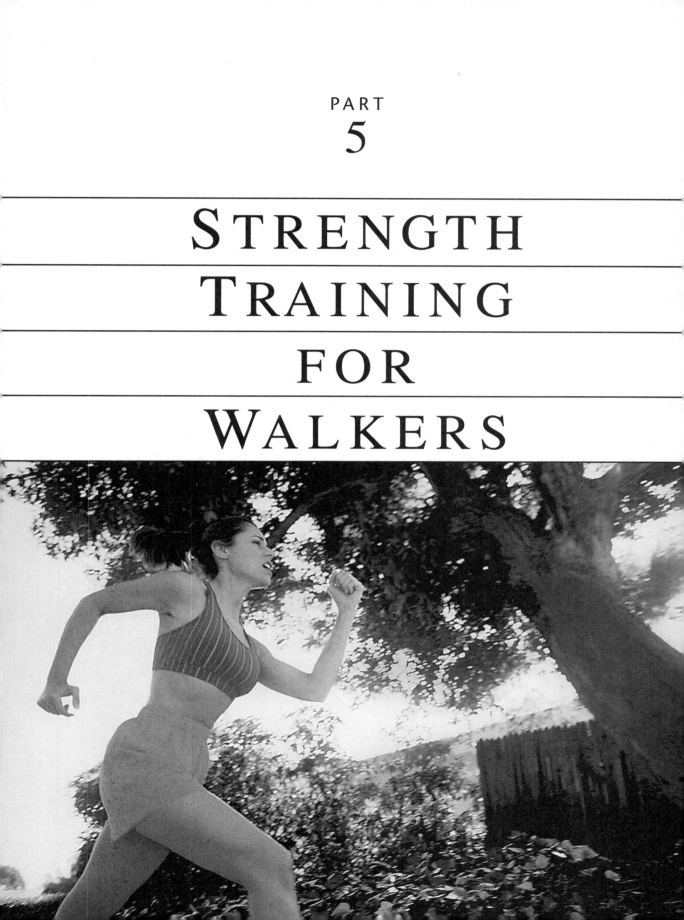

CHAPTER 20

A ROUTINE FOR THE ROAD

Do you want to add some oomph to your walking routine? Pick up your pace? Increase your mileage? Tackle steeper inclines?

The secret to walking faster, longer, and more energetically is a strong, limber body. That strength and flexibility can also help ward off pain in your shins and stiffness in your hips and lower back.

So how do you build such a powerful body? Easy: Just add some simple strength-training exercises to your workouts.

The following modest-but-mighty moves—recommended by walking coach Elaine Ward, founder and director of the North American Racewalking Foundation, and exercise physiologist Doug Garfield, Ed.D., developer of TrainS.M.A.R.T., a program for high-performance athletes—can make a huge difference in the effec-

tiveness of your walking routine. The great thing about them is that they can be done on the go, without weights or other gadgets. The only "equipment" called for is the nearest tree or pole for balance.

You can incorporate these exercises into your workout any way you want. Do them all at once, or split them up between bouts of walking—walk for 10 minutes, do a set of an exercise, walk for 10 minutes, do a set of another exercise, and so on. If you close your eyes while you do the standing stretches, you will improve your balance as well.

To avoid muscle soreness, start with the smallest number of repetitions and work up gradually. Remember, too, that these numbers are only suggestions. If you need to start with fewer reps, that's fine. Allow your body to guide you.

Have fun—and get stronger fast.

PRIME YOUR SHINS FOR SPEED

If your shins scream, "Slow down!" whenever you make an effort to increase your pace, add either of the following exercises to your routine. You don't need to do both unless you have the time and the desire.

HEEL-TOE ROCK. With your weight balanced equally on both feet and your knees bent, gently rock back on your heels and pull your toes off the ground. Then with one smooth motion, rock forward and

roll up onto your toes. Use all of your muscles to perform smooth, controlled movements. Do 12 to 15 repetitions, counting the entire heel-to-toe motion as one.

PAUSE WALK. Swing one leg forward as if to take a step. But before your heel hits the ground, pause with your foot about 3 inches off the ground and your toes pointed toward the sky. Slowly count to three, and as you do, continue pulling your toes back toward your shin. Repeat the pause with each step forward as you walk for 1 minute. Then walk normally for 1 minute. Repeat the entire cycle two more times.

TONE YOUR HIPS FOR POWER

Strong, flexible hip flexor muscles add power and grace to your walk while helping you lengthen your stride. Try the following two exercises to limber up and increase your range of motion. They can also help alleviate any stiffness that you may notice after long periods of sitting.

FIGURE EIGHTS. Stand on one leg, holding on to a pole or a tree for support. With the opposite foot, draw a figure eight in the air, making the top loop in front of your body and the bottom loop behind your body. Gradually increase the size of the figure so that your hip rotates fully in front and back. Do 10 to 20 repetitions with each leg.

HIP STRETCH. This stretch is great for walkers as well as for anyone who has to sit most of the day. Stand tall, with your back straight. Step forward with your right leg, keeping your left foot on the ground. Make sure that your right knee is squarely over the center of your right foot, forming a 90-degree angle. Tilt your hips forward until you feel a mild stretch in your left hip. Keep your left heel flat. Hold for a slow count of five. Step back. Repeat two more times with your right leg forward, then switch legs to stretch your right hip.

TIGHTEN YOUR TUMMY FOR ENDURANCE

Weak abdominal muscles contribute to poor posture and swayback, which can lead to back discomfort, especially on longer walks. These two crunches will help strengthen your stomach muscles and relieve back tension. And, even better, you don't need to lie down on wet grass to do them.

STANDING CRUNCH. Place your palms on the tops of your thighs. Round your back and contract your abdominal muscles. While crunching, slide your hands down your thighs to your knees, applying firm pressure along the way. This intensifies the contraction of your abdominal muscles. Relax. Do 12 to 15 repetitions.

TWISTING ABS. Place the palm of your right hand on top of your left thigh. Round your back and contract your abdominal muscles as you twist down and to the left. While crunching, apply firm pressure to your left thigh with your right hand to intensify the contractions of your abdominal muscles. Do 12 repetitions, then switch sides.

BUILD THIGHS TO CONQUER HILLS

If you walk on level ground most of the time, hills may seem especially challenging. That could be because your quadriceps, the muscles in the front of your thighs, aren't sufficiently developed. Practice these exercises every day, and you'll quickly turn mountains into molehills.

QUADS, PART 1. This is a controlled leg squat. Be sure to do it slowly so it feels challenging. Stand with your feet shoulder-width apart. Moving to a slow count of five, squat down as far as you comfortably can, but no farther than a 90-degree angle at your knees. Make sure that your knees are over but not past your toes and your back is straight. Then straighten up to a count of two. If you reach your arms overhead on your way up, you'll finish each squat by stretching your waist and rib cage. Work up to 15 to 20 repetitions. Always follow this exercise with Quads, Part 2.

QUADS, PART 2. Stand with one foot on a curb, one in the street. Line up the toes of your street foot just below the instep of your curb foot. With your weight on your street foot, squat down to a count of two, then straighten up to a count of two. Again, don't bend your knees more than 90 degrees. You're using your whole body as a weight for your leg. Work up to 10 to 15 repetitions per side.

CHAPTER **21**

A YOGA PROGRAM FOR WALKERS

The older I get, the more I appreciate yoga. All other athletic activities I do, including walking, tend to leave my muscles tight. Yoga stretches my muscles at the same time it strengthens my entire body. It helps me stay flexible, so I move better and feel better, whether I'm fitness walking or just going about my daily business.

These days, I spend some time every morning doing yoga in my living room. Sometimes it's just 10 minutes; other times it's as much as an hour. Depending on how I feel, I may take a brisk walk beforehand, or I may save my walk until afterward.

If I don't have time to do both, or if the weather isn't great for walking outside, I opt for the yoga session. Rushing to fit in my walk can leave me frazzled. Besides, I can usually find time to go for a walk later in the day—and I can do yoga in my pajamas.

Practicing yoga first thing in the morning helps set my pace and my attitude for the day ahead. It puts my schedule, which is usually packed, in

better perspective. It energizes my body and my mind, and that positive feeling can sustain me for hours.

Plus, if I go walking after I stretch out with yoga, my body feels better from the start. I need less warmup time to get into that feeling-great zone.

ADVICE FROM AN EXPERT

For several years now, I've been incorporating yoga sessions into the programs for the *Prevention* Walker's Rallies. Many of these sessions have been led by Suza Francina, a certified Iyengar yoga instructor at the Ojai Yoga Center in Ojai, California, and author of *The New Yoga for People over 50*. She is my very favorite teacher. Rally participants have told me how much they love her detailed yet friendly approach to yoga practice.

I asked Francina to identify the most important, most effective yoga poses for walkers. They're presented in this chapter, complete with how-to instructions. The great thing is that once you begin doing these postures, you should feel a difference almost immediately. "You may not see dramatic changes in your body, but you should feel lighter, freer, taller, and more positive," she says. "You're releasing stress and tension from your body."

And exactly how do these yoga techniques benefit walkers? "If people don't stretch their bodies as they age, their legs stiffen up, and they tend to shuffle," Francina explains. "Often, you can tell someone's age by his or her walk. There's a certain stiffness to it. When you practice yoga, you develop a wonderful, free, fluid stride—like a young person." (You can also use the Dynamic Body Exercises in chapter 38 to ward off stiffness and increase flexibility. Practice one or the other, or both, as I do.)

The great thing about yoga is that you can do it just about anywhere, anytime. It's best done indoors on a level floor, in serene surroundings. But once you are familiar with the basic poses, you can use them to stretch in your kitchen, at your desk, in your backyard, or while watching TV or listening to music.

For standing poses, be sure that you're on a nonslippery surface. For seated and reclining poses, a carpet or a pad works fine. You can even go outside on the grass if you want.

Some of the postures described below call for special equipment such as a yoga strap, a yoga bolster or prop, or a sticky mat (a nonslip mat especially designed for yoga practice). In most cases, you can improvise with something you have at home. If you prefer, you can purchase the equipment by mail from any of the following companies: Bheka Yoga Supplies, Hugger-Mugger Yoga Supplies, or Yoga Props. For the companies' toll-free numbers, call 800 directory assistance.

Ideally, you should stretch at least once every day, for 5 to 10 minutes. If you can, block out time for a few longer sessions each week. Even better, sign up for a class taught by a certified instructor, so you can learn proper movement and form.

Whenever you stretch, listen to your body and concentrate on working those parts that feel most uncomfortable or stiff. You want to do enough different poses that you take your body through its full range of motion. If you experience any unusual strain or discomfort while practicing any pose, stop doing it and seek the advice of a qualified yoga instructor.

Ready? Let's begin!

THE FEET COME FIRST

Remember the old adage "When your feet hurt, you hurt all over"? Well, it has more than a grain of truth. Foot ailments, which often result from years of wearing poor-fitting shoes, can affect your posture and alter your body mechanics. They can also trigger problems elsewhere in your body, including headaches, backaches, and leg cramps.

Sore, painful feet are a primary reason why many people give up fitness walking as they get older. That's unfortunate because the combination of walking and yoga can actually help rehabilitate injured or aching feet. "Walking maintains the overall health of your feet by improving their circulation, strength, and flexibility," Francina explains. "Yoga stretches and strengthens your feet, correcting the damage inflicted by poor-fitting shoes and cumulative wear and tear."

One of Francina's favorite exercises for the feet involves simply spreading the toes. "When I ask beginning yoga students to lift and stretch all 10 of their toes wide apart until they can see daylight in between, they usually look at me in utter disbelief," she says. "But the truth is, we can stretch our toes just like we stretch our fingers. If we went barefoot or wore shoes wide enough to accommodate all 10 toes, we wouldn't lose the open spaces between our toes that we had as children."

When you don't have spaces between your toes, you can't properly balance and support your body. This leads to the underuse or overuse of specific bones, tendons, and ligaments—leaving the rest of your body to compensate.

The three exercises presented below (including spreading toes) help stretch your toes and lift your arches. By practicing them regularly, you can begin to undo a lifetime of damage to your feet. Over time, you may notice that your shoes wear more evenly. That's because you're balancing your stride, walking more evenly on both feet, and experiencing less wear and tear. Your feet will feel stronger and more flexible, ready to carry you for many more miles down the road of life.

Quick Tip

If you can't spread your toes inside your walking shoes, then you need wider shoes. A too small toebox results in the overuse or underuse of certain bones, muscles, tendons, and ligaments. Your entire body must compensate for that.

SPREADING TOES. While seated, spread your toes as far apart as possible. Reach down with your hands and try to make your big toes touch each other. Also separate your little toes away from their neighbors. This lifts and strengthens your arches, which are responsible for holding your ankles and feet in correct position. Hold for at least 30 seconds, long enough to feel that your toes have gotten a good stretch.

ENTWINING FINGERS AND TOES. Sit in a chair or on the floor. Cross your legs so that your right ankle is on your left knee. Take hold of your right foot with both hands. Interlace the fingers of your left hand with the toes of your right foot, sliding the base of your pinkie to the base of your little toe, the base of your ring finger to the base of your fourth toe, and so on. Then spread your fingers wide apart. Extend through your heel and push your toes toward your right knee. Hold for at least 30 seconds. When you release your fingers, notice how your foot appears rosier from the increased circulation. Repeat the stretch with your opposite foot.

If you notice stiffness in any of your toes while doing this exercise, take a few moments to firmly massage them at the base. The more your toes hurt when you spread them, the more they need the massage. Smile and breathe slowly, letting go of any pain or stiffness. Dealing with little pains in your feet will help you avoid greater pains elsewhere in your body.

PEN/PENCIL STRETCH. Sitting on the floor with your legs straight out in front of you, bend your knees just until your feet are within reach. Gently insert pens or pencils of various thicknesses between your toes at the base. Start with pens or pencils that are just thick enough to move your toes apart, especially if your toes are very tight and painful. Save the thickest pens or pencils for your big toes. Leave them in place for several minutes. If done sensibly, this exercise is an effective way to stretch the toes. It's very stimulating.

RELIEVING STIFF SHOULDERS

The cow face pose works the muscles that control your shoulder joints. It's one of the most basic corrective postures for relieving stiffness in the shoulders.

By practicing this posture regularly, you develop greater flexibility and range of motion in your shoulder joints. You also improve your posture, as rounded shoulders return to their natural position. You'll stand taller, and you'll carry yourself more gracefully.

To avoid overstretching your muscles or straining your shoulder joints, you may want to use some sort of strap when practicing this pose. You can buy a cotton strap specially designed for yoga, but a necktie, rolled-up towel, or soft belt will do just as well. Its purpose is to help you approximate the movements of the pose and achieve a comfortable, balanced stretch.

A

COW FACE POSE. Stand or sit in your best, tallest posture. Pause for a moment to observe your breath. Allow yourself to smile. This naturally relaxes your jaw and face muscles.

Stretch your left arm up over your head, then bend it at the elbow so that your palm touches your back between the shoulder blades. Reach across with your right hand to move your elbow closer to your head.

Release your right hand from your left elbow and bring your right arm behind your body. Bend your right elbow and place your right hand, palm facing out, in the middle of your back above your waist. Without distorting your posture or straining, try to clasp your hands together (A).

B

Stretch back with both elbows. Keep your head centered and your face relaxed. Hold for at least 30 seconds, then release and repeat on the opposite side. If one side seems tighter than the other, hold the pose a bit longer or do it a second time.

Note: If your fingers just barely touch, or if your hands aren't close to each other, hold a strap in your left hand and gradually move your hands together (B). You may need to work at this for a few weeks, or even a few months. But with regular practice, you will be able to clasp your hands behind your back.

SILENCING CREAKY KNEES

The health of your knees is affected by the strength and flexibility of your thigh muscles—the quadriceps (at the front of the thighs), hamstrings (at the back), and adductors (along the inside). These muscles can become tight with repetitive activities such as walking. And as they tighten, they pull on muscles around your knees. This compromises the flexibility of your knee joints and makes them vulnerable to injury.

The following exercises gradually stretch and lengthen stiff leg muscles and help prevent knee injury. They're generally safe for everyone, though they should be practiced with a qualified instructor if you have an injured knee. The first time you try these postures, have someone read the instructions to you, so you can concentrate on what you're doing.

STRAP STRETCH. Sit on the floor with your legs straight out in front of you. Lean back on your elbows, then check that your upper body and legs are in line. Lie flat on your back, with your knees bent and your feet flat on the floor. If your head tilts backward, with your chin higher than your forehead, place a folded blanket under your head and neck for support. Allow your back to relax into the floor.

Bring your right knee toward your chest. Loop a strap, necktie, towel, or soft belt over the ball of your foot. Hold the strap with your right hand. Stretch out your left arm, palm facing up, so that it's in line with your shoulder on the floor.

Slowly straighten your right leg. Stretch your toes toward your face to lengthen your calf muscles and Achilles tendons. Move your hand up the strap toward your foot until your arm is straight, as shown. Keep your shoulders and the rest of your back relaxed on the floor.

If your right hand remains far away from your foot, keep your left knee bent. If your hand is high up on the strap close to your foot, or if you can reach your big toe, deepen the stretch by straightening your left leg, extending through the heel.

Relax your face and smile. Let your breath flow freely. Try not to let your hand become tense as it grasps the strap. Hold for about 30 seconds at first, longer as you learn to relax into the stretch. Release your leg, then repeat on the opposite side.

A

HERO POSE. Begin on your hands and knees, with your knees and feet about hip-width apart. Turn your toes slightly inward, pointing them so that the tops of your feet and ankles are on the floor.

If you have difficulty lowering your bottom to the floor from this position, place a stack of blankets, a dictionary, or another firm level prop behind you in such a way that when you lower your bottom, you'll end up sitting near the front of the prop (A). The person in the photo is using a yoga bolster.

116

If you experience any pain in your ankles or discomfort in your feet, you may want to place a folded blanket or rolled towel under your ankles and feet, as shown. Or kneel on a stack of two or three neatly folded blankets, with your feet hanging over the edge. For added comfort, roll up two washcloths or socks and place one behind the crease of each knee. This helps increase space within your knee joints.

From the starting position, slowly lower your bottom toward the floor or prop (if you're using one). If you can't make contact, or if you experience knee strain, add more height to your prop. Place enough support under your bottom so that you can sit upright, with your hands pressing down into your thighs.

B

Hold the pose for 1 minute to start. As your comfort level increases, you can stay in this position even longer. You can also practice stretching your arms upward, which lengthens your spine (B). Simply interlock your fingers, turn your palms outward, and extend your arms forward and upward.

To come out of the pose, return to the starting position, with your hands and knees on the floor.

THE POSE THAT REFRESHES

If you own a dog or cat, you've probably noticed how your pet instinctively stretches its body after a long rest. This natural movement provides the inspiration for the dog pose (hence its name).

The posture is a virtual panacea for people of all ages. It stretches the entire body, from the fingers to the toes. Turning your body halfway upside down reverses the downward pull of gravity and increases circulation in the entire body, including bloodflow to your brain. It releases tension in your neck and strengthens your hands, wrists, arms, and shoulders. It lengthens your spinal column and strengthens your abdominal muscles. It reduces roundness in your upper back by stretching the pectoral muscles on the front of your chest. And it may stimulate bones to retain calcium, helping to prevent osteoporosis. It's like an entire yoga session rolled into one pose.

DOG POSE. Practice this pose on a nonslip surface so your hands and feet don't slide. Begin on all fours, with your knees slightly behind your hips, your knees and feet about hip-width apart, and your toes curled under. Place your hands slightly in front of your shoulders, shoulder-width apart. Spread your fingers wide apart and press both hands into the floor.

(continued)

While exhaling, straighten your knees and push your bottom toward the ceiling so your body forms an upside-down V, as shown. Raise your heels high off the floor, trying to lift your bottom higher and higher. Press your hands deeper into the floor, as if you were pushing the floor away from you. After holding this position for a few breath cycles, try to press your heels toward the floor.

Continue to breathe smoothly and naturally. Keep your face and neck soft and relaxed. Let your head hang down toward the floor. Imagine roots pulling your hands and feet into the earth while your buttocks and tailbone reach toward the sky. Hold for about more five breath cycles—long enough to stretch without feeling strain. Release by returning to all fours. Slowly lower your bottom toward your heels, then your torso and forehead toward the floor.

Note: If you have problems with your wrists, place a folded sticky mat, towel, or blanket under the heels of your hands. This elevates the wrist area and supports it with extra cushioning.

TRAINING FOR THE TRAILS

There's nothing like a hike to get you away from traffic, noise, and less-than-fresh air. But even dedicated city walkers might find themselves nursing sore feet, creaking knees, or an aching lower back after a day on the trail unless they do some prehike training.

This isn't to suggest that hiking is only for the super-fit. On the contrary, anyone who's in reasonable shape can do it. But every activity uses certain muscles, and hiking uses different ones than walking.

I remember hearing from a woman who participated in 10-kilometer Volkswalks (noncompetitive walking events) every weekend. Obviously, she was quite fit. She wrote to me because she was having difficulty navigating hills, which abound on hiking trails. She was in her late sixties, and she had lost strength in her quadriceps muscles, on the front of her thighs. I suggested that she do exercises to build up her quads. She did—and they worked like a charm. Now any 10-K is a breeze for her.

To help prime your muscles for hiking, follow this training routine recommended by exercise physiologist Doug Garfield, Ed.D., developer of TrainS.M.A.R.T., a program for high-performance athletes. Dr. Garfield's strategies can help you conquer any terrain and keep you from feeling overly sore the next day.

For the best results, practice these techniques for at least 2 weeks before you head out on the trail. By that time, you'll be not only stronger but also smarter about the demands of hiking and, therefore, less vulnerable to injury.

GET SET TO GO DOWNHILL

You may not think it, but descending a hill or mountain can be just as physically challenging as climbing up one. Each time your foot strikes the ground on your way down, it absorbs 5 times your body weight. On flat terrain, the impact is considerably less—just

$1\frac{1}{2}$ times your body weight. You need to prepare your body for that extra stress.

"There is nothing like walking downhill to prepare you for hiking downhill," Dr. Garfield says. "It's the eccentric contractions (the lengthening of the leg muscles) that leave you stiff and sore the morning after your hike. To prepare your body for that, you need to find hills to walk down. No treadmill or stairclimbing machine can do it for you."

Try to incorporate walking downhill into the daily workouts leading up to your planned hike. Choose a slope that is paved or at least has an even surface. That way, you work your muscles properly and adequately without putting extra stress on your ankles and knees, which can occur when you're walking on a surface that's rutted, rough, gravel-covered, or just generally uneven.

DO A DRESS REHEARSAL

Another way to thwart posthike soreness is to wear your hiking shoes during your regular walking workout. They weigh more than your regular walking shoes, and they're designed differently, too. They'll take a little getting used to. "Consider this a dress rehearsal for your hike," Dr. Garfield advises. "You'll be much less likely to develop blisters or sore shins from the weight or friction of the boots."

Wearing your hiking boots before you go hiking may also help protect you against backache. "Many people experience lower-back pain after a day of hiking, and they think it's from carrying a pack," Dr. Garfield explains. "But often it's caused by the stress of wearing heavier shoes." The shoes give more momentum to your stride, making it longer. This change can tire out your lower back.

If you plan to carry a daypack when you go hiking, you ought to practice wearing it, too—during your walks around town or on your treadmill. "A pack changes your center of gravity and forces you to use your abdominal muscles more to maintain balance," Dr. Garfield explains. By working up to the approximate weight you'll be toting along on your hike, you'll be accustomed to the pack by the time you hit the trail.

SQUAT, THEN CLIMB ROCKS

For stepping from boulder to boulder and navigating loose accumulations of stone, you need stability in your lower body—your pelvis and hips as well as your knees and feet. This kind of stability comes courtesy of your torso muscles.

According to Dr. Garfield, one great way to toughen your trunk is to do squats. His technique: Pick up a soft exercise ball, the kind you might use in a swimming pool (not a Nerf ball, though). Make sure that it's soft enough to flatten out somewhat when you lean on it. Place it in the small of your back and lean against a wall. Slide down the wall into a squat, as though you were sitting down. Go only as far as you feel comfortable, without straining. Ideally, your thighs should be parallel to the ground, but don't go any lower than that. Keep your knees aligned over your big toes and second toes. Then rise to the starting position. Gradually build up to two or three sets of 8 to 12 repetitions each.

This exercise helps stabilize your torso, pelvis, and hips by teaching you to equally support your weight in all directions as you roll the ball up and down the wall. It also helps strengthen your thighs—and it works fast.

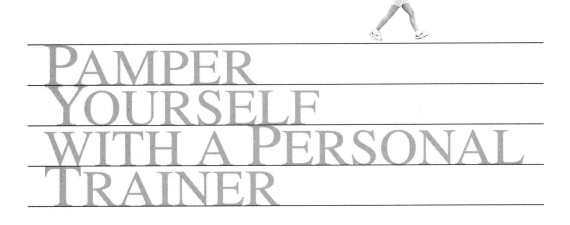

PAMPER YOURSELF WITH A PERSONAL TRAINER

Unless you use an arm-pumping race-walking technique or walking poles, your upper body probably isn't getting much of a workout when you walk. To give these muscles equal time, you need to add strength training to your exercise routine.

Strength training is an integral part of a total fitness program, even for the most dedicated walker. By increasing the strength of your arms, chest, shoulders, and back, you improve your posture and can carry boxes, bags, and other objects with ease. These changes enhance your overall sense of well-being.

Strength training can benefit your lower body, too. For example, if your regular walking route takes you over flat terrain, you're missing out on the buttock- and thigh-toning effects of climbing hills. Exercises that target these lower-body muscles can make a

big difference in your physique. It may enhance your endurance while walking, too.

If you've never lifted weights before, or if you need extra motivation to stick with a strength-training program, consider signing on with a personal trainer. No class can compete with the one-on-one instruction that a personal trainer provides.

This fitness professional can teach you proper lifting technique, whether you're using free weights (dumbbells and barbells) or machines. You'll be amazed at how a slight variation in the way you hold a weight or position yourself on a machine can alter the effectiveness of an exercise. In fact, it can help protect you from injury.

Not long ago, I decided to restart my own strength-training program. But I felt too mentally drained to go it alone. I needed to be told what to do and when to do it. I needed to relax my brain while I fired up my muscles for better fat-burning. I needed to learn new exercises that could trim and tone my body and prepare me for hiking. In short, I needed Aubrey Parsons.

Aubrey is a woman about my age with a body that shows she knows what she's doing. Slim and muscular, she's the embodiment of fitness at 40-plus. Just being around her channeled inspirational messages into my fitness-weary brain. She became my role model.

When I first signed on with Aubrey, we agreed to meet at 7 o'clock two mornings a week for 3 months. (I also did one workout a week on my own.) Here are highlights from some of our sessions. I hope that my positive experience might encourage you to seek out the assistance of a fitness professional.

SESSION 1: STARTING OUT

I arrive at the gym early to warm up on the treadmill. (To avoid injury, you should begin every strength-training workout with 5 to 10 minutes of walking or cycling. This pumps up your bloodflow and primes your muscles for lifting.) Aubrey shows up soon after, and we get right to work.

We start with the machines that work the large muscles of the lower body: squats, leg extensions, and leg curls. As we move from one machine to another, I develop a level of comfort that feels vaguely familiar—like when I was 5 years old and my mom was teaching me how to tie my shoes. Aubrey watches my every move, touching my muscles to show me when I'm doing an exercise right and when I'm not. She counts my repetitions and times my rest periods to the second. All I do is follow her instructions.

For me, this kind of undivided attention is in itself worth the cost of hiring a personal trainer. Women so often take care of others. For this golden hour, somebody is taking care of me. And it feels great!

I leave the gym with quaking thighs and Jell-O arms, having pushed my muscles through three sets of 15 repetitions, even at relatively light weights. Two days later, I'm back—sore, but hungry for more.

SESSION 2: FEELING FITTER

We run through the same routine: lower body first, upper body next, abdominal crunches for the grand finale. Aubrey adds a few new machines. If I tell her that a certain exercise is too uncomfortable, she helps me make adjustments so that the movements feel better. It's bliss to have *her* figure out how much weight I should lift, how high the seat should be, which machine to go to next. I know I need to pay attention so that eventually I can do the exercises on my own. In the meantime, I just let Aubrey baby me.

By the end of the workout, I can sense my body starting to perk up. My posture is straighter. My arms are tighter. Even though there are no visible changes, I feel better all over.

SESSION 3: A SURPRISING FIX FOR SORENESS

I hop out of bed at 6:00 A.M. sharp. I have someplace to go, someone to meet. There is no "Should I or shouldn't I?" Aubrey is expecting me, and I'll be there.

By 6:30, just as the sun begins to rise, I'm in the car and heading for the gym. At one point, I reach up to brush my hair out of my face. That's when I notice the soreness. It took a few days to catch up with me. But the muscles in my arms and shoulders, which don't get much of a workout when I walk, are really achy.

When I arrive to the gym, Aubrey goes easy on me. She tells me to rest an extra day and then do my workout. After 3 days, I still feel pretty sore. I call Aubrey, and she encourages me to move through it.

I go to the gym for my once-a-week

The 10 Biggest Fitness Blunders

THE AMERICAN COUNCIL ON Exercise (ACE) polled its trainers to find out the most common mistakes people make when exercising. At the very least, these errors undermine the effectiveness of a workout. At worst, they may lead to strain, pain, and injury.

1. **Not stretching enough:** Whether you're exercising aerobically or lifting weights, warm up first, then stretch.

2. **Lifting too much weight:** Increase your weight gradually, and you'll avoid setting yourself up for pain.

3. **Not warming up before an aerobic activity:** Don't set the treadmill to your fastest pace as soon as you step on. Gradually increase your speed.

4. **Forgetting to cool down:** Before you head for the showers, cool down by doing some light activity, such as walking slowly. Then stretch your muscles to improve their flexibility. You're actually getting them ready for your next workout.

5. **Exercising too hard:** If you've skipped several workouts, don't try to make up for lost time in one session. You're only setting yourself up for soreness and possible injury.

6. **Drying up:** Drink water—lots of water—before, during, and after your workout.

7. **Leaning on the stairclimber rails:** Yes, you can burn more calories by exercising on a stairclimbing machine than by walking. But if you lean on the handrails during your workout, you're just defeating the purpose.

8. **Wimping out:** While you don't want to push yourself too hard, especially if you're just starting an exercise program, you need to work intensely enough to get results. It's a fine balance—one that's much easier to maintain with the guidance of a personal trainer.

9. **Jerking the weight:** In strength training, you control the weight. Make your moves smooth. If you jerk when you lift, you need a lighter weight.

10. **Pigging out:** If you're at the gym for less than 2 hours, you don't need to supplement your meals with sports drinks and energy bars. A healthy, balanced eating plan and plenty of water will cover your nutritional bases.

solo workout. To my surprise, I feel even better *after* I do my routine. I never expected that what had made me sore in the first place could also help relieve the soreness. It's an important lesson to learn because I get sore easily.

SESSION 4: PUSHING FOR SUCCESS

As Aubrey starts increasing the amount of weight that I'm lifting, I can see the benefit of having a trainer to push me through those last few repetitions. When I get red in the face, break a sweat, and quiver with exertion, I'm ready to give up. Then Aubrey intervenes, telling me in her most serious tone, "Nobody said this was going to be easy! These are the reps that really count!"

I know that if I were alone, I'd wimp out and move on to the next exercise. I'm just not used to pushing myself that hard. What truly surprises me is that when I make up my mind to finish a set, what seemed impossible a few moments before suddenly becomes easier, which just goes to show that attitude is everything.

SESSION 6: A WORKOUT FOR A STRONGER BACK

Today we work on specific strengthening exercises for my lower back, as I've been immobilized by back pain more than once in the past. Aubrey directs me to a contraption in which I position my body at an angle, with my feet propped against stops and my pelvis resting against a pad. I fold my arms over my chest and lower and raise my upper body, like reverse crunches.

I've done these before with ease. But Aubrey points out that I've been using my hip muscles, not my back muscles, to bob up and down. Pushing her fingers into my lower back, she instructs me to push against that pressure. Now I know why these exercises never really helped my back in the past: Because of my form, I wasn't working the right muscles.

SESSION 8: CHANGING FOR THE BETTER

I can't believe that I've already completed 4 weeks of training. I'm noticing lots of positive changes. I stand tall more easily and for longer periods of time, thanks to my stronger back muscles. I bound up stairs with more energy. I carry grocery bags with ease. My shoulders and upper back are broader, which makes my waist look smaller. Because I've gained muscle mass, my clothes fit a little better.

After this session, I go out and buy myself a pair of black Lycra spandex shorts and a bra top. The gym is wall-to-wall mirrors, but I'm ready to give up my bulky sweats for more revealing fitness garb. I can see that my body is slimmer and stronger, and I'm proud of it.

SESSION 16: GETTING OVER THE HUMP

I'm about 2 months into my strength-training program, a critical stage for me. From past experience, I know that this is when I get tired and bored with my routine. I realize that I'm at risk for skipping workouts and possibly giving up strength training for good.

On this particular morning, I lie in bed thinking, "If I weren't meeting Aubrey today, I definitely would not go to the gym. It's cold. It's rainy. It's dark." I'd have no problem staying put, snuggled under my blankets. But because Aubrey is waiting for me (and my payment) at the gym, canceling our session is not an option.

Once I finally drag my butt out of bed and get to the gym, I feel good. By the time I finish my workout, I'm full of energy. I make a mental note to recall this experience whenever I find myself balking at the thought of getting up in the morning.

In the past, when I did strength training on my own, I often skipped the abdominal crunches. They always seemed like drudgery to me. But with Aubrey coaching me, I've worked up to four sets of 30.

I've come to appreciate how crunches benefit my posture and lower back. Now I do them while watching the evening news.

SESSION 24: WHAT A DIFFERENCE 3 MONTHS MAKE

I can hardly believe that this is my last session with Aubrey. She has prepared a chart with all of the exercises I've been doing and the weight I've been lifting, so I can continue on my own. I know I've made substantial gains in strength in the past 3 months. I notice it at odd times, like when I move a piece of furniture or grab two grocery bags instead of one. Friends and family members keep asking me if I've lost weight. The number on the scale hasn't changed, but the sculpting effects of strength training have re-shaped my body.

I hand Aubrey her last check and thank her. I feel a bit like a baby bird getting kicked out of the nest. But I'm confident that I'll stick with my program and continue to progress. When I need a refresher course, I know whom to call.

FOLLOW-UP: STILL GOING STRONG

It's been 3 months since my final session with Aubrey, and I'm pleased to report that I'm still doing strength training. I have cut back my workouts, because I'm now in "maintenance mode." I go to the gym two times a week instead of three, and for each exercise, I do two sets of 12 repetitions rather than three sets of 15. I still feel confident when I go to the gym, because I know what to do with all those machines. And I'm still getting great results from my routine.

For proof, I need look no further than a recent walker's rally. I hiked up long, steep hills carrying a backpack, and I lugged lots of heavy luggage through the airports. Before, that combination would have undoubtedly left my back in knots. But I felt great the entire time, and my back is none the worse for wear.

GAMES WALKERS PLAY

CHAPTER 24

8 WEEKS TO YOUR FIRST 5-K

Mention the word *race* to a group of walkers, and they'll look at you as though you said, "Line up for the firing squad, please." Even the most avid fitness walkers get the heebie-jeebies at the thought of competition.

So why am I bringing it up? Because entering a 5-K can refocus your walking program and reenergize your commitment to getting fit. So, yes, I am luring you to the starting line. Walk this way. . . .

WHAT'S A K, AND WHY 5?

"5-K" is athlete lingo for a 5-kilometer walk/run. Five kilometers equals 5,000 meters or 3.1 miles, which translates to about $12\frac{1}{2}$ times around a high school track. A 5-K is the shortest of the distance races, but it's long enough to be a challenge.

Walk/runs (they're usually called run/walks, but I'm switching the order here) are primarily community-sponsored events that draw folks who enjoy exercising, challenging themselves,

and meeting people. But the biggest appeal of these races is the party atmosphere. There are often pre- and postwalk snacks and drinks, plus T-shirts, awards, and goody bags stuffed with gifts and coupons from sponsors.

While some walkers and runners compete for first-place honors, most sign up for the fun of it. Awards are often handed out just for participating, not only for being the fastest. For example, every 10th walker in a certain age group to cross the finish line might win a prize.

Once you decide to register for a 5-K, you'll reap plenty of benefits well before the race day. Here's why.

• Committing to a 5-K can be powerfully motivating because you'll naturally want to do well. And with the 8-week training program presented in this chapter, you can definitely enhance your performance.

• Setting a goal—namely, to complete a 5-K—renews your sense of excitement about exercise.

- Increasing the intensity of your workouts in preparation for race day builds your speed, boosts your strength and endurance, and maximizes weight loss.

- Concentrating on technique and training rewards you with a sense of pride, mastery, and accomplishment, all of which give you the confidence to try something new and succeed.

Of course, you mustn't overlook the most important benefit of entering a 5-K: having fun! You get to spend time in the great outdoors. You meet scores of like-minded people who share your interest in health and fitness. And if you get hooked on 5-Ks, you'll have plenty of race-day parties to look forward to—not to mention T-shirts.

GOING FOR THE GOAL

Before you start training for a 5-K, find a race that you want to enter and sign up. That makes your commitment concrete.

Look for a walk/run that's happening 8 to 10 weeks from now. Call your local parks and recreation department, YMCA, or running or walking clubs for leads. Also check the local newspaper for announcements.

When you find a 5-K that fits your timetable, mark the date on your calendar. Then register as soon as you can. You may have to pay a small fee, usually $10 to $15, to enter. Consider it an extra incentive to show up on race day.

Once you've signed up, you may want to tell your family and friends about the upcoming event. If they're excited, they can keep you excited— and that makes your workouts a lot easier. For extra motivation, post the race announcement on your refrigerator. Cut out pictures of people exercising and hang them on your bathroom mirror. Buy new shoes or a new pair of shorts. All these things serve as little pep talks as you prepare for race day.

PRIMING YOUR BODY FOR RACE DAY

To help you plan out your training program, I've enlisted the help of Martin Rudow, a former Olympic race-walking coach and creator of the video *Maximum Walking*. Yes, he has trained elite athletes, but he also has helped thousands of ordinary fitness walkers improve their technique and speed.

According to Rudow, the first thing you need to do is assess your current ability to walk a 5-K. As a benchmark, you should have already been walking briskly—fast enough to work up a light sweat, but not so fast that you're gasping for breath—for at least 30 minutes a day, 3 days a week, over the past few weeks. You need to be at this level in order to begin training. If you're not, you need to work up to it.

"To do a 5-K, you should be able to walk for a full hour at a moderate pace, about 20 minutes per mile," Rudow says. "So you want to time yourself walking the entire distance." You can measure out an approximate 5-K (3.1-mile) course yourself, using the odometer in your car, or you can do 12½ laps around a ¼ -mile track. Write your time in your logbook, if you keep one, or on your calendar.

Once you complete the 8-week training program, you should see a significant improvement in your 5-K time. That's because you will have increased your cardiovascular fitness and your muscle endurance.

YOUR 8-WEEK TRAINING PROGRAM

Each week of the training program follows the same pattern: 3 days of workouts at varying speeds, alternating with 3 days of walking at a brisk but comfortable pace for up to 1 hour. One day a week, preferably the one following your hardest workout, is for resting. This reduces your chances of overdoing, which would increase your risk of injury and disrupt your training. If you want, you can use your day off for activities other than walking, such as bicycling and swimming.

Every week, your workouts get a bit more intense as your speed, strength, and endurance improve. Then in the week leading up to race day, your workouts taper off. This gives you an opportunity to rest up, so you're feeling fresh and strong for the big event.

The training program is outlined below in "Time to Train." It consists of these basic building blocks.

The 20s: Warm up by walking at a moderate pace for about 10 minutes.

Time to Train

The following workout schedule can get you ready for a 5-K in just 8 weeks, provided you can already walk briskly for 30 minutes at a time, no problem. Use this schedule as a guide, adjusting it as necessary to accommodate your current fitness level, your personal preferences, your lifestyle, and other factors. Remember, you want a training program that you can stick with. To determine the number of sets to perform for each speed workout (the 20s, 10s, and 5s), refer to the corresponding numbers in parentheses.

Week	Sun	Mon	Tues	Wed	Thur	Fri	Sat
1	Easy	20s (1)	Easy	10s (1)	Easy	5s (1)	Rest
2	Easy	20s (1)	Easy	10s (1)	Easy	5s (2)	Rest
3	Easy	20s (1)	Easy	10s (1)	Easy	5s (2)	Rest
4	Easy	20s (2)	Easy	10s (1)	Easy	5s (3)	Rest
5	Easy	20s (2)	Easy	10s (2)	Easy	5s (3)	Rest
6	Easy	20s (2)	Easy	10s (3)	Easy	5s (4)	Rest
7	Easy	20s (2)	Easy	10s (3)	Easy	5s (3)	Rest
8	Easy	10s (2)	Easy	5s (1)	Easy	Rest	Race day

For the next 20 minutes, walk a bit faster than you normally do. You should feel a little winded but be able to carry on a conversation fairly comfortably. Then cool down by walking slowly for 5 to 10 minutes, or until your heart rate slows almost to normal.

As you progress through the training program, you'll add a 20-minute segment (set) to this workout, with a short rest period in between. ("Rest" means slowing down so that you can breathe easily and evenly, not stopping or sitting.) You'll cool down after completing both 20-minute segments.

The 10s: Walk at a moderate pace for 5 minutes to warm up. Stretch gently, then walk for 10 minutes at a faster pace than in the 20s workout. You should be breathing fairly hard but still be able to get out a few words in conversation. After 10 minutes, slow down and catch your breath. Rest for at least 5 minutes. You'll repeat this cycle up to three times per workout, but don't go for more than that. Remember to cool down afterward.

The 5s: This is the speed-demon workout. Don't panic if you get red-faced, sweaty, and out of breath. That's the idea.

Begin by warming up for 10 minutes, walking at a moderate pace. For the next 5 minutes, walk as though there's molten lava flowing behind you, right on your heels. At this speed, you shouldn't be able to utter a word—and if you can, you're not pushing hard enough. After 5 minutes, slow down and catch your breath. As soon as you're breathing comfortably, pick up your pace again. You'll repeat this cycle as many as four times per workout. Always cool down afterward.

If you're not walking on a ¼-mile track, try heading out for the first half of your workout, then turning around and heading back for the second half. As the weeks go by, you'll find that the halfway mark is getting farther and farther from your starting point. That means you're walking faster.

CAUTION AND COMMON SENSE

Remember to spend a few minutes stretching after every warmup and cooldown. Choose exercises that target your calf and thigh muscles. For some examples, refer to the Dynamic Body Exercises in chapter 38.

If you miss a session here and there, simply pick up where you left off. If you miss a week or more of training, you may have to backtrack a week to resume working out at a comfortable level.

Never do speed workouts (the 20s, 10s, and 5s) on consecutive days or on "easy" days, even if you're feeling great. Doing too much too soon or too fast puts you at risk for soreness and injury. And often you don't know that you're overdoing until it's too late. Remember, you are your only training competitor, and your best time is the one that gets you to the finish line safely and comfortably.

Techniques to Stoke Your Stride

EVEN IF YOU'RE NOT a racewalker, these racewalking-based techniques can boost your 5-K performance.

- Take short, quick steps. Long strides slow you down in the long run.
- Do some fancy footwork. Use the heel-to-toe roll and push off with the back leg.
- Pump your arms. Bend them sharply at the elbows and let them swing from your shoulders like pendulums. Moving your arms in this way helps you get more oomph from your hips, the major power source for walking.
- Control your hips. No need to turn that swing into a waddle. Just imagine your hips as an extension of your thighs. When your thigh moves forward, your hip does, too.
- Stand tall. This gives your waist more room to swivel back and forth with the motion of your hips and legs.

Finally, let your body rule your routine. If you're extremely sore or tired the day after a workout, cut back. Walk only as fast as you can without feeling any kind of muscle or joint pain. If you experience dizziness, chest pain, or sharp pain anywhere in your body, stop your workout and see your doctor. (In fact, anyone with heart disease or diabetes should consult a doctor before starting this training program.)

ON YOUR MARK, GET SET . . . GO!

You've followed the training program religiously, and you're primed and pumped for race day. In your final hours of preparation, read through these tips collected from some walk/run veterans. Their advice can help calm prerace jitters and ensure that your 5-K experience is a good one.

Arrive early. This gives you an opportunity to familiarize yourself with the lay of the land, especially if you're new to the course. It also gives you time to warm up, which can help soothe prerace nerves.

Check in. Find out where to pick up your race number (or to register if you haven't done so already). Pin the number below your chest and leave the bottom flap loose. Someone will tear off that strip as you go through the finish-line chute.

Drink plenty of water. Some experts recommend drinking 12 ounces of water an hour before the race. That's a great idea, but be sure to allow time for a bathroom stop.

Warm up. Walk for at least 10 minutes prior to the start of the race. A cold start could leave your calves cramping.

Set your own pace. Hang back, away from the frontline competitors.

Random Tips of Body Kindness

WHILE YOU'RE IN TRAINING, treat your body with a little extra TLC. You'll feel more comfortable during your workouts, and you'll stay healthy as you progress toward race day.

- Train in the early morning or early evening to avoid the heat.
- Drink plenty of water.
- Wear sunscreen.
- Rub a little petroleum jelly between your thighs to avoid chafing.
- Wear snug-fitting, stretchy shorts that won't ride up between your legs. If you're self-conscious about your figure, slip an oversize T-shirt on top.
- Wear a visor to protect your eyes. Sunglasses are okay, but they can slip down your nose when you get sweaty.
- Smile when you walk. It just makes you feel better!

And don't be afraid to smile and chat with other walkers along the way if you feel like it.

Get your results. After the race, stick around for the awards ceremony and cheer your fellow athletes. Find out your time, no matter where you finished. You want to compare it with your 5-K time from the start of your training program.

Enjoy the postrace revelry. Stick around and mingle. Who knows? You may meet some training buddies for your next 5-K.

CHAPTER 25

MARATHONS: TEAMING UP FOR 26.2

Once the domain of the running elite, marathons are now welcoming walkers to the starting line. Without a doubt, this has contributed to the growing popularity of these events in the United States and around the world.

Some people make marathoning a hobby, entering races in a variety of locales. Others commit to doing one marathon a year.

If you're itching to do 26.2—miles, that is—but you don't know how to go about preparing for such long-distance walking, consider enrolling in the Leukemia and Lymphoma Society's Team-in-Training program. You'll receive the support you need to train for a marathon, and in return, you'll be raising money for a worthwhile cause. It's the kind of experience that can make a difference not only in your life but also in someone else's.

Just ask Marilyn Bukley O'Donoghue, one of thousands of Team-in-Training veterans. "I had never walked more than 4 miles at one time," she recalls. "But I got inspired when I met leukemia patients, who must fight today just to live until tomorrow. If they could get out of bed every day to face the unknown, I could get of bed every day to train."

Over the course of 6 months, O'Donoghue learned techniques that would build her strength and endurance and give her the confidence to start the race. Believing in herself gave her the courage to finish. She completed the 26.2-mile course in 6 hours, 24 minutes, and 41 seconds.

GETTING FIT FOR A GOOD CAUSE

If you're interested in the Team-in-Training program, call the nearest chapter of the Leukemia and Lymphoma Society—there are 58 around the country—to find out when and where the next registration meeting will be. Then mark the date on your calendar and plan to attend.

At the meeting, you'll hear from others who never thought that they could go the distance or raise so much money for a worthy cause. You'll meet your Team-in-Training coach. You'll have the opportunity to ask lots of questions before deciding whether to commit to the program.

If you choose to sign up, you'll receive a special training manual just for walkers, as well as a weekly workout schedule designed to prepare you to go the distance. You'll do the weekly workouts on your own, then meet two to four times a month with your coach and training group. Together, you'll go for progressively longer walks. Training continues for 3 to 4 months. If you stick with the program, you'll be in great shape by race day.

IN STEP WITH

JEANNE TELFARE

A MARATHONER ON A MISSION

MAYBE IT HAD SOMETHING to do with her approaching 46th birthday. Whatever the reason, Jeanne Telfare felt driven to do something worthwhile.

She was familiar with the Leukemia and Lymphoma Society's Team-in-Training program. She would raise money for the organization, and in return, she would receive personal coaching to walk or run a marathon in some exotic locale. "My father had died of a leukemia-related cancer, so raising money for leukemia research meant a lot to me," Jeanne explains. In February 1998, she signed up to train for the Mayor's Midnight Sun Marathon in Anchorage.

"My husband thought I was insane," Jeanne recalls. "For moral support, I turned to *Prevention*'s Walking Forum on the Internet (www.walkingfit.com). I posted a brief message about what I was doing, and I got responses almost immediately. One woman told me that her son had leukemia and that she knew the importance of the Team-in-Training fund-raisers. She thanked me for taking part."

Jeanne began her training in mid-February. She received a workout schedule to follow on her own. And every other Saturday, she met with her training group for walks along the Grand River in Grand Rapids, Michigan.

"We worked out 6 days a week, taking Fridays off," Jeanne says. "By mid-April, we were logging 35 miles a week." And they continued to increase their mileage. By race day, each participant had racked up 547.7 training miles.

The group also did a lot of stretching. "Our coach was emphatic about it," Jeanne says. "But I'm glad because I experienced very little soreness and cramping during my workouts." She also ate lots of bananas (for potassium) and drank plenty of water, following her coach's instructions.

Race day was Saturday, June 20th. Jeanne and the rest of the group got up at 4:00 A.M. to do their final preparations. Their starting time was 7:00 A.M.

As a Team-in-Training participant, your goal is to finish the marathon, not necessarily to finish fast. The average walker completes the course in 8 to 9 hours, which translates to a 15-minute-per-mile pace. Some walkers go much faster than that; others go much slower. If you're interested, it's likely that your coach can show you some tricks and techniques to improve your time.

GO THE DISTANCE ANYWHERE IN THE WORLD

Through the Team-in-Training program, you can take part in select marathons both in this country and abroad. These marathons are walker-friendly—that is, the courses stay open long enough for walkers to finish. Otherwise, the postrace festivities would be over long before you'd get back.

Since the marathons take place in a

Some 500 walkers stood at the starting line that morning. Almost every state was represented. Once the gun went off, the participants moved forward in a close-knit pack. Eventually, they began to spread out.

"Around mile 5, the runners began catching up to us," Jeanne recalls. "They started later, but they'd finish long before we would." It began to drizzle, then shower. Even though clouds shrouded the tops of the mountains, Jeanne found the scenery stunning.

At mile 15, Jeanne and her group stopped to stretch. Soon after, they passed through a residential neighborhood. People lined the streets, waving banners and cheering the walkers on. "When you're tired and hurting, you're perfectly willing to believe people on the sidelines who tell you that you're looking great!" Jeanne says.

The rain, which had stopped for a while, started up again. Jeanne and her group struggled up a steep hill, then crossed onto a beautiful bike path. "By then, I had eyes only for the finish line," Jeanne recalls. "But thoughts of my dad and all the other people battling leukemia flooded my mind, making me push forward, reminding me that I was doing something important."

By mile 23, Jeanne felt herself flagging. Her coach cheered her on: "You'll be fine—only a few miles more!" At last, the finish line came into view. Another ¼ mile, and she was done!

As Jeanne passed through the finish-line chute, she felt proud and amazed at what she had just accomplished. For her efforts, she received a medal and a commemorative sweatshirt.

"I was a bit worried about how I'd feel the next day, but to my surprise, I was fine," Jeanne says. "Even better, the Leukemia and Lymphoma Society raised $25 million that weekend, between the Anchorage and San Diego marathons. And I was there!"

variety of locales, you may want to put off your training until you see a destination that thrills you—like Hawaii or Alaska or Dublin, Ireland. The Leukemia and Lymphoma Society makes all the arrangements for your trip to the host city, and it pays for your training.

In return, you're expected to raise the amount necessary to cover your travel expenses, with any money left over going to leukemia research and support services. Or you can foot the bill yourself. Or you can pay a portion out-of-pocket and the rest through sponsorship. Many people solicit donations through letter-writing cam-paigns. But you have plenty of other fund-raising options as well. The Leukemia and Lymphoma Society can help you out with that.

Keep in mind that you don't have to be in the Team-in-Training program to walk a marathon. You can train on your own or with a buddy or group. Then you just pay the usual entrance fee for the race.

Perhaps the real advantage of Team-in-Training is the camaraderie and mo-tivation that the program provides. Sure, you're getting yourself in shape for the big race. But you're also giving a wonderful gift to those battling a se-rious, often devastating disease.

Park. Choose the plan tailored to the race or event that you're entering, then experiment with it while you're in training. (Since your body reacts differently to foods when you're exercising, you don't want to suddenly change your diet on race day.)

For maximum nutritional value, choose whole-grain versions of high-carbohydrate foods, such as pastas and breads. And be sure to drink lots of water before, during, and after your event.

Right Before	During	After
½–1 cup of sports drink or half an energy bar if you're hungry	No food needed; sports drink if you're tired	Turkey sandwich and fruit; or yogurt, fruit, and a granola bar
Energy bar or sports gel if you need a quick energy boost	Banana, orange slices, or sports drink	Pizza; pasta with turkey meatballs and bread; or a turkey and low-fat cheese sandwich with dried fruit and oatmeal cookies
Energy bar or sports gel	Nuts or trail mix, plus dried fruit; lots of sports drink	Cookies or fruit within 30 minutes of finish; follow with any meal high in carbohydrates and protein

WORKOUT WISDOM FROM A MARATHON PRO

Sheree Meehan is a Team-in-Training coach based in northern California. She has already completed training for four marathons, and she's working on her fifth.

Rather than meeting with her groups once every 2 weeks, as most coaches do, Meehan schedules weekly training sessions. She even works out with some program participants on a daily basis, doing their "buddy walks."

So what does Meehan feel is most important in preparing for a marathon? Practicing good form. "In marathons, most people hit the wall around mile 13," she explains. "Their shoulders droop, and they lean forward from the waist. They feel tired, and they look tired. In my training, I emphasize posture and form—shortening the stride, swinging the arms, standing tall. I make my walkers stop and do stretches en route. They need the break, and they need the stretching and strengthening."

While she is particular about preparation and technique, Meehan stresses that she wants her walkers to have fun. "I want them to stay committed to walking, even after the marathon," she says. "That's why I make sure that they feel good about what they're doing. It's important that they be able to laugh at themselves and have compassion for the struggles of other group members."

With her experience, Meehan has unique insight into the physical and mental demands of walking a marathon. She offers these tips to help you stick with your training program and prime your body for race day, whether you're a first-time marathoner or a seasoned veteran.

Go farther gradually. Especially if you're new to marathoning, your feet aren't ready to cover long distances. Doing too much too soon leads to soreness and injury.

Know your speed limit. Many first-timers don't realize that they need to pace themselves if they want to finish the race. Choose a comfortable speed that you can stick with for the duration of your training walks. You may have to try different paces until you find one that feels good for you.

Slow down to go long. When training for a marathon, you'll be varying your distance from one day to the next. Don't feel that you have to do your long walks at the same speed as your short walks. Eventually, you'll be able to go fast *and* far. But it takes time.

Engage your arms. As you pick up your pace, use a bent-arm swing to help power your stride. Make sure that your arms don't cross the midline of your body or rise above the nipple line.

Rise to the occasion. When you walk, stand tall rather than bending forward from the waist. Poor posture puts pressure on your lower back.

Practice crossovers. Any time your hips feel tight, this exercise can work wonders. Envision a white line running down the center of your path. As you move forward, cross the imaginary line first with one leg, then with the other. This stretches out your hips and helps you engage your entire leg in walking.

Mix up your workouts. If you want to cross-train, choose an activity such as cycling or swimming. "I recommend strength training," Meehan says. "It builds your upper body and supports good posture, which enhances your endurance." Just avoid hiking, inline skating, and anything else that's too close to walking. You'd be working the same muscles, and they need a rest.

Learn to like sport drinks. About halfway through a marathon, these products can provide a much-needed energy boost. If their taste doesn't appeal to you, Meehan suggests diluting them with water.

Treat your feet with TLC. If your feet hurt, they're in need of attention. So stop walking, apply ice, maybe do a little massage. Just give your feet time to rest and recover. Don't make the mistake of thinking that you can out-walk pain. You may end up doing more damage.

CHAPTER **26**

VOLKSWALK: EVERYONE'S A WINNER

From the country that gave the world knockwurst and sauerkraut, Ludwig van Beethoven and Volkswagen Beetles, comes one of the most popular new trends in fitness. It's called Volkssporting.

Yes, Volkssporting.

In German, the word *Volkssport* means "a sport for the people." Volkssporting got its start in southern Germany when a group of recreational sports enthusiasts decided that everyone, not just the athletic elite, should be able to reap the benefits of regular exercise. And they shouldn't have to enter competitions to do it.

Today, Volkssporting is growing so rapidly that it has its own governing body, the International Federation of Popular Sports (IVV), with 26 member countries worldwide. One of these countries is the United States, which boasts more than 500 local Volkssport clubs under the jurisdiction of the American Volkssport Association (AVA).

MAKE YOUR OWN RULES

Technically, Volkssport events could be set up for bikers, swimmers, or cross-country skiers. But usually, they target walkers.

A typical Volkssport walk, or Volkswalk, is 10 kilometers (6.2 miles). Many events also feature a 5-kilometer (3.1-mile) course for beginning walkers. The local Volkssport club handles all the organizational tasks, including plotting the course and setting up checkpoints and water stations along the route.

Volkssport events run an entire weekend. You can participate on Saturday, Sunday, or both days. You must register, but you don't pay a fee unless you want to officially record your mileage or receive an event pin, patch, or award.

Unlike conventional 10-Ks and 5-Ks, Volkssport events have no specific starting time. You just show up, sign in, and start walking. Courses generally remain open for 3 to 5 hours, giving you plenty of time to finish.

SKIP THE EVENT, TAKE HOME THE SPOILS

In one recent year, there were more than 3,000 sanctioned Volkssport walks in the United States. If you want to take part in a Volkswalk, odds are that you can find an event close to your hometown.

But what if you can't make race day or you don't feel like walking with a crowd? You can actually do a Volkswalk on your own. Volkssport clubs all over the country have mapped out courses in their communities and gotten them officially sanctioned as year-round events.

Maggie's Log

VOLKSWALK MADNESS!

THEY CAME FROM ALL over the world to walk. For 2 days in a row, they did just that—10 kilometers, 20, 30, even 40.

Am I talking about Olympians? No. These were Volkswalkers.

In October 1997, they descended on Winston-Salem, North Carolina, for the first-ever Volkswalk held on American soil. The event was sponsored by the American Volkssport Association (AVA) and the International Marching League (IML). I drove for 9 hours just to check it out.

I met people from many different countries. English bobbies striding in full uniform. A Canadian woman carrying a full-size flag from her homeland, accompanied by her black Labrador.

Since I spend lots of time trying to coax people to walk just 1 mile, I was stunned to encounter so many people who found walking a marathon as unremarkable as having afternoon tea. In fact, many folks did 25 miles Saturday *and* Sunday.

These weren't super-athletes by any means. They were ordinary people who love a good, long walk and making new friends while visiting different parts of the world. They ranged in age from thirties to eighties, and they came in all shapes and sizes.

When I asked some of them how long they'd been training for the event, they looked at me with blank stares. "Train for walking? Didn't know we had to, lass." In fact, most of the people I spoke with didn't work out at all during the week. They walked only in Volkswalk events. (Some confided that they didn't like to walk unless they were getting AVA credit for it.)

I must admit, I felt pretty pathetic putting in my measly 10 kilometers each day. My excuse: I had to stay close to the *Prevention* Walking Club booth. But the truth is, I get really sore feet after about 10 miles. I asked a woman from the Netherlands how her feet withstood the 2-day march. She told me that she changed her socks a couple of times during the day and powdered her feet to keep them dry. Her friend just laughed and said that she didn't do anything special. Hardier soles than mine!

I arrived home with a lovely medal to commemorate my walk—and a new admiration for Volkswalkers.—*M.S.*

This means you can go to the site, pick up a map, walk the course, and record the mileage in your distance book. You even get an official stamp in your event book to indicate that you completed the course. (Once you complete your book, you can send it in to the American Volkssport Association for a special award.)

Year-round events usually originate at some location where a box can be placed, such as a hotel lobby, visitors bureau, or park ranger's office. The box contains all the information you need, and it's all on the honor system.

For more information on Volkssport sites and routes, pick up a copy of the American Volkssport Association publication *Starting Point: The AVA Guide to 1,100+ Trails in America*. A new guide comes out every year or so. *Starting Point 2000* lists walking routes by state.

BECOME A VOLKSSPORT VOLUNTEER

If you'd like to get more involved in Volkssporting, contact your local Volkssport club. You'll pay annual membership dues, usually about $10. In return, you'll meet a group of fellow fitness enthusiasts whose primary focus is planning weekend events that attract people from all over the country.

To find the club nearest you—or to order distance or event booklets, *Starting Point* guides, or welcome packets—write to the American Volkssport Association, 1001 Pat Booker Road, Suite 101, Universal City, TX 78148. The organization's toll-free number is available through 800 directory assistance.

CHAPTER 27

PORTLAND TO COAST RELAY: AN EVENT LIKE NO OTHER

Relays haven't yet caught on as a walking event. But they will, eventually. I think they're great because they emphasize camaraderie and teamwork as much as speed. When speed is the sole objective, walking events need to be policed and judged if only to make certain that the walkers aren't running.

The only walking relay that I know of is the Portland to Coast, a sister event to the Hood to Coast Run. The running relay begins at Mount Hood in Portland, Oregon, and ends at Seaside, a resort town on the beach. The Hood to Coast has been around for 17 years. The walking portion came just a few years ago, and already it draws as many as 400 relay teams.

The Portland to Coast covers 125 miles. Each person on a relay team walks two or three 5- to 6-mile sections of the route. Depending on the number of people on your team, you might walk the equivalent of a half-marathon.

STRIDING INTO THE NIGHT

In the Portland to Coast, it doesn't matter much who crosses the finish line first. What's important is participating. I was on one of the walking teams for the 1999 event (it's held in August each year), and I had a blast. At age 47, I wasn't the oldest walker, nor was I the youngest. I met one fellow participant who was in her late sixties. And there were lots of high schoolers taking part, too.

Our team, Buns and Roses, had 12 members. Each of us walked two sections of the route. When we weren't walking, we spent a lot of time sitting in our team vans, waiting for our next turn. (I'd recommend going with an 8-member team and doing three sections of the course instead of two. It's more fun to walk than to sit.)

One of my turns came at about 1 o'-clock in the morning. I remember being scrunched into a ball in the back of a van, listening to the gentle breathing of my four sleeping companions. A few minutes later, I jumped out and scurried to the exchange point, where one of my relay partners handed off the team wristband to me. I proceeded to walk about 6 miles through the dark Oregon countryside—flashlight in hand, reflective vest beaming. I had plenty of time to ponder what possessed me to enter the race in the first place. I was a madwoman!

The night air felt cool and misty. I could see a reflective vest ahead of me and another behind me, each about 100 yards away. Vans passed by occasionally, throwing light against the trees and carving jagged shadows all around me. Just beyond the trees, meadows were bathed in the moon's silvery light, and they seemed to glow brighter when all the artificial light disappeared.

I was startled by how invigorated I felt. The enthusiasm of my teammates had rubbed off on me. I carefully pushed myself to my "edge"—not wanting to overdo and injure myself, but wanting to do my absolute best. Incredibly, I'd been off my feet the entire month before the relay because of heel pain. I'd done some bicycling and kayaking, but no real training. Yet I managed to maintain a 14-minute-per-mile pace—a minute faster than I had

expected. In all the excitement, I hardly noticed my feet hurting.

I think that's the closest I've ever come to identifying with the phrase "Win one for the Gipper!" I was walking not just for myself but for my teammates. And they were doing the same.

PARTNERS IN PERSEVERANCE

Participants in the Portland to Coast come in all shapes and sizes. Most are women, and most are fitness walkers. They have so-so form but lots of heart. They blast out of the exchange points (where one person hands off the team wristband to another) with fire and spirit, going far faster than anyone would guess they could just by looking at them. Every team averages at least 16-minute miles, an impressive pace.

When we weren't walking, my teammates and I got out of the van to cheer other team members at various points along the route. Sometimes we stopped to grab a meal at a local restaurant, though the van was well-stocked with bagels and cream cheese, fresh fruit, Snickers bars, and gallons of water. Sometimes the van driver pulled off the road and

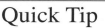

Quick Tip

For more information on the Portland to Coast or to request an entry form, send a self-addressed, stamped envelope to Nationwide Insurance Hood to Coast Relay, 5319 SW Westgate #262, Portland, OR 97221. If you have Internet access, you can visit the relay Web site at www. hoodtocoast.com.

put the van in park, so we could get some real sleep.

Finally, as one of our teammates headed out into the darkness to walk the last section of the course, the rest of us drove ahead to the beach at Seaside. As our teammate rounded the bend and headed toward the finish, the announcer called out our team name, and all of us walked the last 100 yards together. There was plenty of cheering as we crossed the finish line then stood together as a team to receive our event medals. We completed the entire course in 29 hours, 33 minutes.

LOOKING BACK, LOOKING AHEAD

The Portland to Coast Relay is a truly unique event. It's all about working together. People help each other all the way through. When our van got a flat at 2:00 in the morning, the driver of another team's van shone his lights on the tire, gave us a flashlight, and sent out a helper. A bit later, a third van stopped to pick up one of our walkers and our time-keeper, driving them ahead so that they wouldn't miss the next exchange. Word traveled fast that we were in trouble. At the final ceremony, our helpers took home good sportsmanship awards.

Later on, I had a chance to ask other Portland to Coast participants to describe the event. Many of the women likened it to childbirth. It seems awful when you're in the middle of it, but when it's over, you can't wait to do it again.

CHAPTER 28

WALKING THE WANDERWEGS

Walking vacations provide a perfect opportunity for spiritual renewal and mental and physical rejuvenation. I've taken many myself, and I've enjoyed them so much that I've recently instituted a walking tour program. Of all the places in the world that I've walked, Switzerland is one of my all-time favorites for scenery and ease of getting around.

Switzerland is renowned for skiing, but perhaps it deserves recognition for its commitment to walking and hiking. In a country that's half the size of Maine, there are some 31,000 miles of walking trails, and they're maintained all year-round. That's why walkers are just as likely to be out and about in December as in June. Twenty-four hours after snowfall, alpine trails are clear!

Sounds like travel brochure stuff? Perhaps . . . but it's true. When I gathered 20 eager friends and readers to accompany me on a trip to Grindelwald, Switzerland, we experienced firsthand what makes the country a true walker's paradise. Scenery that's easy on the eyes and enlivening to the spirit. Paths that are continuous with few or no cars. No pesky bugs. No poisonous snakes or poison ivy. And safe and spectacular modes of transportation to get you to the most isolated, most breathtaking spots, so you can maximize your walking time in locales with the best views, the cleanest air, and the least human interference.

SIGNS OF THE TIMES

Switzerland has one other amenity that makes it one of the most walker-friendly countries on earth: the *wanderweg* signs. They're posted at all intersections of walking paths and roads, as well as at intersections of what you and I would call sidewalks. Each sign points to a specific destination, but instead of giving the distance in kilometers, it tells you precisely how long you'll need to walk from point A to point B, at the average pace of the local inhabitants. These are not estimates, but tried-and-true times. Imagine that!

The wanderweg signs are yellow. If a sign has a white tip with a red line through it, the path is a designated *bergweg*, or mountain trail. Bergwegs are steep and challenging. Unless you're experienced in alpine hiking, you absolutely need a guide to attempt these trails. (You also need a good pair of hiking boots.)

Even a novice walker can immediately recognize the value of the wanderweg signs. Unless you're aiming for a certain amount of mileage, you probably couldn't care less about the length of a particular trail. What you really want to know is how long you'll need to cover the distance, especially if your planning lunch or bathroom stops. After all, hiking up a steep ½-mile hill could take as long as walking 3 miles across gently rolling countryside.

The signs also direct you to some of the most breathtaking views in the higher elevations of the Alps. My group took full advantage of any and all transportation to reach those altitudes: trains, cable cars, gondolas, and funiculars. (Funiculars are odd little trains that go practically straight up the mountainside on one track. They're perfectly synchronized to pass each other in a short span of double track.) We not only spared ourselves the grueling effort of steep hiking, we got an eagle's-eye view of our surroundings every morning.

ACCESSING THE ALPS

Given the option, I prefer the absolute luxury of a planned walking vacation with an experienced guide. That way, once I'm in my destination, the biggest decision I have to make is what to wear every day. But you could certainly arrange a walking tour of Switzerland on your own by doing a little planning, reading, and talking to travel agents and tourism boards.

Based on my own experience, I recommend taking along at least three items.

An English-to-German dictionary: Unless you know German or one of the many Swiss dialects spoken in the various regions of the country, language may be something of a barrier. Though many Swiss speak English, traveling in a foreign country has its stresses, and not understanding the native tongue is one of them. On my trip, I found myself wishing I had prepared myself with a little friendly German before boarding the plane. It makes a good impression and draws you into a greater awareness of the local culture.

Real hiking boots: While walking shoes are suitable for many trails, hiking boots provide the extra support you need for any ascents or descents that you attempt. Don't cheat yourself

here. One of the people in my group bought an inexpensive pair of boots that left her unable to walk after just 2 days. Buy from a reputable dealer who can fit your foot. Then go walking in your boots many times before you leave on your trip.

A backpack for layers: In general, the temperature in Switzerland between June and October is glorious for walkers: cool mornings, warm afternoons (sometimes 80°F or higher), no humidity. But you need a backpack to carry rain gear and maybe a few other layers, so you're prepared for weather changes as you move through the day and the different elevations.

You don't need to worry about altitude unless you have special health concerns, such as a heart or respiratory condition. The Alps are walker-friendly, with most of the trails less than 8,000 feet above sea level. None of the walkers in my group, who ranged in age from 14 to 78, was bothered by shortness of breath, headache, or fatigue, the classic symptoms of altitude sickness.

While walking downhill may be easy on your lungs, it can be tough on your knees and thighs. My quadriceps muscles were quivering like Jell-O after a 40-minute descent through a steep alpine meadow. If it hadn't been for the cows mooing and their bells tinkling, the stunning view of the snow-capped mountains and the wispy white clouds floating beneath me, I might have been disturbed by my muscle weakness. As it was, I was too close to heaven to notice.

CHAPTER 29

PRESIDENTIAL WALKING AWARD: HOOFING IT FOR HONORS

You're committed to your walking program. You're out there striding several days, if not every day, during the week. So how about getting some recognition for your efforts?

You can if you apply for the Presidential Sports Award for Fitness Walking.

The Presidential Sports Award program debuted in 1972 as a means of motivating Americans ages 15 and older to stay physically active. The program emphasizes regular, consistent exercise—not going super-fast or super-far.

The Fitness Walking Award is one of 51 award categories. To qualify for it, you must walk a total of 125 miles, with a limit of 2½ miles a day. In other words, if you go 5 miles in one workout, only 2½ count toward the award. In addition, you must walk continuously, without stopping to rest. And

you must maintain a 4-mile-per-hour pace (that's 15 minutes per mile).

WORKING UP TO SPEED

If you're not already walking at the required pace, you can work up to it, but give yourself time. Measure out a 1-mile course using your car odometer, and walk it every day or every other day. Never go so fast that you become breathless. Just maintain what feels like a comfortably brisk pace. Your speed will increase naturally.

Remember, you need to maintain your pace for the entire 2½ miles, so there's no point in pushing yourself too hard. You'll only get tired and sore, which will slow you down. Wait until the 15-minute-per-mile pace feels easy to start keeping your logbook for the Presidential Fitness Walking Award. Be sure to warm up and cool down before and after every workout—a few minutes of walking slowly should do the trick.

You can buy special audiotapes to keep you stepping at the proper pace. For example, the Medical and Sports Music Institute of America has produced a tape called *Music-in-Sync, Volume I*. For more information, write to the institute at PO Box 1177, Bloomfield, NJ 07003-1177.

RECOGNIZING YOUR ACHIEVEMENT

To apply for the Presidential Fitness Walking Award, you need to submit a logbook that documents your mileage. (You can create one using forms set up like the one shown below.) Since you'd have to walk 50 times to hit the 125-mile mark—assuming that you're doing the maximum of 2½ miles a day—you should allow at least 2 months to reach your goal. You must complete your walking within 4 months.

Once you've accumulated the required mileage, send your logbook, your mileage verification (the form in "Applying for Your Award" on page 154), and a check or money order for $8 ($10 in Canada) to Presidential Sports Award/AAU, c/o Walt Disney World Resort, PO Box 10000, Lake Buena Vista, FL 32830-1000. In return, you'll receive a personalized certificate of achievement from the president of the United States that's suitable for framing and a letter of congratulations from the chairman of the President's Council on Physical Fitness and Sports. You'll also get a beautifully embroidered Fitness Walking patch to sew on your favorite walking jacket. Wear it proudly to show off your accomplishment!

Your Personal Walking Log

TO TRACK YOUR MILEAGE for the Presidential Fitness Walking Award, make a form like the one below and put copies into a notebook. Then every time you walk, write the date and the distance in your notebook. You'll need to submit these records in order to qualify for the award.

Date	Miles	Date	Miles	Date	Miles	Date	Miles

Applying for Your Award

ONCE YOU COMPLETE THE requirements for the Presidential Fitness Walking Award, make a photocopy of the mileage verification form below and send it in with your logbook.

Date _____ **Miles** _____

    I hereby affirm that I have fulfilled all requirements for the Presidential Sports Award in Fitness Walking. I have enclosed a check for $8, payable to Presidential Sports Award/AAU.

Signature _____

Name _____

Age _____ Sex _____

Address _____ Apt. No. _____

City _____ State _____ ZIP Code _____

Daytime Telephone (____) _____

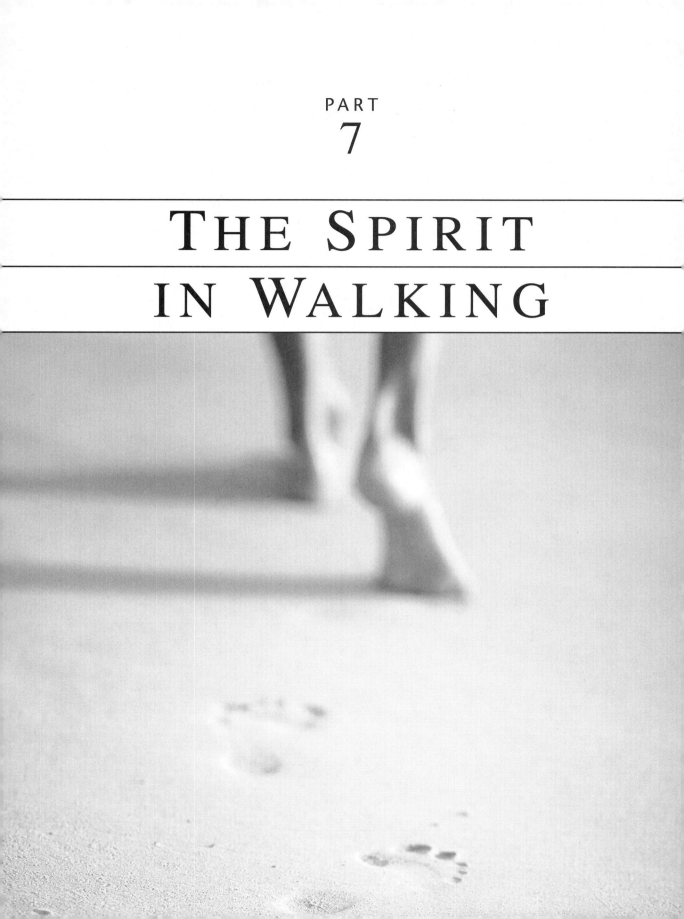

THE SPIRIT
IN WALKING

CHAPTER **30**

SLOW DOWN TO THE SPEED OF WALKING

If you're like most people, you've taken up walking to improve yourself physically, perhaps by slimming down or getting fit. But there's another side to walking, one that supports your emotional and spiritual being.

These days, our lives are set at an incredibly frantic pace. We have so much on our plates that we fear we'll never get everything done. And we wonder when we'll find time to do those things that bring us pleasure and joy.

Even when the world seems to be spinning out of control, walking can restore your sense of inner peace. It gives you a chance to slow down, to relax, to appreciate yourself and your life.

Even if your job is wonderful, your family is healthy and happy, your future seems bright, you can lose touch with the deepest part of yourself unless you slow down enough to breathe deeply, to still your thoughts, to observe the natural world with a sense of wonder. In this regard,

walking can help you reset your internal clock and dispel your sense of urgency. After all, it isn't intended to get you someplace in a super-hurry— unless you're an elite racewalker. By its very nature, it encourages you to breathe more deeply, draining away tension and instilling a sense of calm and contentment.

PLAN A WALKING RETREAT

You can use walking as a sort of mini-retreat. I'm not talking about going away for a week or even a weekend, unless you want to, of course. I'm suggesting that you set aside 1 day for a 3- to 8-hour exploration on foot—far from the demands of work, home, and family.

First, choose a date on your calendar and mark it as your "retreat day." Then discuss your plans with anyone who might be affected by your being unavailable. You want this day to be yours, for your personal walking adventure. (You can invite a friend or family member to join you if you want. But I suggest that you make all the plans so that they suit *you*.)

Next, identify a place that you want to explore on foot. If you enjoy being out in nature, call your local parks and recreation department to request maps of your area. If you love looking at homes and gardens, think of a neighborhood that you'd like to see up close. Try to choose a location that's no more than 15 minutes from your home. You want to spend your time walking, not driving. If you never have to get in your car, all the better.

Tailor the length of your route to your personal limits. You're walking at a leisurely pace, so you can go longer and farther. If you normally walk 2 miles a day, go for 4 to 6 miles. If you usually walk 4 miles, try to go 8 to 10. If you're a beginner, stay under 4 miles.

The night before your excursion, pack yourself a lunch, maybe a sandwich on whole-grain bread, plus fresh fruits and veggies. Make sure that you have a water bottle, too. Put them in a backpack, along with a notepad and pencil in case you want to do some journaling. Other items you may want to carry along: any maps you need; pocket guides for identifying wildflowers, trees, and birds; a magnifying glass for checking out the intricacies of plants; a couple of premoistened hand wipes; and some plastic bags for any garbage you have.

Make sure your favorite walking socks are clean. Pick out a pair of shorts or pants that you can walk in comfortably for hours as well as a cozy jacket if the weather is cool. If it's warm, wear a hat or visor. And don't forget your sunglasses—not only to shade your eyes but also to give you a sense of privacy while you walk.

EXPLORE THE WORLD . . . AND YOUR SOUL

On the day of your journey, plan to get up early, so you can spend a few minutes relaxing and stretching. Stretching is something few people make time for, but it yields great rewards. It leaves you feeling lighter, more flexible, less achy. It makes your walk more refreshing, since you've worked out some of the kinks before you hit the road.

If you have a favorite book of poetry, read from it before you leave home. The sensuous, intuitive language of poetry may put you in a completely different frame of mind than the articles in the morning paper. Afterward, eat a healthy breakfast and drink plenty of water. Then pick up your backpack and head out.

Remember, this is a retreat, not a race. This is to refresh your spirit, to get in sync with your soul and your surroundings. Stand tall while you walk; it makes you feel better about yourself and the world around you. Stop whenever you want to eat a snack or your lunch. Soak up the sun. Stretch again. Savor the moment.

CHAPTER **31**

SKY WALKING: A NEW VIEW OF THE WORLD

So you've already done your walking for the day. Quick—without taking your eyes off this page—try to remember what the sky looked like while you were outside. What was its color? Were there any clouds? What did they look like? Were they moving slowly or quickly?

If you're like most people, you probably can't give a detailed description of the sky's appearance, even though you were surrounded by it, says Jack Borden, founder of For Spacious Skies, a nonprofit organization based in Lexington, Massachusetts. And that's too bad. Because by focusing your eyes on the sky and really studying it, you can boost the destressing effects of your walks.

SEEKING HELP FROM ABOVE

Ralph Waldo Emerson, a 19th-century poet and an avid walker, once described the sky as "the daily bread of the eyes." Borden got a monumental mouthful of it one day 10 years ago, as he rested in a meadow after a long hike. "I looked up, and for the first time in my life, I saw the sky," he recalls.

Realizing what he had been missing, he quit his job as a television broadcaster and founded For Spacious Skies, which is devoted to increasing people's awareness of the sky. Some of what Borden has learned from looking up could add a new dimension to your walking program—and to other parts of your life as well.

LOOKING UP, LOOKING IN

Psychological research suggests that the rewards of really seeing the sky may be greater than just a pleasant feeling from having taken in a nice view. Specifically, sky gazing may sap stress by helping you put your emotions in perspective. As Borden explains, "When you realize that everyone is *in* the sky instead of *under* it, as many people perceive themselves, you get a stronger sense of connectedness."

Ecopsychologist Sarah Conn, Ph.D., agrees that walkers have much to gain by tuning in to the sky. (Ecopsychology is a relatively new field of study in emotional and mental health. It's based on the philosophy that people are connected to more than just the human world and are profoundly influenced by that connection.) According to Dr. Conn, awareness of the sky can help anyone under stress experience their situations in a larger context. They may be able to take that feeling of space outside themselves and somehow translate it to a feeling of spaciousness within themselves.

"In addition, watching the sky and the changes that steadily occur in it can give people a sense that their own feelings move the same way," Dr. Conn says. "Stormy or gentle, feelings all come and go. But above the clouds, the sky is always there, always blue."

GETTING THERE FROM HERE

For some people, a good look up to the heavens is all they need to experience the sky's stress-reducing powers. Others might get better results by using one of these two approaches.

Turn outward. Dr. Conn reminds you to "stay out of your head" when you walk. "One Native American phrase for insanity translates as 'talking, talking, talking, inside your head,'" she notes. "When people keep up this incessant internal chatter, they don't get relief on their walks. I remind them to stop, look, listen, smell, and touch the world around them."

When you're out walking, use all your senses. Taste the air, feel the wind, touch a tree. Try to walk in the same place often, and pay careful attention to the changes that occur from one visit to the next. This includes the changes that take place overhead in the sky. "All this creates a wonderful sense of connectedness and comfort," Dr. Conn says. "The natural world is a place where you don't have to perform. You can act or feel however you want, and the sky is just there."

By walking with awareness of the natural world—of the ground beneath your feet, of the scents, sounds, and smells—you develop a very real protection against stress, according to Dr. Conn. "Stress can move through you more quickly and with greater ease," she explains.

Reframe what you see. It's easy to feel distressed or overwhelmed when some part of your life's landscape is in disarray. Borden recommends an exercise from Apache culture to help you see that any ugliness is only a small corner of your personal picture.

As an example, imagine that you're walking near your town's dump, and you feel overwhelmed by its ugliness. Look out toward the horizon and try to see as much of the landscape as you can, horizontally and vertically. Get the biggest picture that you can without focusing on any one object in particular.

Pretend that your eye is a camera lens. Look closely at the dump through that lens. Then turn the lens toward the sky. As you take in the sky's beauty, you become unaware of the dump. Tilt the lens again until you see only the dump. Then shift back to the big picture, combining the sky and the dump. This is a truer picture of reality—80 percent beauty, 20 percent ugly. You'll feel not only less anxious about the ugliness but also empowered to do something about it if you want to.

Of course, you don't have to limit your awareness of the sky to your walks. Try turning off the television one evening and taking your family outside for some stargazing. Or spend a lazy summer day lying faceup on the lawn, letting the sky sap away your daily stresses. Even these simple acts can be truly potent tools for reframing your thoughts about life.

CHAPTER 32

LABYRINTH WALKING: A PATH TO INNER PEACE

Going around in circles has never been a good thing. It means that you're getting nothing accomplished on a certain project or task.

When you walk a labyrinth, you go around in circles. The difference is, you actually get somewhere. In fact, you follow a path to remarkable stress reduction and relaxation.

Labyrinths are cropping up in parks and on parking lots, in public places and on private property. These intricate courses with ancient roots continue to grow in popularity, as people discover their power to calm the mind and soothe the body. To experience their appeal for yourself, all you have to do is walk between the lines.

Most people think of a labyrinth as a maze from which there is seemingly no escape. But the type of labyrinth I'm talking about is two-dimensional, with no walls to obstruct your vision. It's also unicursal, which means it has a single, winding path that leads to a central point. Follow the path to get to the center, then follow it back to the starting point. No directions, no decisions, and no getting lost.

A maze, on the other hand, has many paths (it's multicursal), and most of them lead to dead ends. Walking a maze is a challenge that can require stamina. Walking a labyrinth requires only that you persist in your journey.

FIND YOUR WAY WITHIN

As with so many things in life, what you get out of a labyrinth depends a great deal on what you put into it, says Robert Ferre, director of the St. Louis Labyrinth Project and author of *The Labyrinth Revival*. "You can skip through the winding paths with childlike abandon, or you can walk solemnly and introspectively."

Many say that walking a labyrinth

calms the body and mind by providing a space that guides a person's focus inward. The rhythmic action of walking can reduce the nervous energy that prevents some people from reaping the benefits of other relaxation techniques. And when you walk a labyrinth, the effortlessness of following the winding path deepens your breathing and helps to release built-up tension.

Some people find inspiration or solve problems on the labyrinth path. Others walk to help them focus at the beginning of the day. Of course, you can experience these benefits on any path. But labyrinth enthusiasts, including art therapist Annette Reynolds, R.N., feel that the intricate courses offer a special format for "going within."

"I've attended classes in therapeutic touch (which some call the laying on of hands)," Reynolds says. "A friend of mine described walking a labyrinth as the laying on of feet. That's how I see it. I've even built one in my garden for my personal use."

A UNIFYING FORCE

Communities are using labyrinths to foster unity by inviting everyone to "walk the path together," a symbolic act of cooperation.

As part of a First Night (New Year's Eve) celebration in St. Petersburg, Florida, organizers created a labyrinth on the site of a demolished downtown building. Their goal was to address racial discord and promote community involvement. "As people walked toward the center of the labyrinth, they were to think about what they would do to help heal the city," explains G. David Ellis, the course designer. "When they got to the center, they tied ribbons to a pole as a symbol of commitment. Then as they walked back, they were to contemplate how to make their pledges a reality."

The event was an enormous success. The labyrinth was packed all evening, and by the time it closed, more than 3,000 ribbons adorned the center pole. It was community art in its highest form.

STAY THE COURSE

If you're a newcomer to labyrinth walking, you may not be sure what to expect from the experience. Ferre advises that you "set aside any preconceived notions or skepticism and be open to whatever happens." And be sure to follow these basic rules of labyrinth etiquette.

1. Begin only at the entry point.

2. Time your start so that people walking ahead of you don't feel rushed or crowded.

3. Walk on the path, not on the lines or markers.

4. Set your own pace.

5. Pass others if necessary, and allow others to do likewise.

6. If possible, sit quietly at the center of the labyrinth before heading back. (At large events, you may be asked to keep moving, since the course can become crowded.)

7. Honor specific requests—for silence, for example.

WHERE TO GO

If you'd like to try walking a labyrinth, here's a small sampling of the courses that are available for public use. Some are open 24 hours a day. You may be able to find one close to home, too. Check with churches and community organizations in your area.

- Aura Soma Lava Rejuvenation Center, Lava Hot Springs, Idaho
- Blue Ridge Wellness Center, Forest, Virginia
- Church of St. Andrew, Marblehead, Massachusetts
- Grace Cathedral, San Francisco (indoor and outdoor)
- Lightgate Learning Center for Body, Mind, and Spirit, Thetford, Vermont
- Raleigh Arboretum, Raleigh, North Carolina
- Sachem Hollow Retreat Center, Block Island, Rhode Island
- St. Paul's Cathedral, Boston (indoor)

CHAPTER 33

WELCOME TO YOUR CREATIVE ZONE

On any given day, you probably face at least one problem or task that demands a bit of creative thinking on your part. Here's an easy way to get those creative juices flowing: Just put one foot in front of the other.

Research has shown that in addition to its myriad health benefits, walking can enhance creativity. In one study, all 63 participants reported a significant increase in the flow of ideas after just 25 minutes of aerobic activity.

Want to brainstorm money-saving initiatives for your boss? Plan a birthday party for your spouse? Redesign your kitchen? Whatever the situation, if it requires brainpower, try foot power.

LET YOUR MIND ROAM FREE

What is it about moving your arms and legs that seems to turbo-charge your brain cells? Scientists theorize that exercise causes the brain to enter a state of relaxation. In this looser mindset, thoughts that would normally be stored in separate compartments instead become blended together. The result is a delicious stew of new ideas.

Creativity coach Julia Cameron, author of *The Artist's Way*, prescribes a daily walk as a potent source of inspiration. "Walking feeds us, image by image. It's one of the most powerful creative tools I know," she says. "With the constant inflow of new images, walking gives us new thoughts that nourish us. It replenishes our over-tapped creative well and gives us a sense of . . . well, wellness."

When you're out walking—away from ringing telephones, pressing deadlines, and other nagging responsibilities—you feel free to let your imagination play. The busy owner of one New York City public relations firm couldn't agree more. "I run a company, and I have a family," the woman says. "When I'm walking, no one is making demands on me. It's amazing what your mind can do when it's not being pushed and prodded in six different directions."

WALKING TO WORK SMARTER

For many people in "creative" professions, walking is a direct path to doing better work. "During one walk, I came up with an entire section of a speech that I was to give at an awards luncheon," says a senior vice president of Minkus and Dunne Communications, a Chicago-based public relations firm.

Paul Levinson, Ph.D., visiting professor of communications at Fordham University in New York City, is the author of 7 books, 30 science fiction stories, and 100-plus scholarly articles. He has done most of his writing since 1993, the year he started walking. He says that's no coincidence.

"Walking opens my mind to ideas that have been nesting in there for years," Dr. Levinson observes. "It took me at least 5 years to write my 1988 book, *Mind at Large*. I completed my latest book, *The Soft Edge*, in 5 months. There's no doubt that walking has made my writing more creative."

PROBLEM SOLVING, STEP BY STEP

Walking can do much more than enhance job performance. For many people, it leads to the discovery of a solution to some professional or personal challenge.

"It doesn't always happen instantly, but over time, you go from worrying about problems to finding ways to address them," Cameron says. "In some cases, the solutions may seem crazy at first. But the more you think about them, the smarter they become."

That New York City PR executive uses her frequent walks through the Big Apple to untangle all manner of perplexing knots, from reorganizing her office staff to deciding what to feed her family for dinner. "You've heard about how your mind can work on problems while you're sleeping? I think the process is analogous to that," she says. "Your mind is working on your problem while you're walking, even if you're not consciously aware of it."

MAKE WALKING A CREATIVE VENTURE

You can't force creativity. But you can give it a gentle nudge by walking. Experts offer these strategies to help stimulate your creative processes.

Exercise every day. Cameron prescribes a 20-minute walk 6 days a week, plus an hour-long walk once a week. "The idea is to stretch both your legs and your creative territory," she says.

Find the right time. Try to do your walking when you can disengage yourself from schedules and structures. "The human mind generally can't switch off old business like a light, so you should walk at a time when you can let go," advises James A. Swan, Ph.D., an environmental psychologist in Mill Valley, California, and author of

Use Your Feet to Open Your Mind

THE FOLLOWING PASSAGE WAS written by creativity coach Julia Cameron for her book *The Vein of Gold: A Journey to Your Creative Heart.* I want to share it with you here, because I feel it so beautifully and accurately conveys how walking can positively influence your powers of creativity.

Walking opens us up. It feeds us. Image by image, it spoons up for us a broth or soup of soul food, which sustains us as we do the work to shape and reshape our lives. In other words, we can walk our way out of "problem" and into "solution."

If I am snagged on a story line, I walk it out. If I am stymied about what to work on next, I walk until it comes to me. When I am tangled in the plot lines of my work or my life, I take a walk and allow the walk to sort things out.

I know that I am far from alone in believing that walking with our soles is really walking with our souls. Our internal horizons stretch with our external ones. We walk into expanded possibility: If we can bear it, the soles of our feet lead us to the feats of our souls.

In other words, walking is a form of meditation.

When we are too heady, too full of the chatter and clatter of our stress-filled lives, our spiritual energy returns to us through our feet. We walk on the ground and we ground ourselves by walking . . .

At least once a week, on one of your daily walks, use the time to exercise your gratitude. Consciously list and vocalize your gratitude for everything about your life that you enjoy. At first, this will require real spiritual exertion and may feel quite difficult. (Also saccharine!) What you are actually doing is gaining altitude so that you can see your life from a higher perspective, where you are able to recognize many more choices.

Nature as Teacher and Healer.

Dr. Levinson agrees, adding that his best creativity-generating walks occur between 10:00 and 11:00 at night. "Afterward, I produce about 2 hours' worth of good writing," he says.

Find the right place. According to Cameron, where you do your walking doesn't matter all that much, as long as it's outside in a place in which you feel safe and comfortable. (While treadmills provide exercise, they don't provide the "image flow" required for creativity.) Head out on your own and see where it leads you.

Attend to your mind. While you walk, focus on what you see, hear, and feel, Dr. Swan suggests. At first you may be restless or feel overwhelmed by the plethora of images that floods your mind. But eventually, your mind will get in sync with the beauty and stimulation of your environment. Over time, you'll find yourself having larger, simpler, and unique creative insights. Step by step, you'll learn to put greater trust in your own ideas. "You'll know they're right because they feel right," he says.

RECONNECT WITH THE NATURAL WORLD

In the past, when I'd go walking, I'd often have so much going on in my mind that I'd hardly notice, much less appreciate, all that was going on in the world around me. Even though I'd be passing through a beautiful pastoral or wooded landscape, I'd be so disconnected from my surroundings that I'd arrive home thinking that I might need to find a more stimulating route.

Thanks to some exercises that I learned from Michael J. Cohen, Ed.D., author of *Reconnecting with Nature*, my walks have taken on a whole new dimension. Now I feel like a kid in a candy shop when I venture outside in the morning.

Dr. Cohen practices and teaches ecopsychology, a new field of study that views people as profoundly affected by the natural world. Through his exercises, he has shown me how to reconnect with nature and, in doing so, to connect more deeply with myself. I've been so delighted and inspired by the experience that I've asked Dr. Cohen to design a set of exercises for you, so you can transform your walks into moving meditations that calm, refresh, and revitalize you.

EXERCISES FOR THE SENSES

The exercises that follow are intended to awaken or sharpen senses that you probably haven't paid much attention to. By using these senses to explore the natural world on a deeper level, you come to realize that you're part of nature, not apart from it. According to Dr. Cohen, this realization helps people learn to make healthier decisions, both for themselves and for their environments.

Ultimately, the goal of the exercises is to help you understand the relationship between your psychological health, your sense of well-being, and the health of the environment around you. You make this critical connection

WALK ON THE
WILD SIDE

LIVING IN PENNSYLVANIA, I have the luxury of ready access to trails of all types. I can do my walking on a canal towpath that runs beside the Delaware River, a partially converted railroad bed, or the Appalachian Trail—each of which is just a short distance from my home.

For me, these trails provide more than a change of scenery in my workouts. They reinforce my health and well-being by allowing me to reconnect with the natural world. They're a critical link in a lifestyle that has become increasingly separated from nature.

Just the other day, I came across a study that confirms my observations. It suggests that walking in nature has even more health benefits than most of us imagined.

In the study, researchers at the University of Michigan School of Nursing in Ann Arbor noticed that of 32 women being treated for localized breast cancer, those who received a 20- to 30-minute "dose" of nature-based activity every week showed improvement in their ability to think clearly, to set goals, and to start a task and follow through. The researchers identified other benefits, too, including a resurgence in energy and optimism that encouraged the women to take on new tasks, like volunteer work, or to learn new skills.

I'm not battling breast cancer, but I'm sure that I can reap the same benefits from walking in nature. That's why I love to take advantage of the many trails running through nearby local, state, and national parks.

Of course, trails don't just happen. They must be built and maintained, and that costs money. A portion of our local, state, and federal tax dollars are earmarked for this purpose. But this financial support can quickly disappear—unless we let our government officials know that the trails are important to us.

This is why the American Hiking Society sponsors National Trails Day, held every June to draw attention to and celebrate America's walking, hiking, and biking trails. Hundreds of thousands of people take part in activities in venues across the country. By joining them, you not only get your weekly dose of nature but also send a message to your government officials that you care about and enjoy having access to trails.

Through this annual event, the American Hiking Society is working toward two goals: to give everyone in the United States trail access within 15 minutes of home and to develop a trail network that could take us wherever we wanted to go, from sidewalk to backwoods. A grand vision? Of course! But one that's worth walking toward, considering its benefits.

For more information about National Trails Day events in your area, you can write to the American Hiking Society, 1422 Fenwick Lane, Silver Spring, MD 20910. For a toll-free number, call 800 directory assistance.—*M.S.*

by becoming aware of all the sensory interactions that exist within the natural world.

Not long ago, I had an experience that demonstrated how dramatically these exercises had enhanced my perception of the world around me. While out walking with my dog, I sensed that we had disturbed another animal. I became aware of a muffled crunching sound coming from the woods on my right. At the same time, a strong, musty odor filled my nostrils. I stopped. Just a few seconds later, a large buck burst through the thicket onto the road in front of us. I'd seen deer on my walks many times, but I'd never noticed them by their smell first.

SAY HELLO TO MOTHER NATURE

The value of the exercises lies solely in your experience of them. If you just read them, they may seem, quite simply, silly. But if you do them and have fun with them, you may find a whole new pleasure and energy in walking outdoors.

Plan to do no more than one exercise a day. "Trying to do all of them in one day dilutes your experience," Dr. Cohen says. "You probably won't sense as much."

If you find that you're not attracted to a particular exercise, put it off for another day or skip it completely. As I worked through the exercises, I found that I didn't trust my own reactions at times. That's when sharing your feel-ings or insights with a friend or a group really helps.

Keep in mind, though, that there are no right or wrong results. Just enjoy yourself!

Explore without your eyes. This is a great technique for awakening your senses before you start walking. Find a spot in your yard or in some natural area where you can stand quietly with your eyes closed. (If it's outside your yard, make sure that it's a place where you feel completely safe.) If you're comfortable doing so, walk around slowly, keeping your eyes closed. Become aware of the input you're receiving from your other senses now that your dominant sense, your vision, is "turned off."

Listen, smell, and—if the area is free of potentially harmful plants (like rose bushes and poison ivy)—touch as you explore your surroundings. Notice as many sensations as you can. Pay attention to your sense of the ground underfoot, your sense of balance, your sense of direction based on the sun or the wind. Notice whether you can feel the presence of trees or rocks around you without touching them. Occasionally open your eyes for just a second and notice how your environment looks. Many people report a heightened awareness of color and shape.

See with your hands. This is one of my favorite exercises. Before you begin walking, go outside and pick up five or six pebbles or small stones of similar shape and size. Mark one with a felt marker or pen. Put the rest in your pocket.

Hold the marked stone in your hand as you walk, learning to recognize it by touch. After 5 to 10 minutes, drop the stone into your pocket with the others and mix them up. Then without actually looking in your pocket, reach in and see if you can pick out the marked stone. Repeat the activity with new stones, or just mark a different stone. What I find so remarkable about this exercise is how different each stone really feels, even though they all look the same.

Connect with your breath. For me, this exercise serves as a great reminder of how much we humans are part of the web of life on planet Earth. It's just as 19th-century American naturalist John Muir once said: "When we try to pick out anything by itself, we find it hitched to everything else in the universe."

For this exercise, all you do is think about breathing. Remember that plants release the oxygen that you breathe into your lungs; in return, you breathe out the carbon dioxide that plants take in.

In your mind's eye, follow your breath as you exhale. Imagine that you can see the carbon dioxide molecules leaving your nose or mouth and flowing into the leaves of the plants nearest you as you walk. At the same time, envision yourself inhaling the oxygen that the plants give off. Take a moment to note how your visualization of this very natural process affects your sense of the world around you.

Acknowledge your appreciation. Think of the wonderful feeling that you get when you say thank you to someone who has given you a gift or a compliment. When you see a beautiful tree and you stop for a moment to experience your appreciation of its beauty, you're sending a mental thank-you to that tree. Can the tree sense your gratitude? I can't say. But try this exercise and notice how it affects your perception of the world around you.

First, suspend any preconceived notions of what's pleasing or attractive. You may be drawn to a certain color, a particular smell, a certain view, or something else. As you become aware of the object or the environment, take a moment to appreciate that it has made you feel good. Dr. Cohen suggests that you even mentally thank whatever has attracted you.

At the end of your walk, write your experience in a logbook. Finish this statement: "I am a person who appreciates and feels supported by . . ." Fill in the blank with what you felt attracted to.

CHAPTER **35**

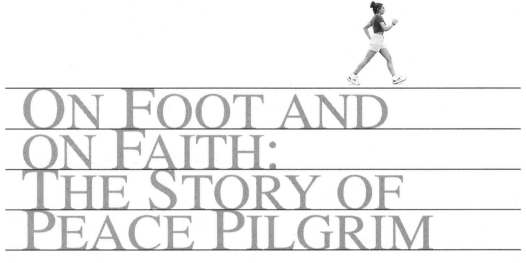

ON FOOT AND ON FAITH: THE STORY OF PEACE PILGRIM

She didn't wear high-tech walking shoes, just plain canvas sneakers. She didn't sport a jacket or hat with a famous logo, just a simple navy blue tunic and pants. No organization sponsored her. No one followed her with a van to pick her up when she grew tired or when the weather turned foul. She traveled alone, on foot and on faith, with a singular purpose: to share her prescription for worldwide harmony. "Overcome evil with good, falsehood with truth, and hatred with love. This is the way to peace," she told anyone who stopped to ask.

In the past century and a half, countless people have walked countless miles on countless missions. Many of these walkers deserve recognition for their feats. But the person who most impressed me was this blue-eyed, slightly wizened marvel who spent al-

most three decades trekking across the United States on foot.

Her name was Mildred Norman Ryder, but she became known simply as Peace Pilgrim. The name captured her essence: She was a woman on a 25,000-mile walking pilgrimage for peace.

In the 1950s, long before T-shirts became billboards for personal politics, Peace Pilgrim realized that sewing a few words to her tunic—"Walking Coast to Coast for Peace"—would be an effective way to share her message with others. But it wasn't her message that fascinated me, at least not at first. It was her medium.

Peace Pilgrim was a phenomenal walker, in every sense of the word. She covered an astonishing number of miles in her lifetime, many more than the 25,000 she originally set out to do.

Even more impressive, she accumulated most of that mileage *after* her 50th birthday. She was vital, energetic, and at peace with herself. She was amazing.

From the moment I heard about Peace Pilgrim, I wanted to know more about her. I hope that you'll find her story just as inspiring as I have.

WALKING TOWARD A VISION

Walking played an integral part in the "creation" of Peace Pilgrim. During what she described as her 15-year preparation period, Peace—then known simply as Mildred—spent time every day walking and drawing inspiration from nature. She said that she received insights on those daily walks, and she worked to incorporate those insights into her daily life. She encouraged others to do the same. "From the beauties of nature, you get your inspiration," she once said. "From the silent receptiveness, you get your meditation. From the walking, you get not only exercise but deep breathing—all in one lovely experience."

In 1952, a year before her first sojourn as Peace Pilgrim, Mildred walked the entire Appalachian Trail, from Maine to Georgia, a distance of more than 2,000 miles. It taught her the necessity of traveling light. "I lived out-of-doors completely, supplied with only one pair of slacks and shorts, one blouse and sweater, a lightweight blanket, and two double plastic sheets into which I sometimes stuffed leaves,"

she said. "I was not completely dry and warm, but I enjoyed it thoroughly!"

Toward the end of her Appalachian expedition, after walking all night, Mildred had a vision of her first pilgrimage across the country. That's when Peace Pilgrim was born.

SPREADING A MESSAGE OF PEACE

Peace Pilgrim's monumental trek across the United States began in 1953 at the Tournament of Roses Parade in Pasadena, California. There, she handed out leaflets and gathered signatures for a Peace Petition, which she delivered to the United Nations after walking coast to coast. Until her death in 1981, she crisscrossed the country seven times on foot, stopping to talk with anyone intrigued by the message emblazoned on her tunic.

Like some spiritual Johnny Appleseed, Peace Pilgrim sowed the seeds of her mission through one-on-one conversations, college lectures, church services, radio programs, and TV interviews. She covered, as she liked to say, "the whole peace picture—peace among nations, peace among groups, peace among people, and, most important, inner peace." It wasn't a new message; she openly acknowledged that. But it was a message that she felt America needed to hear.

Day in and day out, regardless of the season, Peace Pilgrim wore the same outfit. She washed her garments in rest rooms, then allowed them to air-dry on her body. Changes in the temperature didn't slow her down; she said that her body had learned to quickly adjust to weather conditions. She ate only when she was offered food and slept wherever she found herself, which was often in an open field. And she carried only what she could fit into the pockets of her tunic: a comb, a folding toothbrush, her mail, a pen, a map, and, later, copies of her booklet *Steps toward Inner Peace*, which she handed out along her route.

SPEAKING FROM HER HEART

The more I learned about Peace Pilgrim, the more I wanted to read about her. But the more I read, the harder it became to believe that she actually existed. After all, her story seemed so incredible: an ordinary woman, hair already turned silver, walking solo across the country (America, no less— land of the automobile), without a penny in her pocket. Yet thousands of newspaper clippings vouched for what she was doing.

As I followed Peace Pilgrim on her journey and found out more about her lifestyle, I became curious about her message—and about the enthusiasm with which she delivered it. Watching videotapes of her college lectures, I was struck by her presence and presentation. She delivered her speeches like dramatic monologues, raising her eyes to the heavens, waving her arms, clasping and pointing her long, slender fingers to punctuate her message.

Clearly, she spoke from her heart, without a trace of judgment or criticism in her words or tone. And she enjoyed herself.

No question could throw Peace Pilgrim off course. No intellectualization could dampen her enthusiasm. She had found inner peace, and she wanted to shout it from the rooftops. "Only as we become peaceful will we find ourselves living in a more peaceful world," she'd say.

To large cities and to small towns, Peace Pilgrim delivered ideas that would eventually become topics in countless books on self-improvement and spiritual development. "Problems are opportunities in disguise" and "Inner peace is where peace begins" were just two of her mantras.

Peace Pilgrim reached out to people not only through the spoken word but also through the written word. During her travels, she corresponded with thousands of people whom she had met and counseled. She also created a newsletter, called *Peace Pilgrim's Progress*, to keep in touch with her friends while on the road.

At the time, what she said seemed radical. Yet she was so compelling, and she so obviously lived by her beliefs, that thousands of people took her into their hearts and even into their homes.

Eventually, Peace Pilgrim found herself inundated with offers of food and shelter. Her problem was no longer waiting to be offered a meal or a place to sleep but finding a way to graciously refuse many of the invitations. Peace

Pilgrim had traveled far, literally and figuratively.

REACHING OUT TO EVERYONE

In 1964, when Peace Pilgrim had completed 25,000 miles, she decided to change course. The time had come to stop counting mileage. She had been walking mostly along highways so that she could easily chart her progress. But she wanted to meet more people with whom she could share her message. She decided to visit the towns that she had passed by. There, she would find the listeners that she sought.

Along with Peace Pilgrim's change in course came a change in priorities, from walking to speaking. She booked engagements across the country, and she began accepting rides so that she could fit in as many lectures as possible. But she always returned to walking when she had time.

Although Peace Pilgrim believed that people should never look for results from their efforts, she witnessed a change in social and cultural values brought about, at least in part, by her work. In the 1960s, she saw a moral shift away from the belief that war is the answer to conflict. She watched as the fear and apathy of the McCarthy Era gave way to fervent demonstrations for peace. She saw people who had expressed little interest in spiritual growth become hungry for the kind of message that she sought to deliver. The trend toward peace has grown stronger over the years and continues to resonate with all generations.

Peace Pilgrim continued her mission of peace until her death on July 7, 1981. Ironically, she was killed while being driven to a speaking engagement. She left behind no written material other than her newsletters and her booklet *Steps toward Inner Peace*.

When the thousands who followed Peace Pilgrim learned of her death, they joined in spirit to mourn her passing. But I suspect that she would have told them to save their tears. As she said, "The body is just a garment. Death is a glorious transition to a freer life."

In death, Peace Pilgrim was free. But her message lives on in my heart and, I hope, in yours.

To learn more about Peace Pilgrim, write to Friends of Peace Pilgrim, 7350 Dorado Canyon Road, Somerset, CA 95684. You can request a free copy of Steps toward Inner Peace.

GETTING
STARTED
WITH
DYNAMIC
WALKING

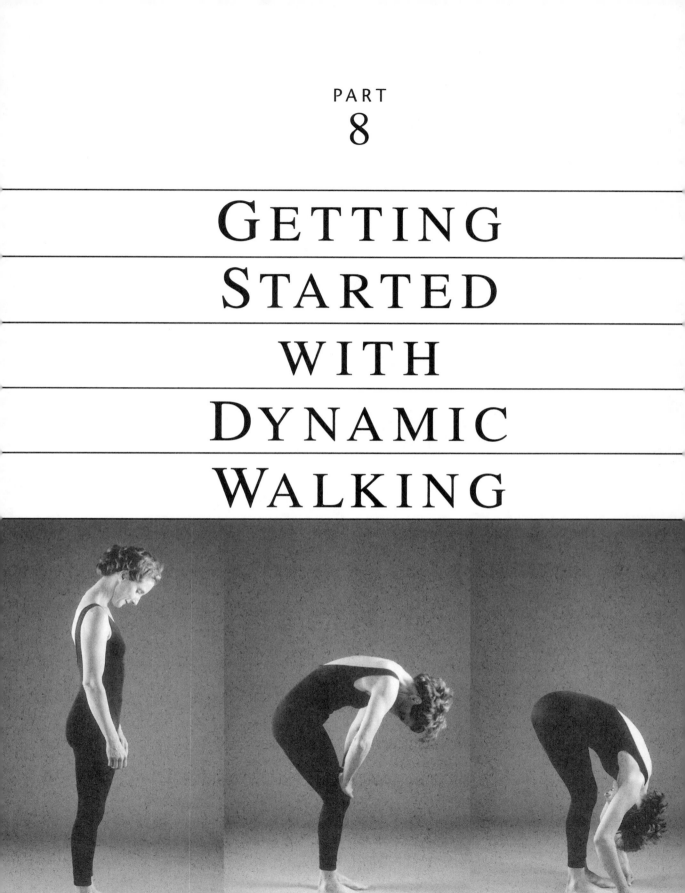

INTRODUCTION

During my 12 years as walking editor for *Prevention* magazine, I've had the opportunity to meet many walking coaches and instructors. And I've been impressed by all of them. But when I met Suki Munsell, Ph.D., in 1993 and began her Dynamic Walking Teacher Training, I knew that I had found a system that could help anyone get more out of walking.

Dr. Munsell is a registered movement therapist with extensive experience in the fields of education, psychology, fitness, dance, and somatic studies (a discipline that examines the relationship of the body to thinking, feeling, learning, and healing). She created and developed Dynamic Walking and the Dynamic Body Exercises after 30 years of studying systems of dance and exercise from around the world.

She trains people to walk with grace and efficiency while slowing and perhaps reversing the aging process, preventing injury, and in many cases, diminishing chronic pain. Using techniques that you'll read about in the next four chapters, she teaches people to modify their habitual movement patterns (their biomechanics) while walking, sitting, standing, and exercising.

Dr. Munsell's approach to fitness has a key element that's absent from most other training programs. She shows her clients how to evaluate their biomechanics to identify the patterns that get in the way of graceful, efficient walking and that may make them vulnerable to injury or delay their healing processes.

Her strategies help restore the body's natural, balanced posture, which enables her clients to walk stronger, faster, and farther. And if her clients do experience any musculoskeletal pain, they're able to heal their bodies and protect themselves against further injury. (Of course, if you have any undiagnosed pain, you should be properly evaluated by a physician before attempting any kind of self-treatment program.)

I have included Dr. Munsell's Dynamic Walking in this book because it's a unique and effective program that anyone can use. What you are about to learn can turn your daily workout into a source of healing, strength, and vitality.

—*M.S.*

CHAPTER **36**

A NEW WAY OF WALKING

At the Dynamic Health and Fitness Institute in Marin County, California, my colleagues and I have spent the past 9 years developing, refining, and teaching a new method of fitness training. Called Dynamic Walking, it shows people how to use dynamic forces, such as gravity, momentum, space, time, and intensity, to get more out of their walking workouts and to prevent injuries caused by faulty movement patterns (or biomechanics).

Of course, you already know how to walk. But without realizing it, you may be hampering yourself with poor posture or gait—perhaps because of stress, strain, or injury, or because you're subconsciously imitating the movement patterns of those around you. As you go through the Dynamic Walking program, you'll learn exercises and techniques that can help you develop good biomechanics. You'll be able to walk faster and get a better aerobic workout without creating undue wear and tear on your joints or muscles.

You may have started a walking program to lose weight, to stay healthy, or to improve your fitness. Whatever your reason, Dynamic Walking can help you reach your goal more efficiently and effectively.

THE KEY TO HEALING

One of the greatest advantages of Dynamic Walking is that it helps you protect yourself against the sort of injuries that occur when you perform a certain motion over and over again with poor biomechanics. These are referred to as repetitive-stress injuries, and they can occur anywhere in your body. When they're related to exercise, they often show up in the lower back, hips, knees, or feet.

Repetitive-stress injuries are among the many problems that prompt people to come to the Dynamic Health and Fitness Institute for help. Some of our clients have chronic back pain or are recovering from some sort of surgery, and they need to go through a re-education process in order to walk pain-free. Other

180   GETTING STARTED WITH DYNAMIC WALKING

clients are athletes who have suffered injuries that put them back to square one in terms of their training. They use Dynamic Walking as a springboard for resuming their respective sports.

What do all of these people have in common? Invariably, they developed problems in the first place because of faulty movement patterns that created a "weak link" in their bodies, predisposing them to injury. By analyzing each client's posture and stride, I can usually pinpoint a biomechanical cause of the person's pain.

As our clients improve their biomechanics, they often experience immediate and long-lasting relief from their discomfort. We have helped many people reduce or eliminate chronic or recurring pain in the back, hips, knees, ankles, feet—even the neck.

Once I teach clients Dynamic Walking, I'll continue to track their progress for several years. Invariably, they report wonderful results. Their postures improve with attention, but without a lot of effort. Their flexibility increases. They're less vulnerable to injury—and if they do hurt themselves, they heal faster. They perform better in other sports, even without practice. Each time they walk dynamically, they reinforce the things I've taught them. Walking dynamically becomes a form of preventive medicine.

My trainers and I also see hundreds of clients who are already pain-free and want to stay that way. These people are interested in improving their health and fitness or perhaps losing weight. They want to learn a safe, reliable walking technique to get the best possible workout. Once they complete Dynamic Walking training, they realize that they have gotten much more from it than they originally expected. They understand their bodies much better and are more sensitive to how they look and feel. They have more pride in their appearance, and they derive more pleasure from their walks.

As you progress through the Dynamic Walking program, you can expect similar results. You'll experience dramatic changes in yourself—not only physically but also mentally and emotionally.

THE PSOAS MUSCLES: A KEY COMPONENT OF BALANCED WALKING

You'll notice that many of the exercises and techniques in the Dynamic Walking program target key postural muscles called the psoas. These muscles extend from the bottom of the diaphragm (which separates the chest from the abdomen) to the top of the inside of each thighbone, or femur. The psoas are hip flexors; they're the major muscles doing the work when you bend your chest toward your thighs or pull your knees toward your chest. They also enable you to swing your legs when you walk.

Unfortunately, when you sit a lot, your psoas muscles become tight. They can pull on your spine, increasing its curves and making you shorter. When this happens, you begin to collapse and slump, which leaves you feeling and looking older. What's more, your breathing becomes shallow, your circulation declines, and many of your muscles and joints don't function properly.

As your psoas muscles tighten, they affect not only your posture but also your gait. They compress your torso so that when you walk, you tend to drop your weight into your hips and land heavily with every step. This causes you to bounce up and down while you're walking, which puts extra stress on your back, hips, and legs. And you take 8,000 to 10,000 steps per day as you go about your daily routine—not even counting your workouts.

With Dynamic Walking, you'll learn to lift out of your hips. This gives your legs room to swing like pendulums, as they are meant to do. (Podiatrists use the term *swing phase* to describe this motion.) The weight of your swinging legs, combined with special stretches called the Dynamic Body Exercises, help lengthen your psoas muscles with every step.

POSTURE: THE BENEFITS OF STANDING TALL

Beyond building your psoas muscles, the Dynamic Body Exercises help realign your entire body and strengthen your core. This is key to rebuilding your posture, another objective of the Dynamic Walking program.

Poor posture is a common cause of back pain, which has reached epidemic proportions in the United States. Back pain affects an estimated 80 percent of Americans at some point in their lives. Many of us in the health and fitness industry have devoted years to studying this public health issue. Back pain robs millions of people of their time, money, and enjoyment of life.

In fact, I first developed Dynamic Walking to help heal my own debilitating sciatica. None of the treatment programs that I tried worked for me. So I created my own.

Like many people, I struggled with poor posture. I've had clients tell me that when they were growing up, their mothers (or grandmothers) were constantly trying to get them to stand up straight. Did that happen to you? While your family surely meant well, they likely couldn't tell you *how* to correct your posture effectively. It took me more than 30 years to figure out.

Through Dynamic Walking and the Dynamic Body Exercises, you'll discover a practical approach to achieving good posture. As you practice these techniques, you'll feel better and more relaxed whether you're standing or sitting. That's because you'll learn to allow your skeletal system, not your muscles, to hold you up. Your muscles will be able to let go of unnecessary tension. Your breathing will deepen as your chest has more room to expand.

Improving your posture doesn't have to be a mystery or an effort. But it does take practice. Using the techniques that I've developed makes it a little easier.

GETTING THE MOST FROM DYNAMIC WALKING

When you walk for exercise, your dynamics should precede your aerobics. In other words, before you try to walk fast to get a good workout, you need to learn to walk correctly, with proper posture and stride. If you take poor posture and stride mechanics and add the forces and pressures that speed creates, your body will suffer. With proper biomechanics, you'll be able to walk faster, and you'll feel good while you're doing it. What's more, you'll be able to walk longer at any speed without getting tired or putting yourself at risk for injury.

In chapter 37, I'll guide you through a 6-week program in which you'll examine your habitual movement patterns and learn techniques for correcting your posture and stride. Even if you have been fitness walking for years, you need to analyze your biomechanics in this way. Once you do, you're ready to learn to walk dynamically.

In chapter 38, I'll teach you the Dynamic Body Exercises, which you'll begin practicing during the 6-week program. The Dynamic Body Exercises go hand in hand with Dynamic Walking. The exercises stretch and rebalance your musculoskeletal system. Then Dynamic Walking "sets" your new posture and stride. If you try to master the walking technique without doing the exercises, you won't get the results you want.

Unfortunately, in the rush to get through their workouts, few people stretch regularly, correctly, or completely. Done carefully and consistently, stretching feels great and helps you maintain your flexibility as you grow older or exercise harder. The Dynamic Body Exercises can help you discover the joys of stretching. They can be done before, after, and even during a walking workout.

In chapter 39, you'll learn a Dynamic Walking routine to use every time you walk. It's designed with respect for your body's natural timing in warming up, cooling down, and stretching. Built into the routine are awareness exercises to help you monitor your progress and keep your workouts safe.

I recommend completing the 6-week program before starting the Dynamic Walking routine. That way, you can concentrate on developing correct posture and stride, then apply those skills to walking dynamically.

As we move on with your Dynamic Walking training, please remember to ease yourself into this or any fitness program, especially if you have been inactive. On the first day, do only half as much as you think you can. Progress gradually from there.

You may experience some soreness from time to time; this is to be expected as you retrain your body to move in different, more efficient ways. If any pain persists or gets worse, by all means see your doctor. Once your doctor rules out any underlying medical problem, you can continue with the Dynamic Walking program.

C H A P T E R   **37**

6 WEEKS TO DYNAMIC WALKING

Welcome to the start of a 6-week program in which you'll learn and practice the three core principles of the Dynamic Walking program. Through the exercises and techniques in this chapter, you'll do the following:

- **Lift**—lengthen your spine and pull up from your hips and your lower back.

- **Stack**—correct your postural alignment, repositioning the building blocks of your body.

- **Build pelvic power**—energize your walk from your pelvis by connecting strongly to the ground through your legs.

Over the next 6 weeks, you'll be working from the top of your body down toward your feet, then back up. The order is critical to your progress.

In weeks 1 and 2, you'll learn how to *lift* your upper-body weight out of your midsection and your hips. This lift,

or decompression, creates more space for your legs to swing like pendulums. The swinging motion, in turn, evenly lengthens and strengthens your psoas muscles. These muscles run down each side of your body, from the base of your diaphragm to the tops of your thighs.

As explained in chapter 36, the psoas muscles are often tight from too much sitting. This can shorten your posture, limit your breathing, and painfully strangle your sciatic nerve.

But as the psoas muscles become longer and stronger, they're able to maintain your pelvis in a neutral position, which is critical in providing postural support for your torso and upper body.

The combination of decompressing and psoas-lengthening makes it easier to *stack*, or realign, the building blocks of your body—that is, your head, chest, pelvis, hips, and legs. In weeks 3 and 4, you'll learn to assess your posture and make any necessary adjustments.

Relieving your hips of upper-body pressure also allows your legs to change their structural alignment, the focus of week 5. Your legs are the foundation of efficient and effortless posture. They must support everything above them, *and* they must move your body around. With Dynamic Walking, your legs will do a better job of providing both stability and action for your body.

In week 6, you'll *build pelvic power* by connecting from your torso through your legs into the earth. Your ground traction will improve, and your legs will grow stronger. You'll also decrease upper-body tension and effort as you trust your legs to do their work. In chapter 39, you'll be adding the power of your arm swing.

THE DYNAMICS OF CHANGE

If you need more than 6 weeks to develop a solid foundation for Dynamic Walking, please be patient with yourself. After all, your current walk has evolved over the course of your lifetime. Changing such a fundamental pattern can seem overwhelming. It's quite normal to feel confused, awkward, and uncoordinated.

Respect the fact that you're making changes in the deepest level of your being, your neurological programming. Be compassionate and persistent, as if training a puppy, and give yourself the time that you need. Even 8 to 12 weeks is reasonable—and you'll be delighted with the results.

Remember, you are deeply identified with your walk and your posture. It's your choice to change them, and you can do so only when you are truly ready. I had one client tell me that correcting his posture made him feel disconnected from his father and grandfather, who also stood with rounded shoulders. Many women say that they first started slumping when their breasts began developing, because they were embarrassed. The human ego has its reasons for wanting to maintain the status quo.

On the other hand, pain is a great motivator for making postural changes. Staying young and vital is another. By progressing slowly and steadily, you allow yourself time to adjust to feeling taller, sexier, or more alive.

Perhaps the most powerful incentive for making the changes that I'm recommending is the increased pleasure derived from moving your body in a smooth, fluid manner, and not just while walking. To help you focus your efforts, I've included with each week's exercises a list of goals as well as a set of what I call kinesthetic images. Remember, to really transform your body, you must develop a new kinesthetic awareness—that is, a new sense of how your body moves.

BUILDING BETTER BIOMECHANICS

When you're ready to begin the program below, think of it as performing an experiment for 6 weeks (or however long you need). Your body may feel uncomfortable on occasion as things shift around. Some of my clients have opted to stop other forms of exercise, especially weight training, during this time. Why work against yourself by strengthening muscles in the wrong position? Give your body time to re-align itself before adding more stress.

As soon as you start week 1 of the program, you may also begin stretching dynamically, as described in chapter 38. If your exercise routine already includes stretching, you need to know that the way you're stretching is part of your habitual movement pattern. It is keeping you in the posture you have now. Think about that. You'll get faster results if you stop your other stretches for a while and do the Dynamic Body Exercises (DBX) correctly and completely. You'll learn biomechanical principles that you can then apply to everything you do, from gardening to driving a car. (Biomechanics refers to your body movement patterns.)

During each week of the 6-week program, I'll ask you to focus on specific Dynamic Body Exercises, practicing them in conjunction with other exercises. By targeting specific aspects of posture and stride, they'll systematically transform your body.

Transforming your body can be an exciting project, like redesigning a room in your home. Keep in mind that your posture affects not only how you carry your weight but also how you look, feel, age, and heal. Watch for these positive changes as you progress through the program.

Knowledge is power. More power to you.

WEEK 1: LIFTING YOUR UPPER BODY

If you notice these signs . . .	C- or S-shaped posture—slumping, collapsed chest, shoulders rolled forward, shallow breathing, bulging belly, swayback; pain in the lower back, hips, buttocks, knees, or heels; feeling like life is an uphill battle
You'll practice these exercises	Side Stroke; Short Shirt Pull; DBX Focus
You'll experience these benefits	Feeling lighter and taller; breathing more fully; experiencing more comfort and less pain; feeling that you've lost weight; being happier
You'll acheive this training goal	Lifting your upper-body weight out of your midsection and lower back

Perhaps you've heard the word *psychosomatic*. It means that your feelings can profoundly affect your body. Indeed, research has shown that negative feelings can produce illness.

The opposite is also true. Alexander Lowen, an early mind-body researcher, discovered that the set (posture) of the soma (body) affects the psyche. He coined the term *somatopsychic*.

You can test Lowen's theory for yourself by doing the following exercise. Begin to slump as you sit reading this book. Continue slumping. Imagine how you'll look in 5 years, in 10 years. How has your breathing changed? How do you feel? What would your life be like if this was your posture? What activities would you have to give up? What would happen to you if you couldn't straighten up? Scary thought, isn't it?

Your body position quite literally affects your outlook on life. Renowned psychiatrist Sigmund Freud once said, "Anatomy is destiny." Perhaps both he and Lowen were warning us that, all too easily, our biology can become our biography.

I've heard it said that while we can't always determine our future, we can determine our habits. Our habits determine our future.

If you experience any of the warning signals listed above, or if you want to avoid them, then practice the following exercises and techniques to decompress your spine. You'll get more lift out of life.

Exercises for Week 1

Repeat these frequently each day this week to build new muscle memory.

Side Stroke: While standing, place your right hand at your left side. Beneath your hand, feel the distance between your rib cage and your hip. Then inhale as you stretch your left arm upward, lifting out of your waist. Feel how you can increase the distance beneath your hand.

Now as you exhale, lower your left shoulder and arm, but maintain that increased space beneath your hand. You're training the muscles around your rib cage to keep you lifted. This will give you more breathing space and reduce the pressure on your lower back. Repeat three times on each side.

Short Shirt Pull: Cross your arms at the wrists and position them at about waist height. Raise your arms overhead, as if pulling off a shirt. Inhale fully, stretching your arms overhead. Lengthen your torso as you reach toward the sky. Resist the urge to arch your back. Keep your head level, with your gaze fixed on the horizon. Exhale and return your arms to your sides while continuing to grow taller through your spine.

Repeat the exercise. Make sure that as you lower your arms, you drop your shoulders like a shirt resting on a hanger. Repeat several more times, imagining that you're pulling off your old body to reveal a lighter, brighter you.

The next time you go walking, do three to six Short Shirt Pulls every few minutes. Notice how the movement alters your walk. Resume your "old" walk and feel the difference.

Practice the exercise frequently during your walking workouts this week, so you retain the lifted posture. Also do a Short Shirt Pull whenever you catch yourself slumping. Don't criticize yourself for slouching; instead, congratulate yourself for being aware of your posture and correcting it.

DBX Focus: Learn how to do the Long Shirt Pull exercise described on pages 209–10.

Kinesthetic Images for Week 1

Practice these frequently each day this week to experience your body in new ways.

Crowning Glory: Lift your head high into an imaginary crown. Balance your head gently at the top of your spine. Make sure that your ears are positioned over your shoulders. Relax your jaw, and relax your face.

Shoulder Shirt: Let your shoulders relax and drop. Imagine them hanging like a shirt on a hanger.

Growing Upward: Whenever you see a tree rising straight and tall into the sky or a flower poised at the end of a slender upright stalk or a person moving with elegant lifted posture, bring that experience into your own body. Imagine that you're riding an upward energy that lifts your body and spirit skyward.

Home Base: Do a Short Shirt Pull. As your arms come down, relax your shoulders completely. Add several Shoulder Rolls (pages 211–12)—up,

back, down, and around—to settle your shoulders like a yoke resting easily on your rib cage. Let the weight of your arms help keep your shoulders relaxed.

Feel the core of your body supporting you. Close your eyes and allow your body to lead you through some spontaneous stretches. This helps you find home base, a comfortable position where your muscles relax and your skeleton supports you.

Goals for Week 1

1. Walk for 10 to 30 minutes, three to five times this week while maintaining an elongated spine.

2. Do 10 to 20 Short Shirt Pulls during each of your walking workouts. Also practice the Short Shirt Pulls frequently during the day to help build and maintain a lifted posture. You're strengthening the levatores costarum muscles, which raise your ribs, to maintain lift.

3. Become aware of when you are lifted and when you are slumping forward.

4. Acknowledge yourself each time you catch yourself in an old habit and you make a positive change.

5. Keep your shoulders relaxed and down while standing taller through your spine.

6. Notice differences in how you carry your weight and how you look and feel.

WEEK 2: LIFTING OUT OF YOUR HIPS

If you notice these signs . . .	Tightness or pain in the lower back or hips; heaviness in the abdomen; shallow breathing; knee or foot pain; slow pace when walking; less get-up-and-go
You'll practice these exercises	Pendulum Arms; Pendulum Legs—Scuff/No Scuff; Nose over Toes to Go; DBX Focus
You'll experience these benefits	Feeling lighter on your feet; walking faster and easier; developing greater flexibility; breathing easier; improving digestion and elimination; feeling more vital and alive
You'll acheive this training goal	Lifting your upper-body weight out of your hips

In week 1, you began learning to send your energy up your spine while leaving your shoulders down and relaxed. Your goals included building important new habits: training the levatores costarum (the muscles that raise your ribs) to maintain lift and training yourself to assume a taller posture whenever you find yourself slumping.

In week 2, you'll be lifting your body up out of your hips. This will create enough space to move your legs like pendulums. Why is this important? Well, have you ever pushed a child on a swing? A swing is a pendulum. After those first few pushes, it moves by itself, with little additional effort to keep it going. The swing moves efficiently because it uses momentum, which is a dynamic force.

You can learn to use momentum to fuel your walk and save energy. You have four pendulums—two arms and two legs—attached to your body. The tricky part is letting go of the tension

you may habitually hold in your shoulders and your hips so that your limbs can swing freely. Ninety-five percent of the people whom I watch walk are not swinging their legs. Instead, they're stepping forward, reaching forward, or falling onto their feet and legs.

Watch for yourself how people walk. Steppers, reachers, and fallers bounce up and down; they're using their leg muscles as springs. The people who swing their legs are gliding. Their walk is smooth at any speed, slow or fast. My husband, Russ, who developed our Dynamic Speed program, has been clocked at an $8\frac{1}{2}$-minute-per-mile pace. And his walk is smooth, never bobbing.

Unless you are among the 5 percent of people who naturally swing their legs like pendulums, Dynamic Walking will be dramatically different for you. The glide feels great, it looks great, it's dynamic. Best of all, it's less jarring to your joints. Since you're averaging

8,000 steps a day, plus 2,000 more for every mile of fitness walking you do, that jarring adds up fast.

Swinging your arms and legs uses dynamic forces wisely. It is economical. You won't be wasting your energy. As a result, you may notice that you can walk farther.

Walking dynamically is a metaphor for learning to use natural resources with more awareness and respect. You'll also be learning to use your muscles differently, so initially you may notice soreness in new places.

Exercises for Week 2

Repeat these as needed each day this week to build new muscle memory. Be sure to practice the first three exercises every time you go fitness walking until you feel yourself gliding easily. If it seems difficult or confusing, don't get discouraged, and don't try too hard. Relaxing into the glide is key.

Pendulum Arms: Stand tall. Bend forward from your hips as if to place both hands on a table. Let your arms hang limp. Reach over with your right hand and push your left arm only once. Let your arm swing until it stops. Do it again. Continue releasing any tension in your left shoulder until your arm is totally relaxed and swinging easily. Describe to yourself how your shoulder feels. Compare as you repeat the exercise with your right arm.

Each time you go fitness walking, let your arms swing relaxed at your sides for at least 10 minutes. Don't

pump them or use them to power your walk—not yet, anyway.

Pendulum Legs—Scuff/No Scuff: Begin with a Short Shirt Pull. Then, while you're standing tall, place your right hand on a support (such as a wall or the back of a sturdy, stable chair) and balance on your right leg. Breathe as you rhythmically swing your left leg back and forth several times from the hip joint. Keep both knees relaxed.

Scuff your left foot on the ground several times as you swing. Then swing without scuffing. Repeat the Scuff/No Scuff twice more. Notice that lifting out of your right hip socket allows your left leg to swing freely and clear the ground. When you scuff the ground, you're settling into your right hip socket. Describe to yourself how your right hip feels. Compare as you repeat the exercise while standing on your left leg.

To transfer this exercise to walking, position yourself with your left side toward a long wall or railing. Practice swinging your right leg (from the hip, not the knee) like a relaxed pendulum. To ensure that you are doing the exercise correctly, reach down with your right hand to pump your leg a few times. If your hip is relaxed, your leg should respond as if you were pushing a swing. Swing your right foot gently into place just ahead of your left foot. This will be shorter than your normal stride length. Step onto your right foot, rolling heel to toe.

Switch sides and repeat the exercise with your left leg. Be careful not to pound your heel. Repeat several more times, alternating legs as you go.

Nose over Toes to Go: Stand with your feet parallel and about one shoe-width apart. Do a Short Shirt Pull. To initiate your first step, lean forward from your ankles—not your hips—until your nose is over toes. This lean positions your legs under and slightly to the rear of your body. Push off from behind with your right leg, allowing it to swing forward, relaxed from the hip, into the Heel-Toe Roll (page 209). Don't think about stepping forward. Concentrate only on the push-off from the ball and toes of the foot that is to the rear of your body.

After your first step, you don't need to continue leaning forward. Do Short Shirt Pulls whenever you're walking, to stand tall and stay lifted out of your hips. If you sink back into your pelvis, you will naturally return to a bouncy stride. If you practice walking dynamically during the day, you'll notice faster results.

DBX Focus: You'll know you've succeeded in releasing shoulder tension when your arms drop and flop at your sides during the Spinal Rotation (page 213). Also practice letting your arms dangle while you're doing the Shoulder Roll (pages 211–12) and the Hamstring Stretch (page 214).

Kinesthetic Images for Week 2

Practice these frequently each day this week to experience your body in new ways.

Limp Limbs: Have you seen someone holding a sleeping child? The child's body, arms, and legs are limp. While you're in bed, practice letting your arms and legs go limp. You may need to squeeze your muscles tight a few times, then relax them with a strong exhale. Proceed up your body, from the muscles in your feet to those in your head. (This exercise, called progressive muscle relaxation, is excellent for releasing tension.) Anchor this new feeling in your body. Think of it as hitting the R key (for "relax") on your "bio-computer." Transfer this new kinesthetic image into your everyday life.

Pendulum Arms and Legs: Have you ever seen a child spin herself around in a circle, her arms following her body? When you're walking, let your arms swing as a result of your movement. Let your legs swing forward passively as a result of your push-off.

Goals for Week 2

1. Lift out of your hips.
2. Swing your legs forward like pendulums as you walk.
3. Relax your hips and the muscles of your pelvic floor.
4. Allow your arms to swing relaxed from your shoulders while you're walking.
5. Increase your daily awareness of tension in your shoulders and your hips. Inhale, exhale, and let tension dissolve.

WEEK 3: ASSESSING YOUR POSTURE FROM THE MIDLINE

If you notice these signs . . .	Backaches; hip, spine, or leg pain
You'll practice these exercises	Dynamic Posture Analysis—Midline; DBX Focus; Dynamic Stride Analysis—Midline; Dynamic Walking Training
You'll experience these benefits	Having less pain; feeling more relaxed and less tense; experiencing less muscle strain; developing better balance; getting a better workout; enjoying more confidence; looking better
You'll acheive this training goal	Improving postural alignment from the front or midline

When infants first begin to sit upright on their own, they hold their spines ramrod straight. Their legs are also straight, extended wide to help create a stable, triangular base. They sit on the floor this way when stacking blocks or dropping colorful rings onto an upright post. Perhaps this is how they learn to stack the building blocks of their bodies before attempting to walk.

During week 2, your task was to incorporate a new awareness—to separate your core from your arms and legs, which could then hang relaxed when you're standing still or swing when you're in motion. To accomplish this, I asked you to continue lifting your torso upward, all the way out of your hips. This allows your legs to swing like pendulums when you walk.

What's more, the upward energy decompresses and elongates your spine, which allows the building blocks of your body to shift more easily into a biomechanically efficient posture. So

your posture better supports you while you're at rest and as you move through your daily activities.

This week, you'll analyze your daily biomechanics and connect this awareness to your walking biomechanics. As an example, one woman came to me with pain in her right hip that was so severe that she couldn't even put on her panty hose. She had sought help from several doctors, but they couldn't tell her what was wrong. After studying her posture in photographs, she realized that she was rotated to her right and sinking (compressed) into her right hip. All day long, she was managing a team of people whose desks were to her right and behind her. With her new awareness, plus walking and stretching dynamically, she relieved her pain.

Have you ever wanted x-ray vision, like Superman? Well, I can't grant you that, but I can teach you to "see" bodies with a greater awareness of the structure that lies beneath.

For example, if your fanny pack, waist belt, or socks are twisting around when you walk, you are probably pushing off harder on one foot. If your shoes wear unevenly, you're likely dealing with unbalanced biomechanics.

Looking at a herd of zebras, you'd have a hard time telling the animals apart as individuals. Their shape and movements make them look almost identical. They must move with respect to dynamic forces to avoid becoming some lion's dinner. It is the law of survival of the fittest. Poor biomechanics might cost zebras their lives. For us humans, it may only reduce the length and quality of life.

The next exercise is the toughest so far. It requires you to look at yourself in a full-length mirror. If you don't already have such a mirror, consider buying one. They're inexpensive and easy to store. You'll need one to track your progress.

I want you to see beyond your immediate reaction to how you look—too heavy, too slumped, too something. Drop all that. Pretend that you have x-ray vision. Look deeper into your musculoskeletal structure.

Exercises for Week 3

Repeat these as needed each day this week to develop new muscle memory.

Dynamic Posture Analysis—Midline: Hang a weighted string down the center of a full-length mirror. Then position yourself in front of the mirror so that you can view your body from head to toe. Find your natural standing posture.

Using the string for reference, observe your body. Does the center line fall straight from your nose to your belly button to between your feet? Do you lean to one side? Do you put more weight on one leg? Is an arm longer, a hip higher, a shoulder lower? Is the space between your arms and your body the same on both sides? Does your clothing wrinkle unevenly or hang differently from one side of your body to the other?

Stand for about a minute, until you feel your body getting tired. Close your eyes and notice in which direction you would most easily shift, twist, or collapse to relieve tightness or tension. Open your eyes and watch closely as you move back and forth between postures. Notice whether different postures make you feel differently about yourself.

Relieve any tension that may have built up from standing by proceeding to the next exercise.

DBX Focus: Do three Long Shirt Pulls (pages 209–10). Begin each one with a Heel-Toe Roll (page 209) to distribute your weight more evenly between your legs. As you roll up, pay attention to how you stack your pelvis over your legs, align your rib cage over your pelvis, settle your shoulder yoke on your rib cage, and perch your head atop your spinal column.

Over the next few weeks, pay attention to the changes you see in the mirror. Close your eyes and feel what has changed. Transfer this new awareness into your everyday life.

Dynamic Stride Analysis—Midline: Whenever you go walking, pay attention to the following (you may want to tape-record these points, so you don't have to memorize them).

- Feet and legs: Look down to observe whether your feet are tracking parallel or pointing in or out. Can you see or feel that you are collapsing to the inside or outside of your feet? Are you on one leg for a longer period than the other? Does one push off harder or step out farther? If you have any pain, analyze which part of your movement hurts.

- Hips: Walk with your hands on your hips, thumbs pointing forward. Notice whether both hips are moving the same or at all. Drop your hands to your sides.

- Arms: Place one hand on your chest for 15 paces. Observe the power of the arm that is swinging. Then change hands for 15 paces. Does one arm seem stronger or more dominant than the other? Switch hands again, this time concentrating on your arm position. Does one arm swing more easily to the front or back? Or do your arms swing equally in both directions? Continue switching until you have a good comparison of the power and tracking of both arms.

- Back: Bring both hands toward your chest as if carrying a package. How does this change your walk? Do you experience pain in your lower back? Drop your arms.

- Head: Notice where you tend to look when you walk. Do you feel any strain in your neck, shoulders, or upper back?

When you are finished, choose three words to describe your most vivid impression of your walk.

Dynamic Walking Training: Whenever you go walking, use your stride analysis to make observations about your body. If one arm swings forward more easily and the other swings back more easily, perhaps your body is rotated. If you feel more weight on one leg, perhaps you're subconsciously favoring that leg or leaning to that side. Your goal is to begin using both sides of your body more evenly when you walk, stand, and exercise.

As you're walking, make the following changes:

- Feet and legs: Walk with your feet pointing straight ahead. Push off equally from the balls and toes of both feet. If one or both of your feet angle out to the sides, practice keeping them parallel for only 1 to 2 minutes at a time, three to five times during your walk. Gradually increase the duration and frequency over the next 3 to 9 months, until you're able to hold your feet in a parallel position without discomfort.

- Hips: Once you're more lifted, the weight of your swinging legs will naturally swivel your hips. Holding back your hips or forcing the swivel causes strain. Just continue to do Short Shirt Pulls while you walk and let nature take its course.

- Arms: Let your arms swing forward and back equally, like pendulums. (In chapter 39, you'll learn the bent-arm technique.)

- Head: Keep your head level, gently perched atop your spine. Let your eyes scan the path ahead of you far to near for safety. As you do the Short Shirt Pulls (10 to 20 per hour), maintain a lift into your crown.

- Breathing: Let your breathing relax. As you continue to elongate your spine, your breaths will deepen.

Kinesthetic Image for Week 3

Practice this frequently each day this week to experience your body in new ways.

Balloon Breathing: As you breathe, notice which area of your body moves.

Then empty your lungs by exhaling forcefully. Often we don't let go of "old" air, so we don't have room for fresh air. As you inhale, imagine your torso filling fully all around, like a balloon. Exhale fully and pause. You'll notice that your body inhales on its own when it needs air. Repeat several times.

Goals for Week 3

1. Be more aware of how you use your body in everyday activities.

2. Stack the building blocks of your body in better alignment.

3. Use both sides of your body more symmetrically when you walk, stand, and exercise.

4. Use your full-length mirror to observe your posture.

WEEK 4: ASSESSING YOUR POSTURE FROM THE SIDE

If you notice these signs . . .	Headaches; eyestrain; shoulder tension; shallow breathing; backaches; hip, spine, or leg pain; poor circulation; depression
You'll practice these exercises	Dynamic Posture Analysis—Plumb Line; Belly Button to Backbone with Heel Press; Psoas Heel Slide; Rib Cage Slide; DBX Focus
You'll experience these benefits	Improving posture; enjoying greater comfort; having less pain; breathing deeper; feeling more relaxed and less tense; experiencing less muscle strain; improving balance; working out more effectively; striding with confidence; looking better
You'll acheive this training goal	Improving postural alignment from the side or plumb line

Several years ago, our local newspaper ran an article on the design of shirts to fit the body of the average older woman. Typically, her shoulders have rolled forward, and her rib cage sits on her hips. This posture is unfortunate and unnecessary, most likely brought on by a combination of poor biomechanics and the brittle-bone disease osteoporosis.

Proper nutrition, weight training, and hormonal balance can prevent osteoporosis. Likewise, good biomechanics can prevent collapse. Whether you're a woman or a man, standing tall communicates to the world your self-respect at any age.

The upright posture is highly valued in cultures worldwide. It's captured in the cave paintings of warriors, the tomb paintings of Egyptian pharaohs, the statues of Greek gods, the erect spine of Buddha, the regal bearings of kings and queens. In the animated film *Mulan*, which is about a young Chinese woman impersonating a man in battle, she prays to bring honor to her family so that her father "can stand tall." In the English language, we refer to people as "upstanding citizens."

Last week, you began to take a deeper look at yourself, to assess how you're growing your body. (As the twig is bent, the saying goes, so the tree will grow.) This week, you'll analyze your posture from the side. You'll need to have a friend take photos of you. It's impossible to use a mirror effectively.

You'll continue to concentrate on stacking the building blocks of your body more efficiently. To do this, you'll learn an exercise to lengthen and strengthen the psoas muscles, which are located deep in your abdomen and connect your spine to your legs.

As you analyze your posture, maintaining a positive attitude can make all the difference. None of us is perfect. We all see things in ourselves that we could correct. Your goal is to correct poor biomechanics. That's different from deciding that you or some part of your body is "bad" or "wrong." Stop saying "my bad leg" or "my bad knee." That only adds insult to injury. It's counterproductive.

Instead, build a more positive, more nurturing vocabulary. Use words like "previously injured" or "recovering." One leg or arm may be "more dominant" or "less dominant" than the other. Parts of your body may be "overburdened" or "underutilized." You may be "carrying more weight" than you want to. Your movement patterns may be "untrained" or "inefficient."

Choose your words carefully and with compassion. They have the power to launch a war or nurture love, to kill or create. Ultimately, they affect your thoughts, your feelings about yourself, and your posture.

Respect your body for the extraordinary gift that it is, and thank it for bringing you this far.

Exercises for Week 4

Repeat these as instructed to build new muscle memory.

Dynamic Posture Analysis—Plumb Line: For this exercise, a Polaroid camera, one that produces its own prints, works best.

Stand as you would at the end of the day, perhaps even closing your eyes to feel the posture you want to have captured on film. Then have a friend take a photo of you from each side.

Looking at the pictures, place a dot on your ear, shoulder, hip, knee, and ankle. (A red permanent ink pen is best for marking photographs.) Connect the dots to see if they're in a straight line, perpendicular to the floor, or if they form a C or an S curve.

Now look carefully at your posture. Are your ears over your shoulders, or is your head forward? Are your shoulders over your hips? Is your upper body slightly behind your lower body, the way a model might walk with her hips pushed forward? Is your back swayed? Is your waistband parallel to the ground or slanted?

Draw a box around your pelvis, using your waistband as the top of the box. Does your pelvic bowl spill forward, creating a belly bulge? Are your knees locked?

Roll down into a Long Shirt Pull (pages 209–10). As you roll up, experiment with restacking the building blocks of your body into better alignment. Repeat twice more. This teaches you how to make your skeletal system bear more of your body weight and how to let your muscles relax. Repeat the Long Shirt Pull frequently throughout the day to maintain lift and spinal flexibility.

Once you've analyzed your photos, label and date them, then store them away for future reference. Some of my clients have new photos taken every 3 to 6 months so that they can see their progress.

If you notice in your photos that you have a C- or an S-shaped posture, practice the following three exercises twice each day this week to build new muscle memory.

Belly Button to Backbone with Heel Press: This floor exercise helps release and lengthen core postural muscles.

Lie on your back on the floor, with your knees bent. Use a towel or pillow to support your neck and head if necessary. Take a few moments to breathe and let your body melt into the floor. Bring your fingertips to your waist to help you notice the space between your lower back and the floor. To close this space, exhale and press your belly button toward your backbone. Press your heels into the floor to hold this position. Remember the connection between feeling your lower back against the floor and pressing your heels against the floor. Breathe in fully and let the space between your lower back and the floor open up again.

Repeat this exercise several more times, pressing your belly button to your backbone and your heels into the floor on each exhale and releasing on each inhale. Enjoy the rocking motion of your pelvis. Notice which muscles in your torso seem to be working.

Don't tighten your abdominal muscles; keep your belly relaxed.

Identify and begin using deeper muscles, especially your psoas. These are your core postural muscles. Stay on the floor and move on to the next exercise.

Psoas Heel Slide: In this exercise, your eventual goal is to straighten both legs while keeping your belly button pressed toward your backbone and your heels pressed into the floor. If you are swaybacked, this will be very difficult at first. Your lower back and psoas muscles may already have shortened. That's what happened to me.

You're still lying on the floor, with your knees bent. On the exhale, slide your left heel *along the floor*, away from your left buttock. Keep your right knee bent, with your right foot comfortably close to your right buttock. Can you continue pressing your lower back against the floor while your left leg is straight?

Bend your left knee, bringing your foot toward your left buttock. Then repeat the exercise, this time extending your right leg by sliding your right heel forward. What happens to your lower back?

Continue alternating legs, sliding one heel and then the other away from your buttocks. Roll your head from side to side, as needed, to keep your neck, shoulders, and upper back relaxed. Breathe deeply; focus on slowly stretching and lengthening the muscles along your back and deep inside your torso.

Always do this exercise with the Belly Button to Backbone. Together, they should take you 3 to 5 minutes. If you have a severe C or S curve to your posture, be sure to do both exercises at least twice a day. Always follow them with the Rib Cage Slide.

Rib Cage Slide: When you carry something, be it a package or a baby, you're likely to push your rib cage too far back behind your lower body. If this posture becomes a habit, it can compress nerves over time, resulting in lower-back and sciatic pain.

If you noticed in your photos that your upper back may be behind your hips, be sure to concentrate on this exercise. It will teach you to move your rib cage into proper position, building a more efficient postural pattern.

The Rib Cage Slide has three parts. First, while standing in front of a full-length mirror, put your hands on either side of your body and extend your fingers so that you're reaching from your lower ribs to your hips. Hold this position while you look in the mirror. Notice where you usually carry your rib cage in relationship to your pelvis.

Next, lie on the floor with your knees bent and your lower back pressed into the floor, as in the Belly Button to Backbone exercise. Again, place your hands at your sides, extending your fingers from your lower ribs to your hips. Notice any difference? The floor is forcing your rib cage more to the front of your pelvis, compared with when you're standing.

Return to a standing position, again noticing where you carry your rib cage. Do a Long Shirt Pull (pages 209–10) to elongate your body. Then do a Heel-

Toe Roll (page 209), pausing when you're back on your heels. Bring your belly button toward your backbone, as though you were pressing into the floor. Feel how this simultaneously slides your rib cage forward. (If you want, extend your fingers at your sides to check this new position.) You need only a slight movement; don't try to lift up your rib cage in front, which would cause you to overarch your back. Continue relaxed breathing as you hold this position for 15 seconds.

Repeat the Heel-Toe Roll for 15 seconds, swinging your arms while you do. Then once again pause with your weight back on your heels. Repeat the Belly Button to Backbone exercise and the Rib Cage Slide. Lengthen your lower back, as though you have a heavy tail that's dropping toward the floor. Do the entire sequence a third time. To release any tension that may have built up in your back, do a Hip Stretch (pages 213–14).

Practice the Rib Cage Slide whenever you notice that your rib cage has dropped back and down. Eventually, as your musculoskeletal system adjusts, this new posture will feel more natural.

DBX Focus: If your posture analysis shows you that your upper body is positioned behind your lower body, then from here on, follow every Long and Short Shirt Pull you do with a Belly Button to Backbone exercise and a Rib Cage Slide. You also need to practice lifting your chin slightly.

Use this new postural alignment whenever you are stretching or walking. If your speed increases slightly while you're walking, then you'll know that you were probably pushing your hips forward before.

Kinesthetic Images for Week 4

Practice these frequently each day this week to experience your body in new ways.

Strong Center Core: If you noticed in your photo that you have a C- or an S-shaped posture, then practicing the Belly Button to Backbone exercise and the Rib Cage Slide will bring your body's building blocks into better alignment. Find a positive image to which you can anchor this new kinesthetic awareness, perhaps a classic Greek column or a redwood tree or even a strong wire coil.

Tail Drop: Elongate your spine from your neck to your lower back. Imagine that you have a heavy tail dropping down toward the ground. If you tend to overarch your back, try wearing a fanny pack with a little extra weight when you walk. When I do this, it reminds me to keep my tail down.

Goals for Week 4

1. After a great workout, close your eyes and notice how good you feel. Give this feeling a name and recall it frequently. This helps anchor in your mind a positive new image of your body.

2. Become more aware of your body language.

3. Notice how your posture affects your mood.

4. Choose the appropriate postures throughout your day to achieve your goals, just as you would choose the appropriate wardrobe to be most effective and comfortable.

WEEK 5: EVALUATING YOUR LEGS

If you notice these signs . . .	Bunions; heel spurs; ankle, knee, or hip pain; iliotibial pain (along the outer thigh); lower-back pain; poor posture
You'll practice these exercises	Shoe Check; Shoe Shopping; Dynamic Posture Analysis—Base (Feet to Hips); Ladder Base into Heel-Toe Roll (or Modified Heel-Toe Roll); DBX Focus
You'll experience these benefits	Increasing comfort; decreasing pain and muscle strain; improving balance; striding with greater ease and strength
You'll acheive this training goal	Improving posture, beginning in your feet

The legs connect the torso with the earth. Without them, we wouldn't have traction on the ground, and we couldn't walk. Often, however, we locate our awareness in our heads and pay little attention to our lower extremities.

Still, we demand a lot from our legs. They hold us up, and over the course of an average lifetime, they carry us some 115,000 miles—more than four times around the circumference of the globe. Fitness walkers, hikers, and runners rack up even more mileage.

We assume that our legs are ready to go anywhere, anytime. We rarely stretch them properly before moving them. Some of us carry extra loads in our work and extra pounds on our bodies. Or we wear poor-fitting shoes.

In fact, we probably think more about our cars than about our legs. We don't service our legs unless they complain, and it surprises us when they do.

Have you ever watched a dance performance—perhaps a ballroom competition or a ballet—and marveled at the strength and precision of the dancers' legs? It took years of dance training before my legs were no longer mere workhorses.

In previous weeks, you learned to lighten the load on your legs and to rebalance the upper-body weight that they must carry. This helps them support you and transport you more efficiently.

Posture begins in your feet. So does powerful walking. When you walk, the most natural biomechanical movement is to roll from heel to toe. Your heel lands slightly to the outside, and you push off between your big toe and second toe. So you're rolling not down the exact centerline of each foot but in a gentle curve from the outside of the heel toward the inside of the ball.

This week, you'll analyze your lower quadrant—your hips and legs, your knees and feet—to discover how to improve your walking biomechanics. This will add miles to your life and joy to your miles.

Exercises for Week 5

Repeat these as instructed.

Shoe Check: Take out your oldest pair of walking shoes and look at the soles. Bare patches on the soles show where you exert pressure. Is the tread worn differently from one shoe to the other? Is it worn unevenly from left to right on each shoe? This information tells a story about how you use your body.

Next, place your shoes on a table and look at them from the front. Is one toebox creased or crumpled differently than the other? Bend down so that you can view your shoes at eye level from the back. Are they different heights? If one shoe appears flatter than the other, it means you're carrying more body weight on that leg.

Connect this information with what you learned from your stride analysis and posture analysis in weeks 3 and 4. Each time you buy new walking shoes, take a moment to check your old shoes.

It's another way to monitor your biomechanics to be sure that you're using proper form.

If you wear orthotics (specially designed shoe inserts), you might want to remove them for short periods—say, 10 to 20 minutes—during your workouts. This gives your musculoskeletal system a chance to realign itself. If you don't have any pain, you can gradually reduce the amount of time you're wearing orthotics, either while walking or while going about your daily activities. This systematic approach to weaning off orthotics was suggested to me by my colleague Harry Hlevac, D.P.M., a biomechanicist and author of *The Foot Book.*

Shoe Shopping: Unless your shoes are less than 2 months old and still fresh, buy new ones this week. The old pair is worn in a postural pattern that will keep you from making the changes you desire. Buying new ones will help you put your best foot forward. Find a shoe salesperson who has been trained to fit shoes and who will help you select just the right size and style for your feet. (For more shoe-buying strategies, see chapter 8.)

Dynamic Posture Analysis—Base (Feet to Hips): Stand in front of a mirror in your normal posture without shoes. How far apart are your feet? Are they parallel, or does one foot or both feet point out at an angle? While a slight outward turn is normal, ideally your feet and knees are symmetrical and directed straight ahead. Bend your knees. Do they come over your toes, or are they more to the inside or outside of your feet?

Stand up straight. Are your knees locked? Is your weight distributed evenly between both legs? Do you fall to the inside (pronation) or outside (supination) of one or both feet? Your goal is to be equally balanced on both legs, with your knees unlocked.

Put on your walking shoes. Look at your feet, knees, and legs in the mirror. Place a small piece of masking tape or a round sticker in the center of each kneecap and in the center of each foot, behind the toes.

Next, place your fingers on the front of your hipbones. Slide your fingers to the inside of these bones. Under your hands are the balls in the ball-and-socket joints of your hips. Point your fingers straight down toward your feet. Ideally, the pieces of tape or the stickers on your feet and knees are in straight vertical lines beneath your fingers.

Drop your arms but continue looking in the mirror. Imagine each leg, from hip to foot, as the upright of a ladder. Ideally, the rungs between your hips, knees, and ankle joints are parallel. Proceed to the next exercise.

Ladder Base into Heel-Toe Roll: Still in front of the mirror, stand with your feet as parallel as is comfortable and one shoe-width apart. This position provides maximum stability and biomechanical support for your joints. Your goal is to line up your hip, knee, and ankle joints from one side of your body to the other, creating a Ladder Base. Retraining your standing posture with your legs one shoe-width apart will help ensure a fluid stride.

From the Ladder Base, begin the Heel-Toe Roll (page 209). Swing your arms easily to add momentum to your roll and to improve your balance. Keep your knees relaxed. Pay attention to rolling down the center of your foot, just as you need to do when you're walking.

Practice rolling your feet with your knees tracking under the balls of your hips. As you roll forward, the tape on your knees should stay in line with the tape on your feet. Watch yourself in the mirror.

If you habitually lock your knees, practice this exercise for 1 to 2 minutes. Repeat it several times a day, especially when you find yourself standing in line. It will help you build dynamic strength in your knee joints so that you won't feel the need to lock them for support.

Modified Heel-Toe Roll: If your feet aren't parallel or your knees aren't tracking over your toes, you have a choice. If you're over age 60 and you're not experiencing any musculoskeletal pain in your body, you can continue walking just as you are. Otherwise, you can correct your walk by practicing the Modified Heel-Toe Roll. This exercise can be especially helpful if you've been experiencing musculoskeletal pain in your spine or lower quadrant.

As you roll from heel to toe, slowly turn your toes inward, then outward, then inward again. Make sure that your knees are tracking over your toes and your feet are parallel. Practice this for a minute at a time, three to five times during your walking workouts.

Gradually add more of these 1-minute intervals to your walks, provided you're not experiencing any pain. It's important not to force your legs into this new position too quickly. You could develop joint pain unnecessarily. Based on your age and flexibility level, your musculoskeletal system may need many months to re-align properly. Give it the time it needs.

DBX Focus: Concentrate on your foot position whenever you're practicing the exercises in chapter 38.

Kinesthetic Images for Week 5

Practice these frequently each day this week to experience your body in new ways.

Ladder Base: Bring this image of your hips, knees, and ankles being in alignment into your body as you stand and walk. Stand tall from your hips upward. Extend your energy from your hips downward through your legs and into the earth.

Power Legs: Continue to be aware of the power in the legs of dancers and athletes. Bring the perception of strength into your legs, especially when you're pushing off during your walks.

Rocking Horse: While walking, picture the bottoms of your feet as being curved like the base of a rocking horse. Roll down the center of each foot from heel to toes, as described earlier.

Goals for Week 5

1. Become aware of how you use your legs while walking, standing, and sitting.

2. Slowly bring your legs into a stronger, more biomechanically efficient posture.

3. Listen carefully to your body.

4. Make changes at a speed that achieves your goals without creating stress.

WEEK 6: HARNESSING PELVIC POWER

If you notice these signs . . .	Can't elevate your heart rate for an aerobic workout; slow pace when walking
You'll practice these exercises	Force Field/Kick Sand; Power Surge/Pelvic Push-Off; DBX Focus
You'll experience these benefits	Increasing your walking speed; building more thrust for speed bursts; feeling more grounded; improving balance; strengthening your legs; contouring your buttocks
You'll acheive this training goal	Building pelvic power

If legs are the workhorses of the body, then the pelvis is the engine that gives them power. We can only build strong legs and a strong walk by connecting with our core.

While in Japan one summer, I trained in the traditional Japanese arts of tea ceremony, calligraphy, Noh (masked dancing), *budo* (swordplay), and flower arranging. Each class began by focusing attention in the center of the body. The center, often referred to as the *hara*, is the point of consciousness from which all movement flows. It is also the center of balance. Whether I held a sword, a fan, or a calligraphy brush, connecting with my center empowered all of my actions.

Over the past 5 weeks, you've become more aware of your postural habits in your daily activities, improved your biomechanics, and sharpened your walking technique. You've learned how to avoid potential injuries and to fall in step with Mother Nature's design. Your efforts so far have been rewarded with increasing elegance, efficiency, and ease when you move.

You're now ready to begin building power and speed in your walk. In week 6, you'll learn to direct your core strength through your legs into the ground beneath and behind you. By focusing your energy, you'll build thrust, like a rocket.

Exercises for Week 6

Repeat these frequently each day this week to build new muscle memory.

Force Field/Kick Sand: Picture a circle beneath your body, with two-thirds of the area being directly under and behind your body. This circle represents the force field where you'll have the greatest contact with the ground and therefore the greatest thrust.

To increase your push-off power, practice standing tall on one leg. With the other leg, scrape the ground as if to kick sand beneath and behind you, like a dog digging a hole. Use your whole leg from the hip, not just your knee. Feel the action up into your buttock. Repeat six times on each side.

Apply this push-off power when walking. Walk tall. Keep yourself directly over your force field for maximum traction and speed.

Power Surge/Pelvic Push-Off: You'll need a partner for this exercise. Have the person place a long, wide band low across your pelvis, at your hipbones. As she holds the ends behind you, walk naturally for 30 seconds. Then she adds resistance by pulling on the band.

Keep your upper body relaxed. Don't muscle up in your arms and chest or tighten your jaw. Sink into your legs and push off from behind, as if kicking sand. Continue for another 30 to 45 seconds.

At this point, your partner should let go of one end of the band. When she does, don't slow down. Surge forward with your newly discovered push-off power. Use your ankles fully as you roll your feet forward. Walk dynamically for 30 seconds. Then repeat the exercise.

DBX Focus: Concentrate on the hip and leg stretches (DBX #6 through #13) in chapter 38.

Kinesthetic Images for Week 6

Practice these frequently each day this week to experience your body in new ways, especially while you are walking.

Power Surge: Picture a racehorse at the starting gate. When the bell rings, the horse surges forth. Notice how its hooves throw dirt to the rear as it speeds along.

Power Legs: Continue to observe the legs of dancers, athletes, and running animals. Feel their agile power in your legs. Watch martial artists like Jackie Chan and Michelle Yeoh. They maintain their balance in their centers at all times. When they deliver a blow, energy shoots outward at lightning speed from their cores through their extremities. Their legs are powerful in action, stable at rest, like tamed tigers. Cultivate greater awareness of your own leg power.

Goals for Week 6

1. Discover how your legs can more fully support you in all positions.

2. Build leg strength as you get in and out of a chair, bed, or bathtub.

3. Use your whole body when walking. Connect the power from your pelvis to your legs.

4. Thrust the ground away from you as you walk.

5. Roll your feet forward, using a full range of motion in your ankles.

THE DYNAMIC BODY EXERCISES

In the previous chapters, you learned the basic movement patterns of Dynamic Walking. You analyzed your daily activities and observed your own habits to learn how you've bee'n growing your body. You began using gravity and other dynamic forces more consciously, as tools to rebuild your body. Now you're going to learn to apply those same forces to a more complex activity: stretching.

The 14 stretches in this chapter—I call them the Dynamic Body Exercises—have actually been a lifetime in the making. Long before I imagined that movement therapy would become my life's work, I was captivated by the grace and joy of a body in motion.

As a child, I began dancing, and I have continued ever since. I remember performing in a recital at age 5, enrolling in ballet classes shortly thereafter, winning an *American Bandstand* jitterbug contest at age 10, and attending classes in social dance as a teenager. In my lifetime, I've studied a variety of ethnic dance forms, from African to Noh, the Japanese art of masked dancing. My husband and I have even developed our own Latin fusion dance style.

For more than 25 years, I have been a student of Anna Halprin, an award-winning dancer and choreographer. When I first began my training, Halprin encouraged me to work with children, just as she had. For 7 years, I taught movement education in a Montessori school that my son was attending. I engaged my students in a variety of activities, including yoga and mime, soccer and swordplay, puppetry and masked dancing.

Maria Montessori, an Italian physician and educator, established the Montessori school system on a foundation of fun plus fundamentals. Her philosophy inspired my curriculum. For example, I taught my students roller-skating, an activity that they loved (fun) and that helped them improve their posture (fundamentals). It required that they use both legs equally, glide balanced on either leg, move forward and backward, relax their upper bodies, and build lower-leg strength. My students learned to apply their roller-skating skills to other activities; they played broom hockey and choreographed dance routines on skates.

When I moved on to teaching college students and eventually to teaching adults, my experiences gave me the opportunity to watch for the universal movement patterns common to all age groups. By studying disciplines as diverse as belly dance and yoga, tai chi and cha cha, I was able to identify a common alphabet of movements from which each person builds his body language and each culture its unique dance expression.

For example, my research taught me that the human spine is capable of five primary movements: bending forward (forward flexion), bending backward (hyperextension), bending to either side (lateral flexion), twisting to either side (rotation), and being straight (extension). The spine is healthiest when stretched in each of these positions equally and regularly, on a daily basis. All dance forms, all sports, every expression of body language derives from these five spinal positions. They're some of the most basic links among humans of all ages and ethnic backgrounds.

GETTING BACK TO BASICS

Based on what I've learned over the years, I'm convinced that this common alphabet of movements is essential to a healthy body and a peaceful soul. It is what led me to create the Dynamic Body Exercises, or DBX.

Learning the DBX is like learning your ABCs. The exercises provide the foundation not only for walking but also for more complex activities such as swinging a golf club or planting a garden. In the first few weeks of practicing the DBX, you'll learn to stretch your spine evenly in all directions; to elongate your body to feel lighter and more lifted; to breathe more fully; to stretch your five sets of leg muscles; to maximize the range of movement in your spine, shoulders, and hips; and to improve your postural alignment.

Within a couple of months, as you rebuild your posture, you'll find a "home base"—a quiet, calm center where your skeleton supports you more easily, a place of peace in gravity. You may also notice a decline in the habitual tension patterns that color your thoughts and feelings.

Many people have asked me how the DBX differ from yoga. Both exercise systems build conscious (somatic) awareness and use breathing patterns to dissolve stress, increase vitality, and generate tranquillity. Personally, I prefer the DBX because they're more practical and more connected to my everyday life than yoga. I demand a lot from my stretching—a quick, commonsense routine that I can apply to my daily activities.

Through the DBX, I've learned how to avoid injuries and how to improve my strength more rapidly when weight training. The exercises have also helped me to heal my sciatic pain, improve my sports performance, and work more easily at my computer. So if anything, the DBX is a practical, everyday yoga—a mind-body technique that teaches me how to move through life with greater energy, efficiency, elegance, and ease.

The 14 stretches in the DBX are designed to complement Dynamic Walking. When used together, the two maintain the musculoskeletal system in a balanced state. The stretches change alignment; Dynamic Walking sets the new alignment.

Over time, repeating this pattern—change, set, change, set, change, set—coaxes the body into a more dynamic posture. You're poised for movement and poised at rest.

MAKING THE MOST OF YOUR WORKOUTS

When you perform the Dynamic Body Exercises, always think *FIT*—as in *F*requency, *I*ntensity, and *T*ime. These three elements help determine the effectiveness of your workout and, ultimately, of the DBX.

The guidelines that follow will help you determine how often, how hard, and how long to exercise. Just remember to stay conservative, starting slowly and easily and working up gradually. Injury always sets you back.

Frequency: For the best results, practice the DBX at least once per day for the first several months, and at least three to five times per week thereafter. You may also use the exercises as follows:

- After any stressful or unbalanced activity
- Every hour when you're seated for long periods of time
- After 5 to 10 minutes of exercise and again at the end of the workout

If it's cold or windy outside, you may want to do the DBX indoors before you begin your workout. Then repeat them once you get home.

Intensity: When you begin doing the DBX, you may notice soreness in some new places. This is an indicator that you're making the necessary structural changes for your body to realign itself. Over time, the discomfort will go away.

Keep in mind that there is a difference between soreness and pain. Exercise should never be painful in any part of your body. If any movement hurts, immediately stop what you're doing and consult your doctor.

Time: Hold each DBX stretch for two or three breath cycles (one inhale and one exhale per cycle), or 20 to 30 seconds. Initially, the entire DBX sequence will take 12 to 15 minutes to complete. But once you become accustomed to the exercises, you'll be able to do them in 8 to 10 minutes.

Before I explain how to perform the individual DBX stretches, I want to spend some time on the ins and outs of breathing. The rhythm of your breathing should coordinate with the rhythm of the activity you're performing—in this case, the DBX. Begin and end each exercise with an awareness of your breath. Exhale fully when you're about to enter the effort phase of the movement and whenever you compress your torso. Also exhale when you want to release deeper into a stretch.

When you're inhaling, allow your torso to expand and stretch in all directions, like a balloon filling with air. Be sure to keep your shoulders down and relaxed. Use each inhalation to refocus on your form. And always inhale when returning to an upright position (spinal extension).

DBX #1: THE LONG SHIRT PULL

Everybody loves this exercise because it feels so good. And the more you do it, the faster you'll build a lighter, lifted, and younger-looking body. Adapted from ballet, the Long Shirt Pull improves postural alignment and stretches your body from head to toe. It incorporates two of the five basic spinal positions: forward flexion and extension.

THE HEEL-TOE ROLL. This movement prepares your body for the rest of the exercise. Begin by standing with your feet together. Envision your feet separated by the width of one shoe. Move your feet apart that distance, keeping them as parallel as is comfortable (A).

Roll from heel to toe, rocking back and forth down the center of your feet (B, C). Imagine that your feet are curved like the base of a rocking horse. Equalize pressure on the inside and outside edges of both feet. Widen your toes as you roll onto the forefoot. Try to maintain your feet in a parallel position, but don't force them. Keep your knees gently flexed or soft. Watch in a mirror or look down to make sure that your knees are tracking over your toes. Allow your arms and shoulders to swing effortlessly.

Stop rocking and equalize the pressure on both feet (D). Move on to the Roll-Down.

(continued)

THE ROLL-DOWN. Tuck your chin to your chest (E). Exhale and slowly roll down toward the ground (F). Keep your knees relaxed and aligned over your middle toes. If you have lower-back problems, rest your forearms on your thighs for support and stretch from there. Inhale, exhale, and relax while your arms and head dangle loosely (G). Inhale and exhale again, releasing all tension. Proceed to the Roll-Up.

THE ROLL-UP. From the Roll-Down, very gently cross your arms at the wrists (H). Imagine that you're pulling a shirt up and off your body. Inhale as you roll up, with your arms relaxed, your elbows leading, your hands gliding along the front of your body (I). Lift the imaginary shirt up over your head, stretching upward (J). Keep your head level. Don't arch your back. Move on to the Returning to Extension.

RETURNING TO EXTENSION. Grow taller through your spine as you release your arms and shoulders. Keep your pinkies in your peripheral vision (K). As you continue moving your arms down to your sides, feel your shoulders drop into a settled place, like a shirt hanging effortlessly on a hanger (L). Look around. Notice if you feel taller. Repeat twice more.

DBX #2: HYPEREXTENSION

This backward-bending stretch is one of the five spinal positions. You may already be using this position to wash your hair in the shower. Do the stretch gently, especially if you have lower-back pain. Use your breathing to relax into it.

Raise your arms upward, lifting your torso (A). Arch your back, looking up and behind (B). Do not drop your head backward onto your shoulders. Stay lifted out of your lower back and your hips. Hold for two or three breath cycles. Return to a standing-tall position, then bring your arms and shoulders down. Let them hang relaxed at your sides (C). Move on to the Shoulder Rolls.

DBX #3: SHOULDER ROLLS

Have you noticed that the first six letters of *shoulder* spell the word *should*? Perhaps that's because when we "should" ourselves (as in "I should have done that"), our shoulders seem to rise up around our ears.

Many of us carry tension in the shoulder yoke, the area around and between the shoulders. We tend to round our shoulders as we go about our daily business—whether we're sitting at a computer, washing dishes, or driving a car. Doing this exercise can help you relax your shoulder yoke, release tension, and improve posture.

If you tend to carry your head forward, Shoulder Rolls are critical. Your head and neck cannot return to proper alignment until your shoulders are back and down. Although this exercise does not stretch the spine, it's included here because shoulder tension affects posture and spinal health.

When you start doing Shoulder Rolls, be gentle until you find your range. Your goal is to dissolve shoulder tension and allow your shoulders to rest relaxed on your rib cage, like a shirt on a hanger.

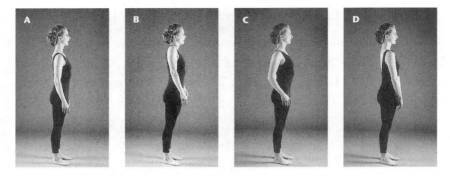

Stand tall, with your arms hanging at your sides (A). Roll your shoulders up (B), back (C), down (D), and around. Synchronize your breathing with your movement, exhaling and inhaling fully for two or three breath cycles. Wiggle your jaw to create a yawn, which can relax your jaw, neck, and shoulders. Move on to the Lateral Stretches.

DBX #4: LATERAL STRETCHES

Many of us have a stronger arm and a dominant side to our bodies. Stretching the muscles on either side of your torso releases tension in your spine and balances your body, left to right. If you tend to carry one shoulder higher than the other, you may find that Lateral Stretches, together with Shoulder Rolls, help to level them out.

Reach overhead (A). If it's comfortable, entwine your fingers. Stretch toward the right, exhaling and lengthening both sides of your torso (B). Stay evenly balanced on both feet, pressing your left foot deep into the ground. Be careful not to twist, arch backward, or compress your spine. (Practice against a wall to find the correct position.) Extend out through your arms and the top of your head. Breathe deeply as you release into the stretch. Find those muscles deep in your abdomen that pull you back into an upright position. Be aware of restacking the building blocks of your body. Repeat, stretching to the left side (C). Repeat to both sides once or twice more. Return to a standing-tall position to begin the Spinal Rotation.

DBX #5: SPINAL ROTATION

Life doesn't always take you in a straight line. Sometimes you must navigate around corners and obstacles. This exercise makes daily activities that require you to twist your torso easier. It also makes your stride more graceful. When you walk tall, the swinging of your arms and legs naturally creates a gentle spinal rotation that massages your spine, shoulders, and hips.

When doing this exercise, notice if it's easier to rotate in one direction than the other. Balance your efforts to improve your musculoskeletal health.

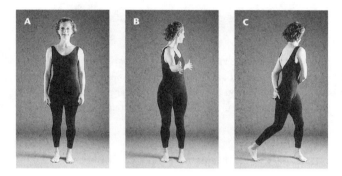

Stand tall, with your feet parallel and your knees slightly bent (A). Allow your wrists and arms to float upward, to shoulder height. Raise your shoulders as you inhale, then drop them as you exhale, keeping your arms outstretched to your sides. Repeat.

Pivot your head from one side to the other, looking from one hand to the other. Then gently rotate your upper body, following each hand, in turn, as it moves behind you (B). Exhale as you turn, inhale as you return to center. Allow your whole upper body to enjoy the movement. Look as far behind you as possible on one side, then the other.

Widen your stance and rise up on one toe, then the other, as you rotate around (C). Relax your shoulders and let your arms drop against your sides. When you hear your arms make contact, you'll know that you have let go of the tension in your shoulders. Allowing your arms to swing free is one goal of this exercise. After 20 to 30 seconds, move directly into the Hip Stretch.

DBX #6: HIP STRETCH

Adapted from Latin dance, this exercise can help you develop independent hip action (meaning each hip moves separately from the other) and keep your pelvis young. The hip motion is vital to a natural, fluid stride. It also improves balance and prevents falls on stairs.

The Hip Stretch feels great on your lower back. If you tend to arch your back, repeat the exercise frequently during the day, especially after standing or sitting.

This stretch can be difficult for men, since their hips are often narrower and tighter than women's. If it's hard for you, prepare for it by standing with your feet together and your hands on your hips. Lift, then lower one hip at a time. You can lift your heels in turn, if necessary. Slowly widen your stance, maintaining your hip motion until you are in a slightly squatted position.

Bend at your hips and knees to drop into a squat. Place your hands on your thighs, with your fingers pointed inward (A). Keep your back straight and your shoulders down and relaxed. Lift and lower each hip by imagining that you are vigorously scratching your backside on a tree (B, C). Exhale and inhale fully in rhythm to your movements. Proceed directly into the Hamstring Stretch.

DBX #7: HAMSTRING STRETCH

This is the first of five stretches that target the leg muscles. The hamstrings are located on the back of each thigh. These muscles can be tight if you sit a lot, if your lower back is swayed, or if you stand with your knees locked or your feet wide apart. In my experience, men tend to have tighter hamstrings than women.

Turn to your right. Fold your arms and bend over to place them on your right thigh, just above your knee (A). As you exhale and relax, allow your upper-body weight to slowly straighten your right knee (B). Your right foot is pointed forward, while your left foot is at a 45-degree angle. Your left knee, whether it's bent or straight, is aligned over your left toes.

Continue relaxing into this position, without pushing, through three breath cycles. As your right knee straightens, you can either drop your arms (C) or keep one hand on your shoelaces. Roll up enough to pivot to your left side to stretch your left hamstring. Be sure to keep your neck relaxed, your head dropped, and your eyes looking back behind your legs.

Repeat the exercise to your left side. Then move directly into the Calf Stretch.

DBX #8: CALF STRETCH

Your calf muscles are located in the back of your lower legs. They're connected to the bottom of your feet by the Achilles tendons. Keeping your calf muscles stretched can help you avoid plantar fasciitis, a troublesome foot condition that can cause severe heel and sole pain.

From the Hamstring Stretch, roll up, supporting yourself with your left hand on your left knee if necessary. In this position, turn your right heel out so that your right foot is pointing forward, parallel to your left foot. Keep your head, neck, torso, and right leg in one long line, as if you were a plank leaning against a wall. Do not arch your back or stand upright from your waist. This puts too much pressure on your lower back. Keep your lower left leg perpendicular to the ground and your right heel pressed down. Hold this position for three breath cycles, or 20 to 30 seconds. Move on to the Soleus Stretch before repeating this stretch facing to the right.

DBX #9: SOLEUS STRETCH

Underneath the calf muscle lies the soleus muscle. It, too, can contribute to plantar fasciitis if it isn't stretched regularly and thoroughly. It tends to tighten up in women who wear high heels.

To stretch the right soleus muscle, push off on your left foot and step backward so that it's slightly in front of your right foot. Tuck your buttocks and lower yourself as if to sit, as shown. Any pressure should be behind your knees, not in your kneecaps or quadriceps (the muscles on the fronts of your thighs). Keep both knees flexed. You'll feel the broad band of your right Achilles tendon flatten out. Keep your upper body lifted, your lower back lengthened. Exhale and inhale deeply three times.

Pivot to your right. Step forward with your right foot to stretch your left calf muscle (follow the instructions for the Calf Stretch). Then push off on your right foot and move it backward so that it's slightly in front of your left foot. Repeat the Soleus Stretch, this time working your left soleus muscle. Move on to the Shin Stretch.

DBX #10: SHIN STRETCH

The shin muscles run along the outside of the shinbone, in the front of the lower leg. They are small muscles that build strength slowly when you walk (running doesn't develop them at all). They can burn when you walk briskly or when you perform the Heel-Toe Roll if you aren't used to the exercise.

This stretch works *only* when done correctly. So pay attention to proper form. This is one of the most important stretches you can do after a walking workout.

Stand tall, with your feet one shoe-width apart. Do a Heel-Toe Roll (see page 209) until you're in a balanced position, then stop.

Cross your left foot over your right, drawing your left toes back along the outside of your right foot. Turn your left foot under so that your toes are pointing behind you, as shown. Bend your knees so that your right knee presses into your left calf. Breathe deeply, holding this position for three breath cycles, or 20 to 30 seconds. You may feel the stretch in your left shin, ankle, toes, or arch—they're all connected. Repeat on the other side.

DBX #11: QUADRICEPS STRETCH

The quadriceps muscles, located at the fronts of your thighs, can get tight from excessive sitting and poor walking technique. As the longest muscles in your body, they work with your hamstrings to help you maintain balance.

If you have poor balance, use a tree or a low fence for support when you do this stretch. You can also improve your balance by keeping your feet from falling to the inside (pronation) or the outside (supination) while walking. Wearing shoes with good support can help.

Stand on your right leg and swing your left leg like a pendulum (A, B). Drive the movement from your hip, not from your knee. Notice how you can swing your leg without scuffing the ground. That's because you're standing tall on your right leg.

Reach back and grab your left foot, or your pants leg, behind you. Pull it toward your left buttock (C). Keep your knees relaxed and your pelvis tucked under. Breathe deeply for 20 to 30 seconds. Move immediately into the Ankle Stretch. You'll stretch your right quadriceps a bit later.

Note: If you have knee problems, you can work your quadriceps in another way. Position yourself next to a sturdy, stable chair, with your right hand on the chair back for support. Standing on your right leg, begin swinging your left leg. Extend it far enough behind you that when you plant your left toes and bend your right leg, you feel a stretch in your left quadriceps muscle. Continue for 20 to 30 seconds.

DBX #12: ANKLE STRETCH

By rolling your foot from heel to toe with each step, you keep your ankles limber and your lower legs in good condition. If you stop rolling and start walking flat-footed, you may look and feel years older.

From the Quadriceps Stretch, release your left leg and let it swing forward. Catch and tuck your knee to your chest (A). Lengthen your lower back and keep your torso erect. Drop your arm while keeping your left leg in place. Slowly circle your ankle in all directions (B). Move immediately to the Psoas Stretch.

DBX #13: PSOAS STRETCH

The psoas muscle is one of the most important postural muscles and one of the longest in your body. It extends from the top of the inside of your thigh all the way up to your diaphragm, which separates your abdomen from your chest.

This stretch lengthens the muscle and trains it to hold your pelvis in a neutral position. This builds core strength and lower back support.

From the Ankle Stretch, lower your left leg to the ground (A). Continue to grow taller through your spine. Press your belly button toward your backbone, as if you were pressing your lower back against a wall (B).

Now go back and repeat the Quadriceps Stretch, Ankle Stretch, and Psoas Stretch for your right leg.

DBX #14: THE LONG SHIRT PULL

Finish the DBX series with three Long Shirt Pulls (see pages 209–10) to balance the building blocks of your body. Notice how you feel compared with when you did your first Long Shirt Pull.

CHAPTER **39**

YOUR DYNAMIC WALKING ROUTINE

Walking is a deeply nurturing activity. Its simplicity allows it to fulfill many purposes. It can provide time alone, time with a buddy, time to commune with nature, time to solve problems, time to explore new terrain, time to exercise, time to be with your kids, time to be with your dog, time to get errands done, time to travel to your next destination.

No matter why you're walking, you'll enjoy it more once you learn to do it dynamically. You'll be more deeply in tune with your body, so you'll avoid injury and get maximum benefit from every workout.

In this chapter, you'll build on what you've already learned about Dynamic Walking, applying all the fundamentals of good form to your daily walks. You'll learn awareness exercises that not only help you monitor your progress but also keep you safe during your workouts. You'll warm up and cool down safely by progressing through a variety of gears, just like an engine. And by using an efficient arm

swing and other new techniques, you'll ultimately transform your walk into a fluid glide.

For each gear, I've included an approximate time frame so you'll have some idea of how long you'll need to perform the various exercises and techniques. Eventually, you'll discover your optimum time in each gear. For some walks, you may opt to stay in first gear. For others, you may hold steady in second or fourth, depending on how fast you want to travel and how many calories you want to burn.

FIRST GEAR: WARMING UP

Begin walking at a slow pace, with your arms long and swinging freely at your sides. This gives your shoulders an opportunity to unburden their load and relax. Stay lifted out of your hips to allow your legs to swing like pendulums.

Your arms will start swinging naturally, in cadence with each step. Don't force them to move. Don't carry anything in your hands. Wear a fanny pack to hold your keys, I.D., water, and the like.

While in first gear, you'll do a series of scans: the Body Scan, the Environment Scan, and the Technique Scan. You can remember them with this simple mnemonic: Together, they'll make you feel *bet*ter (as in *B*ody, *E*nvironment, and *T*echnique).

The Body Scan

This exercise gets you out of your head and into your body—fast.

Part A: Scan each part of your body, from your feet to head. Pay attention to what you're feeling. If you notice any areas of discomfort or pain, rate each area on a scale from 1 to 10, with 1 being the most comfortable and 10 being the least. Remember this number for comparison at the end of your walk.

When you fail to acknowledge your aches and pains, you may subconsciously compensate for them, which can get you into trouble. But by paying attention to any discomfort, you can consciously experiment with the exercises you are learning to make yourself feel better.

Part B: Evaluate your vitality level, rating it on a scale from 1 (least vitalized) to 10 (most invigorated). Remember this number for comparison at the end of your walk. Depending on your goals, the outside temperature, and other factors, walking can either invigorate you or drain you. Noting how you feel, either mentally or in a logbook, can help you sort out cause and effect.

The Environment Scan

This exercise takes you outside yourself and connects you with the sights, sounds, and smells of nature.

Part A (the Eye Scan): Using only your eyes, continuously scan the path in front of you from far to near, the way you might study the road while driving. Make scanning a habit. Memorize the path. This allows you to spot obstacles and oncoming traffic well before you meet up with them. You'll feel safer because you're less likely to trip and fall. Your body will relax, your head will remain lifted and level, and you'll walk tall. Looking down strains your neck, shoulder, and back muscles and restricts breathing.

Part B: Once you've memorized the path, you are free to scan the rest of your surroundings—to enjoy the beauty of nature, to soak up the vitality of the air, and to appreciate your being alive and the gift of walking the earth. Repeat the Eye Scan frequently. It's an important practice, especially when you're increasing your speed, hiking on uneven terrain, or walking on a crowded street.

The Technique Scan

This exercise brings you back to your body and sets your intention for your training walk.

Part A: Do several Short Shirt Pulls (page 187) as you walk. Bring the lift into your torso. Stretch tall out of your hips. Become aware of the weight of your arms and legs. Let them swing like pendulums from your shoulders and hips. Use their momentum to power your walk. Use your ankles through their full range of motion. Imagine the bottom of each foot curved like a rocking horse. Roll along the length of your foot, from heel to toe. As you roll onto your forefoot, be sure to relax and spread your toes. Clenching them could cause bunions.

Balance your right and left sides, distributing your weight equally between your right and left legs. If you have new shoes, they should help stop you from collapsing your feet toward the insteps (pronating) or to the outside (supinating). Balance your arm swing, too. A dominant arm swing or leg push is a repetitive stress that could eventually twist your spine.

Practicing the Heel-Toe Roll (page 209) has made you more aware of the position of your knees over your toes. By making sure your knees track correctly, you diminish wear and tear on these joints, so they're good for more mileage over the course of a lifetime.

Part B: If you followed the 6-week program outlined in chapter 37, you've already done several analyses of your posture and stride. Mentally review what you discovered about your body. For example, you may have realized that your upper body was positioned behind your lower body. If so, you

practiced the Rib Cage Slide (pages 198–99). Do that now as you walk. Notice your results.

Every week, choose only one or two corrections on which to focus while you walk. Write your results in a walking log. By concentrating on only one or two things per week, you'll feel less overwhelmed and better able to track the changes that are occurring throughout your body.

DBX STRETCH BREAK

If you're like most people, your body needs 8 to 10 minutes to warm up. So once you've warmed up in first gear, stop and stretch using the Dynamic Body Exercises in chapter 38. Stretching now will help dissolve the habitual tension patterns that you've brought with you on the trail. It will also bring your body back into balance. You'll probably notice a dramatic increase in the speed, ease, and efficiency of your walk. (If it's cold or windy outside, stretch gently at home before beginning your workout.)

After stretching, resume walking in first gear. Quickly repeat the three scans to observe any changes and to refocus your intentions.

SECOND GEAR: PICKING UP THE PACE

In first gear, your arms were swinging at your sides. In second gear, they'll be bent at the elbows and pumping. But if you move them into position before your legs are fully warmed up, two things could happen: You may never release your shoulder tension, and you may not get maximum effort from your legs. It's your legs' job, not your arms', to power your walk.

In second gear, you want to increase the power of your push-off. First, you need to find your optimum stride length. To do this, practice walking with a too long stride (overstriding) for 30 seconds. Notice how you bounce and how that feels in your joints and lower back. Now switch to tiny steps for 30 seconds. Feel the tension in your hips and notice the lack of a pendulum swing in your legs.

Next, lengthen your stride slightly, still keeping your feet in the Force Field (page 204) beneath and behind you. Take shorter, quicker steps with a rapid turnover. Practice the Kick Sand exercise (page 204). Remember the feeling of the Pelvic Push-Off (page 204) and use that to power your walk.

Once you've maxed out the power of your legs, your arms will naturally bend at the elbows to create a shorter, more efficient pendulum. The arm stroke itself is very clean and precise. Your arms swing naturally from your shoulders, with each one bent at about a 90-degree angle and moving in a fist-to-hip, elbow-to-hip pattern. Don't cross your arms over the center line of your body or pump them up and down to burn extra calories. This creates shoulder tension and is counterproductive.

To propel yourself forward, put power into the backward phase of the arm stroke. Imagine flames shooting from each elbow equally. Relax and recover on the forward phase of the swing.

Stay in second gear for 2 to 5 minutes before moving on to third.

THIRD GEAR: PRIMING YOUR HIPS

You'll spend only 20 to 30 seconds of your walk in third gear. It warms up your hips in preparation for fourth gear, when you really pick up your pace.

Begin with a walking Short Shirt Pull (page 187) to increase the lift out of your hips. Then slow your pace to keep from tripping. Visualize a line down the center of the path you're on. Cross each foot *over* the line to make your hips swivel. (This is a training technique used by racewalkers.) You can clasp your fingers together at waist height to help maintain your coordination.

FOURTH GEAR: HITTING TOP SPEED

As you move into fourth gear, stop crossing your feet over that imaginary center line, but keep the image of the line in your mind. The inside edge of each foot will just touch the center line.

As you approach your top speed, the momentum of your legs will naturally swivel your hips. People who carry more weight around their hips swivel more easily than those who are thin. Nevertheless, if you stay lifted out of your hips, your legs and feet will naturally fall into a more proper alignment along that center line. In fact, one of my clients, who had difficulty flexing her ankle and lifting her toes because of an injury, was able to avoid chronically stubbing her toes by swiveling her hips, which brought her foot into proper position.

While you're in fourth gear, quickly repeat the Body Scan, Environment Scan, and Technique Scan. Occasionally take short, quick steps to increase your steps per minute and to become more aerobic. Resist taking longer strides. A bouncy walk could cause heel and knee pain.

If your shins start burning, stop to do the Shin Stretch (pages 215–16). Then proceed at a slightly slower pace and build slowly in intervals. Interval training involves alternating periods of brisk walking with periods of recovery. In this case, walk fast for 1 to 2 minutes, then slow down for 1 to 2 minutes. Repeat this pattern three to five times. By gradually increasing the exertion phase and decreasing the recovery phase, you can safely build power and speed. Slow down if you begin to lose form.

Within a few months, you'll be able to stay in fourth gear for at least 20 minutes, all the while maintaining speed and proper form. Once you have mastered the Dynamic Walking technique (or your weight has stabilized if weight loss is your goal), you may

prefer to do most of your maintenance walking in second gear.

WINDING DOWN FROM YOUR WALK

Once you've finished your walk, downshift into first gear and cool down for 5 minutes. Do a final Body Scan, paying special attention to any areas of your body that were painful or tense when you first started out. Notice any change in how you feel. Reassess your vitality level, too.

Reserve the last segment of your workout to repeat the DBX exercises. Eventually, you'll be able to do the entire series in just 8 to 10 minutes, as each muscle group learns to relax and stretch quickly. If you forgot to do your final scans while you were cooling down, now is a good time to fit them in.

TUNING IN TO YOUR INNER COACH

Now that I've showed you the principles and techniques of Dynamic Walking, I want you to continue your training with another coach, the most important coach you'll ever have. She's the one living inside you. She's available to you 24 hours a day at no charge, and she knows your habits intimately. Her wisdom can help you persevere in any somatic fitness program (meaning, a program that cultivates inner awareness, as this one does). Ask for her advice whenever you need it.

Especially when you're starting

your training, your ego may step in and want to do things another way. It can fill your head with thoughts like "I don't really need to work out today" or "It's not really hot—I can leave my water bottle at home" or "I've got to fit into those jeans, so I'll push myself just a little harder." Eventually, your inner coach will be empowered enough to challenge these thoughts and make decisions that are in the interest of your whole body. Give her time to find her voice. A patient, positive, nonjudgmental attitude works best when building skills to last a lifetime.

CHANGING PAIN TO PLEASURE

Just as your inner coach can help you learn and hone your Dynamic Walking technique, she can also teach you to listen to your body "speaking" to you through sensations of pain and pleasure. These are normal, healthy messages—a sort of biofeedback.

One of the goals of Dynamic Walking is to decrease pain and increase pleasure for a lifetime through correct alignment and biomechanics. As you progress, don't be alarmed if you experience discomfort in new places. As your musculoskeletal system rebalances, as your body transforms, pains may shift around.

Experiment with the exercises I've given you and observe the results. Reread the instructions often to make sure that you're performing the movements properly. Over time, your efforts will be rewarded with greater pleasure—and a happier body.

Something else will happen that's just as magical: As you continue walking dynamically, your stride will transform into a glide—elegant, efficient, and easy. When the glide takes over, you feel as though you can go on forever. Your body may feel more fluid and integrated, too. You'll move in a smooth, relaxed manner at any speed, in any situation, even when entering a room full of people. You'll feel more confident, more in control. And that will have a positive impact on all areas of your life.

Happy trails. Walk with beauty.

—*Dr. Suki Munsell*

To learn more about Dynamic Walking, or to request information about other fitness programs and training, contact the Dynamic Health and Fitness Institute by calling (888) 852-6717. Or visit the institute's Web site at www.dynamicwalking.com.

PART
9

EVERYTHING ELSE YOU NEED TO KNOW

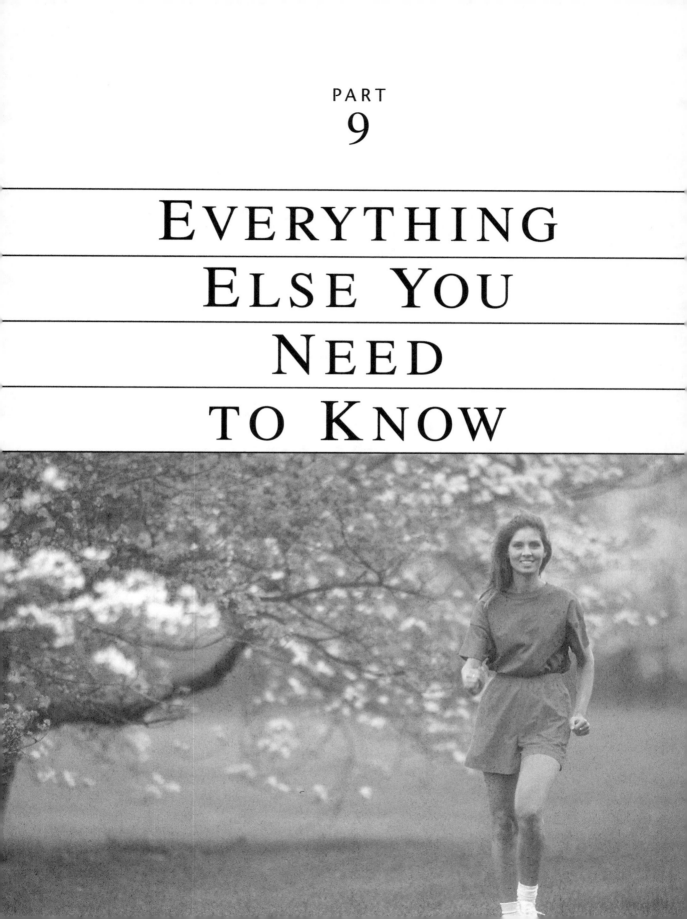

CHAPTER **40**

COMMON QUESTIONS ABOUT WALKING

Over the years, I've received thousands of letters from people wanting to know more about specific walking-related issues. Now the queries arrive via the Internet as well. With the click of a mouse, folks from all around the world can ask me anything on the subject of walking.

Many questions come up over and over again. They're the ones featured in this chapter. As you read through them, perhaps you'll find information that you can apply to a situation or problem that you're experiencing.

BACK TO BASICS

Q: *What's the best time of day to walk?*

A: It varies from one person to the next. To me, any time of day is perfect!

In the summer, I love to walk in the mornings, when it's nice and cool and the sun is up early. In the winter, I usu-ally try to walk on my lunch hour, since that's the warmest part of the day. The fresh air revitalizes me for the afternoon, plus I get a healthy dose of vitamin D from the sun's rays.

The question is, when are you most willing and able to walk? That's the best time for you.

Q: *Should I eat before I walk?*

A: Again, it varies from one person to the next. I almost always eat something before I leave on my morning walk. I just feel better. But if I'm planning to go at a brisk pace or to do some interval training, I'll keep my breakfast small and simple—maybe a piece of fruit and a glass of juice, or some low-fat or nonfat yogurt. The human body doesn't particularly like digesting food and exercising hard at the same time.

That said, a leisurely stroll after a large meal may enhance digestion and burn a few extra calories. But walking before a meal works just as well, provided you don't have any problems with your blood sugar.

And if that meal happens to be breakfast, be sure to drink a nice, tall glass of water before you head out. Your body may be somewhat dehydrated after a night's sleep.

Q: *What's the simplest way to determine how fast I'm walking?*

A: The easiest way to gauge your speed without wearing a pedometer—or getting in your car and measuring mileage, which can be pretty difficult unless you walk along a street—is to count your number of steps per minute. The experts use this number to calculate pace, based on an average stride length of 2½ feet. (Stride length is the distance from the heel of one foot to the heel of the other foot when you're taking a step.) They've already done the math for you.

- 70 steps per minute equals 30 minutes per mile, or 2 miles per hour.

- 105 steps per minute equals 20 minutes per mile, or 3 miles per hour.

- 140 steps per minute equals 15 minutes per mile, or 4 miles per hour.

If you pay attention to your steps, after a while, you'll be able to estimate your pace fairly accurately without bothering to count. You'll just know what a 20-minute mile or a 15-minute mile feels like. At least I do.

Q: *How many calories do I burn by walking a mile?*

A: The average 150-pound person burns between 80 and 100 calories per mile. That number can change depending on your height, your weight, your fitness level, whether you're walking on hills or level terrain, what you're wearing, the outside temperature, and many other factors.

If your goal is to lose weight, forget about the numbers. Instead, develop a healthy eating plan that you can live with, and incorporate as much physical activity into your daily routine as possible. Walk for at least ½ hour a day. If you can do more, great! Maybe you can squeeze in ½ hour in the morning and another ½ hour in the evening. Then during the day, take as many short walks as you can, indoors or out.

Become aware of how much time you spend sitting, and make an effort to fill some of those minutes with physical activity. At work, for example, pace around while you're talking on the phone and use the restroom on another floor or in the farthest corner of your building. That way, you know you're burning more calories throughout the day. The exact number doesn't really matter.

SHOE SAVVY

Q: *My walking shoes have two sets of eyelets. Which should I use?*

A: That extra set of eyelets allows you to fine-tune the fit of your walking shoe. If you have a narrow heel, lace both sets of eyelets to tighten the top of your shoe. This keeps your heel from slipping, so you don't develop blisters. You may have to experiment to get the lacing just right.

Q: *I walk early in the morning, so my walking shoes always get wet. They're still damp the next day when I go to put them on. Any suggestions?*

A: Ideally, you should have two pairs of walking shoes, so you can alternate between them. That said, stuffing newspaper inside your wet shoes can help soak up moisture, so they might be dry by the next day. Just don't put wet leather shoes near the heat. Drying them too fast causes them to shrink or crack.

Q: *When should I get new shoes?*

A: Replace your walking shoes every 6 months or 600 miles, whichever comes first. At that point, it doesn't matter if the shoes still look great. They've lost a lot of their cushioning power. Be kind to your feet, and you'll keep walking forever.

FOCUS ON FITNESS

Q: *How can I evaluate my fitness level as a walker?*

A: James Rippe, M.D., author of *Dr. James Rippe's Complete Book of Fitness Walking*, has developed a special formula to help walkers assess their fit-

ness. Find a flat 1-mile loop. Warm up for 5 minutes, stretching your calves and hamstrings. Then walk the mile as quickly as you can without running out of steam. Compare your time against the benchmark for your age group.

- Under 30: If you can walk a mile in 13 minutes, you're in great shape.
- 30 to 39: Doing a 14-minute mile puts you in the "great shape" category.
- 40 to 49: Cover a mile in just under 15 minutes (14 minutes, 42 seconds), and you're at the top level of fitness for your age group.
- 50 to 69: Doing a 15-minute mile is excellent.
- 70 or over: If you can walk a mile in 18 minutes, 18 seconds, you're very fit for your age.

If you exceed the ideal time for your age group by 3 to 6 minutes, you're not in the best shape aerobically. But don't worry—just keep walking. Regular, consistent exercise can lower your time.

Q: *Is it possible to do too much walking? Can I overtrain?*

A: If you're new to walking, build up your time and mileage gradually. After all, you want your feet to toughen up and your muscles to get used to the exertion. You may not actually hurt yourself, but if you feel stiff and sore, it may keep you from going out again.

If you're walking regularly and

you're really picking up your pace, you can just as easily overtrain. Here are some indicators that you may need to reduce your intensity or distance or even take a day off once in a while.

- Your daily walks seem to be getting harder instead of easier.
- You feel more tired than usual during the day.
- You have difficulty springing out of bed in the morning.
- You have trouble falling asleep or sleeping soundly.
- You begin eating less or eating irregularly.

If you cut back on your walking routine and your symptoms persist, see your doctor. There may be an underlying medical problem that's making you feel bad.

STAYING INJURY-FREE

Q: *My hands swell when I walk. Is this a problem? It feels funny, and I don't like it.*

A: Swelling in your hands is normal. When you swing your arms, the blood rushes down into your fingers. It isn't harmful, but it could be uncomfortable, especially if you wear rings. It's a good idea to take off your rings before you go walking.

If the swelling bothers you, try squeezing your hands into fists from time to time while you walk. This helps push blood back from the fingers. Some people carry small rubber balls to squeeze. Keeping your elbows bent as you swing your arms can also minimize swelling. But unless you're race-walking, the bent-elbow technique can feel rather silly.

Q: *Whenever I start walking, I get side stitches. What causes them, and what can I do about them?*

A: A side stitch—a sudden, stabbing pain in your side—results from a spasm of the diaphragm, the muscle that separates your chest and abdomen. It's crying out for oxygen because your expanded lungs and contracted abdomen are blocking normal bloodflow. This sounds serious, but it's not a big deal.

At the first sign of a side stitch, stop walking. Using three fingers, massage the area where the pain is most severe until you feel relief. Do not hold your breath. As your breathing slows to its normal rate, the pain should subside. Then you can resume your walk. Like any muscle, your diaphragm cramps when it isn't warmed up properly. So remember to warm up before you head out. Walking slowly should do the trick.

Q: *Help! I'm having pain in the front of my lower legs. What is it?*

A: It sounds like shinsplints, a common problem among beginning walkers. It results from doing too much too soon. Your shin and calf muscles cramp from overuse, and you notice a burning pain in your shins.

To avoid shinsplints, increase your distance and pace gradually, and always take time to warm up before doing any speedwork. If you've already overdone it, try slowing your pace. If you're still in pain, try stretching your calf muscles. Stand facing the nearest wall or tree, then lean forward, putting your palms against the wall or tree and keeping your heels flat on the ground. Or sit on a bench with your legs straight out in front of you and flex your feet toward you. Still in pain? Hobble home and apply ice for 15 minutes. Be sure to wrap the ice in a towel, to protect your skin from the cold.

Q: *I have heel pain. What should I do?*

A: Heel pain becomes increasingly common with age, especially among the over-40 crowd. Often it results from a condition called plantar fasciitis—that's inflammation of the plantar fascia, a sheath of connective tissue that runs along the bottom of the foot. As this tissue becomes overstretched and inflamed, it produces sharp pain, especially first thing in the morning when you get out of bed. (I know because I've had it.) The pain eases as you walk around, but it can come back, especially if you sit for a long time.

As you get older, your body's tissues become less pliable. That's why stretching is so important. For heel pain, stretching your calf muscles may help. If it doesn't, you may need better walking shoes or special shoe inserts (called orthotics) to keep your ankles from rolling inward (overpronating), which may overstretch and inflame the plantar fascia.

If simple stretching doesn't relieve your pain within a week or two, schedule an appointment with a podiatrist. You need to find out what's causing your pain. If you keep stretching and tearing your plantar fascia, you may develop heel spurs, painful bony protuberances from the heel bones.

Whatever the source of your heel pain, it needs time to heal. Just be patient. Your podiatrist may want to give you cortisone shots, but they're only a temporary solution. Getting them repeatedly may cause tissue damage over time.

Q: *How can I avoid blisters?*

A: A bad case of blisters can knock a beginning walker right off her feet. More experienced walkers who step up their workouts or switch to hiking can encounter problems, too. Here's how to keep your feet blister-free.

• When you feel a "hot spot" on your foot, act right away. Take off your shoe and apply moleskin or an adhesive bandage over the affected area.

• Make sure that your shoes fit both feet. Often one foot is larger than the other. The friction created by wearing the wrong-size shoe—whether it's too small or too large—can lead to blisters.

- Wear high-tech socks made from fibers that wick away moisture. Skip the cotton and look for synthetic blends such as CoolMax or Wonderspun.

SAFETY FIRST

Q: *There are some nasty-looking dogs in my neighborhood, and they're not always chained or fenced in. What can I do to protect myself?*

A: You're right to be concerned. Even dogs that seem friendly around their owners can become aggressive when they're protecting their turf from strangers. If you can take another route, do so. Or call local authorities—either your town's animal-control officer or the police—to find out the provisions of municipal leash laws and to report any violations.

If you must walk by a property with potentially dangerous dogs, be sure to carry something for protection. Tie a sweatshirt around your waist, wear a fanny pack, carry an umbrella or a walking stick—anything that you can put between yourself and a dog, in case one tries to bite you. The dog won't care if he gets you or the object in your hand. As he bites down on the object, keep tension on it and back yourself to a place of safety, like inside a car or behind a fence. Then let go and wait for him to leave.

Never stare down a dog. Instead, stand still and try to stay calm. Say, "No!" in a deep, firm voice. If the dog stops in his tracks, yell, "Go home!"

If a dog knocks you down, curl into a tight ball and protect your head and neck with your hands. Wait for the animal to leave, then slowly move to safety. Running will only attract the dog's attention.

Report any attack to your local animal-control office immediately. Even if the dog bit your fanny pack and didn't harm you, he's dangerous, and his owner should be notified.

Q: *I like walking on an outdoor track near where I live because I don't have to contend with dogs or cars, but I get bored. Any suggestions?*

A: An outdoor track can be lots of fun for walking. It's a great place to interval train—speed up for one lap, slow down for the next. You can listen to music during your workouts since you're out of harm's way. (If you're completely alone, you might want to keep one ear free, so you can hear a stranger approaching.) You can practice special techniques, like walking with your feet parallel to one of the white lane lines or crossing each foot over the line to stretch out your hips.

Wear a watch or a stopwatch to monitor your pace. If you walked a 15-minute mile last week, can you shave a few seconds off your time this week? Write down your times, so you can track your progress.

When you're on a track, you can really let your mind wander since you shouldn't have to watch for obstacles.

Carry a little tape recorder to record your brainstorms or to make tapes to send to relatives or friends. If you're comfortable walking with someone, just having a buddy can distract you from the monotony of going around in circles.

PAIRING UP TO WORK OUT

Q: *My wife and I like to walk together, but she has trouble keeping up with my brisk pace. I don't want to give up our time with each other, but I do want to get a workout. What should I do?*

A: Your situation is quite common among walking couples. Each person has a different pace or a different stride, so one gets bored slowing down or the other suffers trying to keep up. There isn't any perfect solution, but since you're the faster partner, you could wear a weighted vest or backpack while you're walking. Or you could try using a PowerBelt. It's a device that you wear around your waist, with handles to pull for an upper-body workout. Just pumping your arms helps to rev up your heart. (For more information on the PowerBelt, see chapter 17.)

Perhaps the best suggestion is for you to do most of your workout first, then join your partner for your cooldown. You'll be relaxed and in a great mood by the time you're finished walking, ready to share quality time with your partner.

Q: *I want to start a walking club in my area. Where do I begin?*

A: My first question to you is, do you really want to add this kind of complication to your life? Most people I know prefer to walk either alone or in pairs. Getting an entire group together on a regular basis is just too difficult.

On the other hand, you may find some interest in walking classes. Many people are willing to pay a nominal fee to have someone motivate them to walk. If you're willing to lead a class, all you need is a watch, a cell phone, CPR certification, and some enthusiasm. You don't have to know racewalking technique, although good posture is definitely a plus.

To find your recruits, place an ad in your local newspaper or post a notice at your church or YMCA. Explain that you'll lead walks at a particular time, from a designated starting point, a set number of times a week for a fee of $3 to $5 per session. (If you're experienced in racewalking technique or you have some sort of training certification, you may want to charge more.) You'll have the walking group you wanted in the first place, and as a bonus, you'll be getting paid for your efforts.

The catch is, you're responsible for everything, including getting your walkers back to the starting point on time, making sure that they stay within their target heart-rate ranges, and leading them in stretches before and after every workout. You may want to have water bottles or light snacks available, too.

As you can see, this approach takes work. But to me, it seems a lot more plausible and inviting than trying to recruit members for a walking group.

TREADMILL TIPS

Q: *Do I get as good a workout when I'm on my treadmill as when I go outdoors?*

A: All treadmills are different. Some give very accurate indications of your speed, while others don't. On my treadmill, I feel like I'm walking 4 miles an hour even though the speedometer reads 2.5.

What's more, when you're on a treadmill, the walking surface is continuously pulling away from you. As a result, you're not getting the solid push-off from your back foot that you do when you're walking outside.

But the real issue is that you're probably using the treadmill for a certain reason, perhaps you don't feel safe walking outside, or the weather is keeping you inside. What's important is that you're moving your muscles, burning calories, and getting a great workout.

Personally, I wouldn't want to do all my walking on a treadmill. The benefits of walking outside in nature are just too great to ignore. So make sure that you exercise outdoors whenever you can.

Q: *I feel dizzy when I get off my treadmill. Is there something wrong with me?*

A: Absolutely not. When you're walking on a treadmill, your body gets confused because it's moving but the scenery isn't changing. So once you return to terra firma, your body thinks it should keep going, even though you're standing still. To minimize dizziness, try slowing your treadmill to a very easy pace before you hop off. Then walk around for a few minutes until your sense of equilibrium returns.

WHAT I WOULD HAVE MISSED

A long time ago, I received a poem from a reader detailing all the things she would have missed if she hadn't gone walking. This idea struck such a chord with me that over time, I found myself reacting to many of my observations on my morning walk with the same thought: "Look! I never would have seen that if I'd decided not to walk today!"

It turned out to be a fun way to motivate myself and others. Now I make a point of sharing interesting things about my morning walks with my friends. For me, sharing my experiences reinforces the value of walking, beyond the health and fitness benefits that I write about daily. And perhaps it makes my friends think in the same way I do: "If I don't walk today, what will I miss?"

To that end, I thought I'd share one summer's worth of memories with you because I enjoy doing it and because I want you to know more about my reasons for walking. Maybe by thinking, "What will I miss?"

you'll be inspired to walk on those days when you need a little extra motivation.

A SEASON FOR THE SENSES

That year no one planted corn in the field behind our house. Instead, it grew thick with wildflowers and emerald green grasses that undulate in the wind. The field belongs to my husband's family. It's about 5 acres, all gently sloping uphill. At the top of the hill, there's a breathtaking view. I can see all the way to Little Gap and Delaware Water Gap, two landmarks in the Appalachian mountain chain. From up there, the sky seems wider and deeper, the air fresher. It's quiet, yet it's humming with life.

My husband mowed a private walking path for me, encircling the field. I love not having to walk on the macadam road. Three times around makes a mile, according to my pedometer. I could also walk into an adjacent vacant lot that's meticulously mowed and cared for, like a green without a golf course.

In the early spring, I was highly aware of the birds' songs. It seemed like there were more birds than ever. I loved trying to identify the various calls as I walked. What conversation was I interrupting? Or instigating?

One morning, while walking with a friend, we came upon a flock of 12 turkeys and their young, all pecking and waddling their way through the brush. They hardly seemed to notice us.

Another morning, while walking with my dog, Petey, I heard a rustling sound and looked up to see four raccoons scampering up a tree. They stopped and looked down at Petey, who was completely oblivious to them. Then they locked eyes with me and scampered higher and higher into the branches.

One afternoon, I stood at the top of the hill and watched a thunderstorm roll across the valley. The lightning crackled through the clouds. The valley darkened and brightened in a patchwork of light. The air changed from sultry to crisp. The scents intensified.

Early in the summer on my weekend walks, I carried a small pail to collect blackberries, raspberries, and mulberries. The hedgerows were full of them! I used them to make pancakes and cobblers (low-fat, of course).

A neighbor scattered wildflower seeds along the hedgerows, and the colors changed with the seasons. In early spring, the white and yellow daisies dominated, along with purple thistles. Then the golden Gloriosa daisies burst forth, mixed with delicate Queen Anne's lace. Finally, the purple coneflower took over. If I didn't walk for a few days, the meadow would be completely redecorated by the time I returned.

One day, I even discovered a new path. Someone had mowed a trail through the deep woods. It curved around gnarly trees and broken-down remnants of apple trees. Vines hung everywhere, and butterflies flitted in and out of the speckled sunlight. I felt like I'd entered an enchanted forest. (In reality, it was a path for a dirt bike.)

THE LITTLE THINGS MATTER MOST

As that sweet summer passed, my attitude toward my walks became one of excitement and expectation rather than obligation. What would I see today? What gift of nature was waiting for me on that hillside? It was a delightful reprieve from the shoulds and the have-tos.

As you go walking, observe and appreciate the many surprises that await you in the great outdoors. Don't worry if you don't live in the country, as I do. It doesn't matter whether you see a flock of wild turkeys waddling along, a mother bending to kiss her child goodbye outside a school bus, or a puddle shimmering in the sunlight. Give yourself the opportunity to absorb and savor your surroundings, whatever they may be.

USING A WALKING LOG

Whether you're an experienced walker or just starting out, this log is your daily reminder to get out there and do it! To uphold your commitment to health and fitness, plan your schedule in advance, and then place a checkmark when you've met your goals. But if you miss a goal or a walk, don't feel too bad about it—just recognize it and try to understand why you found other things to do. Maybe you had an emergency or a heavy workload that day. Or maybe you found excuses you can remedy simply by better planning. Reviewing your progress over the months and seeing all the miles you've walked is a great motivator for those times you may start to get tired of your daily walks.

This log can also be a diary of sorts, helping you to remember your favorite walks in the months or years down the road. In the "Comments" section, be sure to record not just how you felt physically on the walk, but also how

you felt mentally. If you walked alone, with a friend, with your spouse, or with your dog. If the sun was shining and the birds were singing. Or if a car splashed you on a rainy day, soaking you head to toe, and you could do nothing about it but laugh. These are the things walking memories are made of.

Be sure to refer to your comments from time to time to see patterns emerge: What made your walks easier—walking with your friend? What made them harder—walking with your dog who likes to stop and sniff everything? Finding the answers to these questions will only make your walks more rewarding.

We've given you 2 weeks of blank entry pages to get you started. Make sure you make photocopies of the blank entries so you can continue to log your walks over many weeks, months, or even years.

Enjoy your walking!

MONTH November

DAY	DISTANCE	HOURS	ROUTE	COMMENTS: EXPERIENCES, BODY RESPONSE, WEATHER
SUNDAY 2	6m	2 hrs.	The long loop down Gafney Hill and up Died's Road	Beautiful, sunny day! Took the steep hill slowly. Only had to stop once to catch my breath. Stretched!
MONDAY 3	–	1	–	Woke up late! Tried to use the stairs at work whenever I could.
TUESDAY 4	3m	.45	Short loop on Cate Pass, up Texas Rd	Pushed a little. Used racewalk technique. Shins slightly hurting. Must stretch more.
WEDNESDAY 5	2m	.30	Route from new building - downtown and back	Lunchtime walk with Bob. Fast - but we could still talk. New work bottle at work.
THURSDAY 6	3m	.45	Palmer Bike Park at 7am - Lots of walkers!	Practiced strengthening exercises for racewalking. Was able to try further without shin pain.
FRIDAY 7	2m	.40	Lunchtime route	Leisurely pace with friends. Drizzle - but cool
SATURDAY 8	(13m)	(1½)	From The Cottage to Bethlehem and back	Bike ride! Nice change of pace. (Sore thighs, though.)
WEEK 14	16	44.40 M TOTAL		
+ previous Year To Date total	111	254.20 M		
Year To Date	127	30 hrs TOTAL		

Maggie Spilner has been keeping a walking log for years. Here she shares seven typical entries.

MONTH			ROUTE	COMMENTS: EXPERIENCES, BODY RESPONSE, WEATHER
DAY	DISTANCE	HOURS		
SUNDAY				
MONDAY				
TUESDAY				
WEDNESDAY				
THURSDAY				
FRIDAY				
SATURDAY				
WEEK 1 + previous Year To Date total		TOTAL		
Year To Date		TOTAL		

MONTH			ROUTE	COMMENTS: EXPERIENCES, BODY RESPONSE, WEATHER
DAY	DISTANCE	HOURS		
SUNDAY				
MONDAY				
TUESDAY				
WEDNESDAY				
THURSDAY				
FRIDAY				
SATURDAY				
WEEK 2			TOTAL	
+ previous Year To Date total				
Year To Date			TOTAL	

PHOTO CREDITS

INDEX

Underscored page references indicate boxed text. **Boldface** page references indicate photographs.

Underscored page references indicate boxed text. **Boldface** page references indicate photographs.

Underscored page references indicate boxed text. **Boldface** page references indicate photographs.

Endorphins, 23, 29, 62

Entwining Fingers and Toes, **114**, 114–15

Environment Scan, 219, 222

Escalators, climbing, <u>56</u>

EVA, 39–40

Events. *See* Races

Exercise. *See also* Aerobic exercise; Dynamic
     Body Exercises; Strength training;
     Stretching; Yoga program
  arthritis and, 20–21
  for back, 126
  brain activity stimulation by, 16
  in cancer prevention and treatment, 4–6
  in cold weather, 71
  for diabetes, 15–18, <u>17</u>
  expanding horizons of, <u>22</u>
  for heart health, <u>8</u>, 12–14
  hiking program, 119–21
  immune stimulation from, 3–4
  incremental, <u>85</u>
  insulin and, 16, 18
  intensity of, 89, 90
  mindful, 29
  mistakes during, <u>125</u>
  resting pulse rate and, 8
  for the senses, 169–72
  timing of eating and, 13, 18, 57–58, 64
  total-body, 95
  for trimming intra-abdominal fat, 9–10
  weight loss and, 18, 81, 88–92

Exercise ball, 120

Exercise plans
  Get-Started Plan, 82
  Maximum-Calorie-Burn Plan, 84–87
  Plateau-Busting Plan, 82–84

Exercises, strength training, 110, **110**
  Figure Eights, 110, **110**
  Heel-Toe Rock, 110, **110**
  Hip Stretch, 110, **110**
  Pause Walk, 110, **110**
  Quads, Part 1, 111, **111**
  Quads, Part 2, 111, **111**
  Standing Crunch, 111, **111**
  Twisting Abs, 111, **111**

Exerstriders, 91, 95–96

Eyelets, in shoes, 228–29

Eyes
  environment scan with, 219
  exploring without, 171
  protecting from allergens, 78

Eye Scan, 219

F

Face, protection in cold weather, 75

Fanny pack, 48, 219

Fat, body
  burning with long slow distance exercise, 88
  intra-abdominal, 9–10

Fat, dietary, 97, 100

Feet
  blisters, 68, 120, 231–32
  care of, <u>18</u>, 18–19, 142
  curvature of, and shoe fit, 42
  in Dynamic Walking, 194
  flexibility of, and shoe fit, 39, 42, 43
  heel pain, 147, 231
  measuring, 42
  problems with, and shoe size, <u>45</u>
  type of, and shoe fit, 42–43
  yoga exercises for, 113–15, **114**

Fiber, dietary, 100

"Fight against Fat" program, 35

Figure Eights, 110, **110**

Fitness. *See also* Exercise
  blunders in, <u>125</u>
  evaluation of, 229
  health protection from, 7–9

5-K, 131–36
  assessing ability to walk, 132
  benefits of, 131–32
  cautions for, 134–35
  clothes for, <u>136</u>
  motivation for, <u>131</u>, <u>132</u>
  race day, 135–36
  signing up for, 132
  techniques for, <u>135</u>
  tips for, <u>136</u>
  training for, 132–34
  workout schedule, <u>133</u>

Fluid intake
  on race day, 135
  in warm weather, 69

Foot. *See* Feet

Force Field, 204, 221

For Spacious Skies, 159

40-30-30 diet, 97

Framingham Cardiovascular Institute, 8

Frequency, of Dynamic Body Exercises,
  208

Friction, protection from, 68–69

Friends of Peace Pilgrim, 176

Frostbite, 72

<u>Underscored</u> page references indicate boxed text. **Boldface** page references indicate photographs.

Underscored page references indicate boxed text. **Boldface** page references indicate photographs.

<u>Underscored</u> page references indicate boxed text. **Boldface** page references indicate photographs.

M

Magnetic resonance imaging (MRI), <u>25</u>
Magnets, therapeutic, 22
Mall walking
  benefits of, 55, <u>57</u>
  boosting calorie burn in, <u>56</u>
  heart disease and, 13
  motivation and, <u>57</u>
  in multistory facility, <u>56</u>
  safety during, <u>57</u>
  weather conditions and, <u>57</u>
Marathons, 137–42
  diet for, <u>140–41</u>
  goal in, 139
  pace in, 139, 142
  physical and mental demands of, 142
  training for, 137–38, 141–42
Masks
  for cold weather, 72
  ski, 75
  surgical, 78
Maximum-Calorie-Burn Plan, 84–87
Maze, 162
Meats, in diet, 101
Medial support, 40
Medical and Sports Music Institute of America, 153
Medications
  antihistamines, 77
  anti-inflammatories, 24
  for diabetes, 16, <u>17</u>, 18
  for high blood pressure, 10
  nitroglycerin, <u>12</u>, 14
  pain relievers, 21, 24
Meditation, 29, 31, <u>168</u>, 169
Mile, calorie burning in walking one, 228
Mindful exercise, 29
Modified Heel-Toe Roll, 202
Molds, 76, 77, <u>78</u>
Monofilament test, <u>18</u>
Montessori school system, 206
MoonWalkers, 58
Morning, walking in, 56, 227
Motivation
  for 5-K, 131, 132
  for mall walking, <u>57</u>
  for marathon, 140
  pairing up for, 60, <u>61</u>
  personal trainer and, 122
  walking club and, <u>91</u>
  walking log for, <u>5</u>

walking team and, 105–6
  for weight loss, <u>98–99</u>
Movement education, 206–7
MRI, <u>25</u>
Muscles
  abdominal, 111
  adductors, 116
  back, 24, <u>25</u>, 26, 27
  calf, 215, 230, 231
  diaphragm, 230
  hamstrings, 116, 214
  hip flexors, 181
  levatores costarum, 189
  pectoral, 117
  psoas, 181–82, 184, 198, 217
  quadriceps, 111, 116, 118, 151, 216
  relaxation of, progressive, 191
  shin, 215, 230
  shoulder, 115
  soleus, 215
Muscle soreness
  avoiding, 109
  in strength training program, 124–25
Muscle spasms, back, 24

N

National Allergy Bureau of the American Academy
    of Allergy, Asthma, and Immunology, <u>78</u>
National Strength and Conditioning Association
    (NSCA), <u>123</u>
National Trails Day events, <u>170</u>
Nature, walking to reconnect with, 169–72, <u>170</u>
Neuropathy, diabetic, <u>18</u>
New Age Health Spa, <u>9</u>
Night, walking at, 58
Nitroglycerin, <u>12</u>, 14
Non-insulin-dependent (type 2) diabetes, 18
North American Racewalking Foundation, 109
Nose Over Toes to Go, 191
NSCA, <u>123</u>
Nurses, heart disease study on, <u>8</u>
Nurses' Health Study, 16
Nutrition. *See also* Diet
  carbohydrates, fats and proteins in, 97
  for marathons, <u>140–41</u>

O

Obesity, as risk factor, 7
Orthotics, 44, 231

<u>Underscored</u> page references indicate boxed text. **Boldface** page references indicate photographs.

<u>Underscored</u> page references indicate boxed text. **Boldface** page references indicate photographs.

Underscored page references indicate boxed text. **Boldface** page references indicate photographs.

<u>Underscored</u> page references indicate boxed text. **Boldface** page references indicate photographs.

Underscored page references indicate boxed text. **Boldface** page references indicate photographs.

<u>Underscored</u> page references indicate boxed text. **Boldface** page references indicate photographs.